From We Will to At Will

"A must-read not only for veterans and military spouses, but also for employers and HR professionals looking to take advantage of the capabilities veterans/military spouses bring to the workforce."
  —Gen. George W. Casey, Jr.,
  (Ret.), U.S. Army

"I know the value our veterans and military spouses bring to the workplace, and Justin skillfully communicates that message to HR professionals across all industries and effectively bridges the gap to veteran hiring, career development, and growth."
  —Joseph M. DePinto,
  President & CEO, 7-Eleven, Inc.

"As the ranks of transitioning veterans swell, Justin delivers a vital and comprehensive guide for understanding today's veterans, cultivating a military-friendly work environment, and managing the hiring process."
  —Diana Drysdale,
  President, PSEG Power Ventures, PSEG Power

"Finally! The definitive book on veteran employment written by the definitive leader in the space."
  —Jack Fanous,
  Founder & CEO, JobPath

"The solutions for effective veteran-hiring programs are spot on and easy to relate to, understand, and most importantly, implement!"
  —Lt. Gen. Mike Linnington,
  (Ret.), U.S. Army

"The combination of best practices and thought leadership with expert insight makes this an invaluable resource for HR professionals, veterans, and spouses."
  —J. Patrick Law,
  Chairman of the Board, Defenders of Freedom

"Packed with insightful firsthand experiences from dozens of companies, nonprofit organizations, and governmental agencies, this is a must-read handbook for anybody making the transition from the military to the private sector."
  —Charles Sevola, Jr.,
  Vice President & Head of Prudential Veterans Initiative

"By drawing on his own experience and inspiring story, Justin delivers a compelling guide for hiring veterans and the benefits service backgrounds bring to organizations."
  —Linda Woodruff,
  VP Human Capital and Motivation, Human Resources,
  Panasonic Corporation of North America

FROM WE WILL TO AT WILL

FROM WE WILL TO AT WILL

A Handbook for Veteran Hiring, Transitioning, and Thriving in the Workplace

Justin Constantine

with Andrew Morton

Society for Human Resource Management
Alexandria, Virginia www.shrm.org
Strategic Human Resource Management, India
Mumbai, India www.shrmindia.org
Society for Human Resource Management
Haidian District Beijing, China www.shrm.org/cn
Society for Human Resource Management, Middle East and Africa Office
Dubai, United Arab Emirates www.shrm.org/pages/mena.aspx

This publication is designed to provide accurate and authoritative information regarding the subject matter covered. It is sold with the understanding that neither the publisher nor the author is engaged in rendering legal or other professional service. If legal advice or other expert assistance is required, the services of a competent, licensed professional should be sought. The federal and state laws discussed in this book are subject to frequent revision and interpretation by amendments or judicial revisions that may significantly affect employer or employee rights and obligations. Readers are encouraged to seek legal counsel regarding specific policies and practices in their organizations. This book is published by the Society for Human Resource Management (SHRM). The interpretations, conclusions, and recommendations in this book are those of the author and do not necessarily represent those of the publisher.

This publication may not be reproduced, stored in a retrieval system, or transmitted in whole or in part, in any form or by any means, electronic, mechanical, photocopying, recording, or otherwise, without the prior written permission of the publisher, or authorization through payment of the appropriate per-copy fee to the Copyright Clearance Center, Inc., 222 Rosewood Drive, Danvers, MA 01923, 978-750-8600, fax 978-646-8600, or on the Web at www.copyright.com. Requests to the publisher for permission should be addressed to SHRM Book Permissions, 1800 Duke Street, Alexandria, VA 22314, or online at http://www.shrm.org/about-shrm/pages/copyright--permissions.aspx. SHRM books and products are available on most online bookstores and through the SHRMStore at www.shrmstore.org.

The Society for Human Resource Management is the world's largest HR professional society, representing 285,000 members in more than 165 countries. For nearly seven decades, the Society has been the leading provider of resources serving the needs of HR professionals and advancing the practice of human resource management. SHRM has more than 575 affiliated chapters within the United States and subsidiary offices in China, India, and United Arab Emirates. Please visit us at www.shrm.org.

Library of Congress Cataloging-in-Publication Data has been applied for and is on file with the Library of Congress.

ISBN (pbk): 978-1-586-44507-2; ISBN (PDF): 978-1-586-44508-9;
ISBN (EPUB): 978-1-586-44509-6; ISBN (MOBI): 978-1-586-44510-2

Printed in the United States of America

PB Printing   10 9 8 7 6 5 4 3   61.14519

Table of Contents

Foreword

THE JOURNEY TO "VETERAN-READY"

Each year, more than a quarter of a million former service members embark on a journey—both literal and figurative—as they transition from the "we will" culture of the military to the "at will" reality of the civilian workforce. This handbook was designed not only to inspire us as employers to hire veterans, but to empower us to create organizational cultures where veterans can thrive. *From We Will to At Will* takes us on our own journey of cultural and organizational understanding as we transform our workplaces from "veteran-friendly" to "veteran-ready."

Over the last few years, the SHRM Foundation has worked to create a measurable impact on the hiring and retention of former service members, gleaning valuable lessons along the way. Through partnerships and research, we've learned that, although veterans are a key element of a diverse and inclusive workforce, distinct challenges remain. Do veterans feel included, engaged, and capable of reaching their full potential in today's workplace? Too often, the answer is no. A sobering 65 percent of veterans depart from their first nonmilitary job within two years.

From We Will to At Will tackles this challenge head on, outlining a holistic approach that goes far beyond translating military résumés and applying particular interviewing techniques. While these fundamentals are an integral part of hiring veterans, this handbook goes much farther, providing case studies, call-outs, and data; state-of-the-art resources and tools for recruiting and hiring; and fresh insights into the veteran experience. It demystifies military culture, explores hidden barriers to inclusion, and presents new approaches for helping veterans—and their families—continue their mission of service within our nation's workplaces.

As SHRM's CEO, I met Justin Constantine in early 2018, and he impressed me immediately with his passion and willingness to collaborate to forge monumental change for working veterans. His own service to his country is neither measured by his time in uniform alone, nor defined solely by his heroic and inspirational experiences in combat. Like so many veterans in communities across our country, Justin is far from finished fulfilling his life's purpose. *From We Will to At Will* is a testament to the humility, selflessness, and commitment that exemplifies a Marine officer. He has created a candid, straightforward, and vital resource for anyone looking to create a meaningful veteran-hiring program—one that goes far deeper than "goodwill" and is rooted firmly in good business.

The journey *From We Will to At Will* is not as far as organizations and veterans may assume, and the rewards are immense for both. Tapping the talent of these uniquely prepared individuals enhances every workplace culture, and HR can—and should—lead these efforts.

Johnny C. Taylor, Jr., SHRM-SCP, is President and Chief Executive Officer of SHRM. He currently serves on the corporate board of Gallup and on the Board of Trustees of the University of Miami. He is an advisor to Safe Streets & Second Chances and a board member of Jobs for America's Graduates. In a 2018 White House ceremony, President Trump appointed Mr. Taylor Chairman of the President's Advisory Board on Historically Black Colleges and Universities.

Acknowledgments

Justin:

To Dahlia—you were the cornerstone of my recovery and have been an incredible partner over the last twelve years.

To my many friends and collaborators in the veteran space—thank you for your continued work to ensure our efforts and sacrifices are not forgotten.

I want to thank especially thank fellow veteran Andrew Morton. He and I have been connected for decades—from the rugby fields of James Madison University to both serving in Iraq—unbeknownst to each other at the time. Reconnecting a year and a half ago, we joined in this effort to create this handbook and I could not have done it without him. He's my brother in arms and my brother in this work.

Andrew:

I've experienced no shortage of remarkable moments in my life, and collaborating on this effort ranks amongst all of them for three very specific reasons. First, it afforded me the opportunity to give back in some way to a profession that serves as readily as we do in uniform—HR. Thanks to all of you for guiding so many of us to our next purpose-driven opportunity after our time in uniform is done. Secondly, it allowed me to reconnect with a life-long friend who's a hero. Justin—thanks for your generosity, support, and friendship! Finally, it reminded me every day of how blessed I am to have the most amazing kids in the world. Luke, Catie, and Jude—through deployments in years past and late nights and weekends during this effort, you've always been there for me! You are my mentors and my inspiration! I love you will all my heart!

Preface

*There is, I am convinced, a sea of goodwill out in the
country of people and places yearning to help. We need
to tap into it. We need to make that connection.*

—Admiral Mike Mullen, Chairman of the Joint
Chiefs of Staff, Memorial Day, 2008

FROM A VETERAN-FRIENDLY TO VETERAN-READY WORKPLACE

A quarter of a million service members transition from the military each
year, joining millions of their fellow veterans in the civilian workforce in
communities across the country. Over the last fifteen years alone nearly
2.5 million veterans of the wars in Afghanistan and Iraq have returned home
to what Admiral Mullen describes as the collective "sea of goodwill."[1] This
sea is an incredibly powerful part of helping them transition.

These immeasurable acts of kindness from millions of Americans and
thousands of private and public sector organizations have given today's generation of veterans and their families an unprecedented level of support.
Nevertheless, while we've made significant strides across so many areas, businesses, support organizations, and veterans still struggle with perhaps the
most impactful aspect of any postmilitary transition: finding meaningful
employment opportunities for veterans.

Much has been written, studied, and researched regarding the challenge
of employing veterans. And still, for so many veterans, bridging the divide
between the "We Will" environment of the military and the "At Will" reality of the private sector can be as daunting as many of the missions they've
faced in uniform. In many ways, the research tells us what we already may
know: while veterans are outstanding employees in many respects, there are

challenges inherent to hiring, engaging, and retaining these employees as organizations navigate the path from veteran friendly to veteran ready.

The purpose of this book is to provide research-based information, case studies, and proven best practices to empower HR and employers to develop scalable and sustainable veteran-hiring programs. With learning points, real-world tips from employers, and insights to both the culture and the mind-sets of today's veterans, our goal is to help you

- Demystify both the culture and mind-set of today's veteran;
- Understand the business case for and the business of hiring veterans;
- Manage the hiring process from resourcing to recruiting, and from offer to onboarding; and,
- Cultivate a military-friendly culture and work environment that leads to engagement and retention.

While this book is primarily written for businesses, hiring managers, and HR professionals, veterans and their families will also benefit from the case studies and resources, and perhaps most importantly, they can relate to the personal insights about what it's like to transition to life after military service.

To be clear, this book is not a war story—it's about a journey where ordinary men and women, many of whom served in extraordinary circumstances, are now returning to a life where the mission is quite different and circumstances have certainly changed. What has not changed, however, is the collective desire to make a difference and the need for a sense of fulfillment, regardless of what that new mission may be. The book is written by veterans, informed by their transition experience, combined with lessons learned, case studies, and best practices from organizations of all sizes. HR professionals are and will continue to be on the front lines of changing lives and giving veterans opportunities to serve long after their mission in uniform is complete. This book is for HR and informed by HR.

Additionally, this book was not written to elicit sympathy or instill patriotic overtures around the principles of veteran-hiring. Hiring programs that are born of goodwill may be noble in their intentions, but they are not sustainable. Additionally, no veteran wants to be hired simply because of their veteran status, and no organization can afford to hire employees, veteran or otherwise, who don't contribute to the bottom line. The good news is that we know there is a strong business case for hiring veterans across all industries, regardless of skill sets. The challenge, however, is that many organizations do not take a holistic approach to their practice of hiring veterans, and ultimately they either can't find or attract the veteran candidates they want, or they cannot retain the ones that they have. This begs the question: How do organizations achieve long-term, scalable success in hiring, engaging, and retaining this talented and diverse cohort?

FOUR PHASES TO TAKE COMPANIES FROM VETERAN FRIENDLY TO VETERAN READY

First, it starts with finding common ground. Demystify veterans by debunking long-established stereotypes that organizations have about veterans, and that veterans have about the civilian workforce. We start that process in the very first chapter, "Military 401." Then, throughout the rest of the book, we examine the key components of the four phases of veteran-hiring programs (see Figure P.1).

Phase 1: Discovery

During this initial phase, organizations assess the *why* (business case) of their veteran-hiring initiative while gaining an appreciation for veteran culture and examining how their organization's culture is, or is not, aligned with the veteran's culture. Veterans must examine why they are departing military service and be self-aware enough to know what they are able and willing to commit to during their postmilitary career. All too often both organizations and veterans skip this essential phase and go right to the résumé and the job fair stage of this process, which ultimately leads to challenges with fit that negatively affects engagement and retention.

Phase 2: Search

Once both the organization and the veteran have developed an appreciation and a better understanding of their goals and objectives, it's time to refine the job and candidate search. Organizations must attract and assess veteran

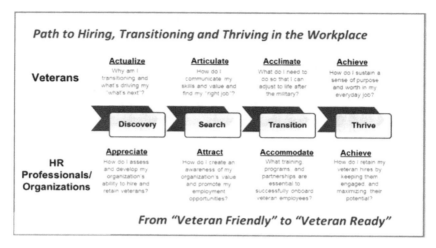

Figure P.1. The four phases to go from veteran friendly to veteran ready

candidates in a way that accounts for their soft skills, while veterans must articulate their value both on their résumé and during the job interview process. We examine each of these facets of the employment process in multiple chapters, answering questions such as, How do I find and attract veteran talent? How do I wade through their résumés and interview them in a way that accounts for their unique background?

Note: Many of the challenges regarding fit and retention are by-products of either the veteran or the organization not fully appreciating the importance of the first two phases. Not unlike dating and marriage, if you don't examine what you're looking for and who your partner truly is, it's unlikely that the relationship will be successful.

Phase 3: Transition

"Congratulations, you got the job!" quickly turns into drinking from the firehose. Any HR professional knows how critical onboarding can be, and it's especially important while welcoming vetrans to your organization, as HR, hiring managers, and supervisors all play a vital role in accommodating these unique attributes and challenges. Meanwhile, the veteran must quickly acclimate to the realities of their postmilitary career and adapt to their new normal in the same way they adapted to the first phase of life in uniform.

Phase 4: Thrive

Essentially, this phase is an opportunity for both the organization and the veteran to excel given all the effort and resources that have been put in place leading up to this moment. Organizations, large or small, can leverage any number of internal and external resources to keep the veteran engaged, and the veteran must continue to assimilate to their role, and advocate and communicate when there are issues along the way. Ultimately, if both the organization and veteran get to this stage, they've put a significant amount of time and effort into this process and while there may be periodic issues (as with any other employee-employer relationship), the prospects for long-term engagement and retention are high.

The most impactful veteran-hiring programs go well beyond the job fairs and résumé-building seminars, and address the true challenges of this transition in the long term. From "we will" to "at will" may seem like a long journey for many veterans, but there is significant common ground between organizations and veterans along the way.

Purpose, passion, and a cause greater than ourselves—these are the things that make life worth living for so many of us, veterans and civilians. Whether you're a teacher, a doctor, a Soldier, or a parent, so many of us thrive when we have that reason to get up in the morning. One part sacrifice and many more parts reward. Parents who find themselves in the empty nest, a teacher who retires from the classroom, and a veteran who takes off the uniform—these are the moments of our lives when we may feel furthest from our intended purpose, both lost and vulnerable. Yet, if we can still find ways to serve, to give of ourselves, we retain our identity in the most meaningful of ways. And that is exactly what successful veteran-hiring programs do!

ENDNOTE

1.   John W. Copeland and Colonel David W. Sutherland, *Sea of Goodwill: Matching the Donor to the Need*, white paper, Office of the Chairman of the Joint Chiefs of Staff Warrior and Family Support, May 17, 2010, http://fifnc.org/programs/Sea_of_Goodwill.pdf.

Introduction

I cannot see out of my left eye. I am missing most of my teeth and the end of my tongue. I cannot run, because the doctors removed several of the bones in my legs to reconstruct my upper and lower jaws. I also suffer from post-traumatic stress disorder (PTSD) and a traumatic brain injury (TBI). However, I think any company would be lucky to have me as one of their employees, primarily because of the skills I developed while serving in the Marine Corps.

Let me put my injuries in context. I joined the Marine Corps after my second year of law school. However, when I deployed to Iraq in 2006, it was not from the Judge Advocate General (JAG) Corps. In the Marine Corps, all the officers learn the basics of many different jobs, so I volunteered for deployment as a civil affairs team leader. In that role, I had the honor of leading a team of eight Marines and a navy corpsman as part of a Marine infantry battalion located halfway between Fallujah and Ramadi in the Al Anbar Governorate. As a civil affairs officer, I was to develop contacts and contracts with the local population to help rebuild the basic infrastructure needed for any city: clean running water, functioning electricity, drivable roads, and much-needed schools.

Unfortunately, fall 2006 was an extremely volatile time in Iraq, and the insurgency there was at the height of its power. Convincing the local Iraqi people to work with us to rebuild their cities was virtually impossible. By day, we would be advocating for what they needed and how we wanted to help. By night, members of the insurgency would visit them with death threats if they cooperated with us.

Because I worked closely with the battalion commander, he put me on his jump team. This team was composed of about a dozen Marines and would go out "across the wire" together about four or five times per week. This meant that we left the base and ventured into places where the opposition might be established or entrenched. On October 18, 2006, we were on a regular combat patrol and we had just gotten to an area where we knew an enemy sniper was active—he had already killed a few of our Marines in the preceding few weeks.

We actually had a reporter with us that day. Through later conversations with that reporter, my brothers-in-arms, and some of the doctors who treated and saved me, I learned what happened that day—I do not remember most of it, and only snapshots here and there of the next few weeks. I remember our patrol brief that morning, and then waking up almost a week later on an airplane. From the stories I heard, I know that earlier that day we stopped at an Iraqi police station that had been shot up by insurgents the night before. We wanted to show the Iraqi police how to defend their position better. We also stopped at one of our forward operating bases to check on our Marines, and I remember noticing that the reporter was kind of just standing around—an easy target for a sniper. When we got out of the vehicle at our next stop and started walking away from the Humvee, I told him that he needed to move faster or he might get shot. Based on that, he took a big step forward, just before a round came in right where his head had been and hit the wall next to us. Before I could react, the next shot hit me behind my left ear and exited through my mouth, causing incredible damage along the way.

Fortunately for me, Corpsman George Grant is an amazing young man. As blood was pouring out of my head and what remained of my face, he performed rescue breathing and an emergency tracheotomy on me. While the sniper was still shooting at us (in fact, they also shot the Marine behind me), Corpsman Grant saved my life. He was also wearing 65 pounds of protective armor in over 100°F, like we all were that summer. In the face of overwhelming adversity, and with complete disregard for his own life, George was able to focus entirely on me and keep me alive. In the absolute chaos going on around us, he conducted such a perfect tracheotomy that my plastic surgeon at the military hospital thought another surgeon had performed it.

After a lengthy recovery period, I returned to work for the federal government as an attorney, working for the Department of Justice on Capitol Hill and then for the Federal Bureau of Investigation. I also worked for the US Chamber of Commerce Foundation's Hiring Our Heroes program for four years, and started my own business. At every position, I continued to receive strong performance reviews and periodic promotions. Most of what I learned in the Marine Corps applied to my jobs outside the military—I showed up to work early, volunteered to help with ancillary duties, listened to others, enjoyed working on teams and issues much larger than myself, and took great pride in my work. The vast majority of our veterans and military spouses bring these same skill sets and much more to the workplace, and more and more companies are recognizing that.

We wrote this book not only to explain the business case for hiring veterans and military spouses, but because a review of the market identified that no single comprehensive resource existed for recruiters, HR professionals, middle managers, or corporate executives who wanted to understand every aspect of a successful veteran-hiring program. We know that oftentimes HR professionals are empowered to implement veteran-hiring initiatives but feel a little intimidated because veterans are coming from a culture they know little about. This book is designed to make you far more comfortable reading military résumés, interviewing veterans and their spouses, and onboarding in a robust manner that results in great retention rates and job satisfaction.

We also recognized that as intimidating as this may be for employers, it is equally intimidating for our veterans and military spouses. Many of them struggle to describe their military duties on their résumés in a way that corporate America can understand. Many have never sat through an official job interview before, or are not sure where to go to find companies that want to hire them. Therefore not only is each chapter of this book chock-full of guidance and resources for employers, but we have also included material from a wide variety of sources that will greatly benefit veterans and military spouses in their transitions so they can thrive in the civilian workplace.

As you will see in this book, you will benefit not only from *our* thoughts and experiences on various topics related to veteran employment, but also from the input of over fifty corporations, nonprofit organizations (NPOs), and government agencies. Many companies and groups are doing fantastic work when it comes to hiring veterans and military spouses, and they have provided learning points, best practices, case studies, and pitfalls to avoid, all to support other employers as well as job seekers.

Of course, veterans are just like any other demographic group—we are composed of people from all backgrounds, and thus it can be a little challenging to paint with a broad brush. So we also included chapters on three specific groups that we felt merited a little extra focus. The first group is our wounded warriors and disabled veterans, because there are a lot of misconceptions out there, especially when it comes to PTSD and TBIs. The second group is our women veterans, too often forgotten and with their own specific variables in careers. As you will see in that chapter, we relied heavily on input from organizations that focus specifically on this particular group. Lastly, as a veteran entrepreneur, I thought it was important to include a chapter on that particular group, not only to provide resources and guidance for the hundreds of thousands of veterans and military spouses who want to start their own businesses, but also because including our businesses in your supply-chain diversity programs is an incredible way to support veterans.

Ultimately, we hope this breaks down some of what is referred to as the civ-mil divide: the gulf that seems to exist between the military community and civilians. This is not an intentional disconnect, but a lack of communication often caused by stereotypes and misinformation. And we believe this is a two-way street—just as we encourage employers to take steps to learn more about the military culture and our veterans (and why they are often such great corporate assets!), we want our veterans and military spouses to learn more about life outside of the military so they can hit the ground running and truly thrive in the workplace.

At the end of the day, you should hire veterans not because it is the "right thing to do," but because of the return on investment your organization will see from doing so. We aim to make that hiring and retention experience as easy as possible for you here. As a veteran with a good career, I am very engaged with my friends, family, and community, I contribute in myriad ways to society, and I help others as much as I can—imagine an America where every veteran had those same opportunities.

CHAPTER 1

Military 401

BEYOND INSIGNIAS, MOTTOS, AND SKILL SETS—UNDERSTANDING THE CULTURE AND MIND-SET OF TODAY'S VETERAN

Most Americans get their view of the military from movies, from the news, hearsay, from watching whatever, rather than personal understanding or connection with Soldiers.

—General Mark A. Milley, Chief of Staff for the United States Army

BRIDGING THE CULTURAL DIVIDE

In February 2017, as part of its broader initiative in support of integrating and engaging veterans within the workforce, the SHRM Foundation assembled a diverse group of businesses, thought leaders, and stakeholders from across the public and private sectors with one very specific objective: identify the challenges to integrating and engaging veterans in the workforce as well as the solutions to those challenges. After a comprehensive facilitator-led process that actively involved the nearly sixty assembled participants, several things came to the surface, but the most prevalent and pressing of these top-level findings was this: if HR professionals and businesses are to be successful in recruiting, engaging, and retaining veterans, they must develop a much deeper understanding of military culture and the military perspective. That burden of responsibility, however, does not rest solely on the shoulders of the employers. Veterans must also develop an appreciation of corporate culture and the business perspective to effectively transition from their time in uniform and adapt to a professional career after military service.

There's no doubt that developing and articulating transferable skill sets is a key component to any veteran-hiring program (see Figure 1.1). However, an appreciation and understanding of military culture is what truly determines the long-term success of any veteran-hiring and retention initiative.

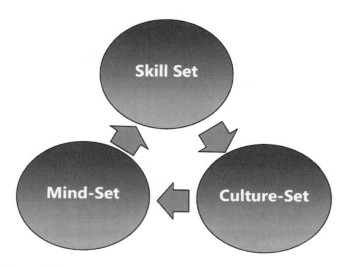

Figure 1.1. Beyond skill sets

We've titled this chapter of the book "Military 401" for a very specific reason. Many veteran-hiring resources focus on providing employers with lists of military service–related mottos, duty descriptions, and rank insignias. While these pieces of information are certainly valuable, we felt that it was necessary to move from this "Military 101" to the graduate 401 level by demystifying who veterans are and what they can and will bring to your organization. By focusing on the culture and mind-set of these men and women, organizations can bridge the cultural divide between employers and veterans. Based on the vast "sea of goodwill" described in the preface of this book, there's never been a greater appreciation of the service and sacrifices of veterans. The challenge, however, is to translate that appreciation into understanding, as goodwill is not a good foundation of any long-term, sustainable, and business-focused veteran-hiring program.

In this chapter, we lay the groundwork for many of the subsequent chapters of the book by providing readers with both insight and context to the central question: Who is today's veteran, and what can they bring to my organization?

So much of the success of recruiting, transitioning, and retraining veterans is contingent on an appreciation of who you're hiring—beyond myth and misperception. While it's impossible to collectively define all 18.5 million veterans in one broad brush stroke, it is possible to dispel many long-established stereotypes by providing analytical and anecdotal insights into the culture, demographics, and mind-sets of today's veterans. However, before all of that, it's important to understand the context of the very decision that brought that veteran employee to your doorstep—the decision to leave military service.

LEAVING THE HUDDLE IS NOT EASY—BUT NEARLY 250,000 DO IT EVERY YEAR

Successfully transitioning to civilian culture is challenging for many reasons. One of these reasons is that for many who have served—regardless of the length of service, branch, or specific occupation—the military is ingrained in who they are. That sense of belonging and camaraderie has been compared to the transition many professional athletes experience at the end of their careers. Former NFL quarterback Peyton Manning, who spent eighteen years in the NFL, recently reflected on what he missed most about the game he played his entire adult life: "The huddle. Not the touchdown passes, Super Bowl victories—I miss the huddle."[1]

Later in the book (Chapter 6), we explore how you can build a program that helps your veteran employees recapture that "huddle," but for now it's important to realize that many veterans looking to become a part of your organization are leaving a part of who they are behind. And while many do so readily, they may not have a full appreciation of the impact of that decision until they are well into the next phase of their professional lives.

For most veterans, our time in uniform is defined by both passion and purpose and there's a sobering reality that strikes us as we wear it for the final time, transitioning from the "we will" culture of the military to the "at will" reality of the civilian workforce. It's not the rank on the collar or the awards across the chest that define that experience; rather, it's the collective sense of belonging and feeling of making a difference that some veterans worry they may never recapture. That's why picking the job that's *right* rather than one that's *right now* is so very important. Serving in an organization that understands and appreciates the challenges of assimilation and the inherent value veterans bring to the organization makes all the difference in the world.

Most service members who transition do so of their own accord, in their own time, and the overwhelming majority do so long before retirement. In fact, according to Department of Defense statistics, in 2015 only 17 percent of service members departed with a retirement pension.[2] So, given that few reach that retirement milestone and most know they are leaving a part of them behind, the question remains: Why do service members leave the military?

Of course, the military is an extremely diverse organization, full of individuals who all have unique perspectives on life, and each person makes decisions based on their own set of circumstances. Nevertheless, here are three reasons that many veterans cite:

1. **Stability over Service**—Since September 11, 2001, roughly 2.7 million service members have been deployed to combat operations in Iraq

and Afghanistan combined. This does not account for the hundreds of thousands of other active duty, Reserve, and National Guard service members who've been forward deployed to other overseas duty stations and military posts in support of more than a decade and a half of continuous combat operations. The long-term effects of this "optempo" (operational tempo) have certainly had an impact on many who've served in our all-volunteer force during this unprecedented period. Perhaps, even more importantly, this pace of deployments has influenced military families: the adage is that recruiters enlist Soldiers, Marines, Sailors, and Airmen; recruiters *reenlist* families. So many veterans have had to make the choice between serving their country and managing the effects of multiple deployments on their families, and over recent years, several military careers have been cut short by the reality of needing to choose stability over service.

2. **Bureaucracy and Opportunity**—Despite the fact that it is the best trained, best resourced, and most professional military in the world,[3] there are certain constraints felt by the US Armed Forces. While there is a very specific career path for the professional development of both enlisted service members and officers alike—across all branches—the reality is that there is not a significant amount of individual flexibility, in either the timetables or the opportunities for advancement. In short, while high-achieving service members value their opportunity to serve their country, they feel at times that the built-in bureaucracy of the services stifles their professional growth.

3. **Time for a New Challenge**—Beyond deployments, family considerations, and opportunities for career growth, there are veterans who quite simply find themselves looking for a new challenge. The very spirit that inspired them to join the military in the first place causes them to accept a new challenge outside of uniform. In fact, most service members want to do something very different from what they did in uniform when they transition, whether that's getting an MBA and starting a corporate career, teaching middle school, or starting their own business. These veterans have fulfilled their goal of serving their country and are ready for that next purpose-driven mission.

A quarter of a million veterans transition each year. They head to universities, trade schools, private companies, the government sector, and nonprofits, and start their own businesses. All of their new career journeys are simultaneously unique and similar. Now that you have a better understanding of the reasons they've decided to transition from military service, it's time to take a closer look at who today's veteran workforce really is.

How do we educate and empower both the veteran and the organization to take advantage of opportunities and create hiring programs that are good business for everyone? We start by breaking down the barriers of communication and dispelling the myths and misperceptions these barriers have created. Then, we find common ground where businesses, hiring managers, and HR professionals see veterans for who they are: ordinary human beings who've earned and learned some remarkable skills through extraordinary circumstances, and who now aspire to bring those skills into the everyday workplace in a meaningful way. If you label veterans "heroes" based solely on our appreciation for their service in uniform, you effectively keep them at arm's length and are no closer to appreciating the everyday value they can bring to your organization. At the same time, if veterans continue to feel that they are misunderstood (as 70–80 percent indicated in a recent University of Southern California study[4]) and their skill sets are underappreciated, then they too will perpetuate this continual cycle of misperception. Both parties have a responsibility to find common ground. While the divide in communication and understanding certainly exists, it's certainly not born of ill will, and that's news that should inspire veterans and organizations alike.

UNDERSTANDING TODAY'S VETERANS: EIGHT FACTS TO BREAK DOWN BARRIERS AND STEREOTYPES

Like any large and historically significant organization, the US Armed Forces has its own unique culture, language, and way of doing business. Given that at any point in time, less than 1 percent of the country's citizens are currently serving in the military, exposure to this language and culture is quite limited. In fact, much of the country's understanding of the military is driven by movies, TV shows, and short sound bites from various news sources. For organizations to effectively transition from veteran friendly to veteran ready, hiring managers and HR professionals need to have a deeper understanding of the institution and the people who've served within its ranks. Here are eight facts that demystify both the culture and the institution.

Fact 1: Only 14 percent of the active duty military are combat specialists.

In many cases, the civilian world only sees tactical training, a by-product of a purposeful attempt to market and project our military's strength. These combat specialties, however, are only a small percentage of the overall military, with nearly nine in ten occupational specialties directly linked to similar and transferable civilian occupations. Whether it's an HR professional, mechanic, medic, construction engineer, or any of the several hundred administrative and support jobs, each of these military specialties has an everyday, routine business application to them that may not be glamorous but is certainly transferable to the civilian workforce. While there are some challenges in terms of gaining civilian credentials and licenses, those who have served in these roles are able to continue in them as they transition to the civilian workforce.

In the everyday world of employment there's not always a crisis to solve or a war to win, and believe it or not, it's the same in the military. A significant amount of time is spent doing the mundane everyday tasks that civilians do, but the unique bond between service members is what makes even the most mundane tasks meaningful. Yes, every Marine is a Marine first, and every Soldier is a Soldier first, on through the branches; they are all prepared to serve in combat regardless of their occupational specialty. However, they are also highly trained and highly versed in nearly all the roles civilian organizations are recruiting for.

Fact 2: As the nation has grown more diverse, so have the armed forces.

In today's workplace, organizations large and small across all industries strive to create both a diverse and inclusive workplace. Based on historical numbers or perceived stereotypes, many recruiting this diverse workforce assume that the military is not the place to start. That assumption couldn't be further from the truth. The reality is that as the private sector has focused on these diversity initiatives, so has the military. During what's called the post-9/11 period of military service—2001 to at least 2018—the demographics of those who serve our military have changed significantly, with a more ethnically diverse cohort than ever before. According to Department of Defense statistics, racial and ethnic minority groups made up 40 percent of the active duty military in 2015, up from 25 percent in 1990.[5] As a frame of reference, in 2015, 44 percent of all Americans ages 18 to 44 identified as racial or ethnic minorities. African-American people account for 17 percent of the active duty military—four percentage points higher than their share of the US population ages eighteen to forty-four (13 percent). The percentage of Hispanic service members has increased by 33 percent over the last decade as well, probably a by-product of both the increasing population and a historically strong tie between military service and Hispanic culture.[6] Organizations that are committed to recruiting an ethnically diverse workforce should know that the military has followed suit, or, as it has in previous generations, led the way in providing equal opportunities for a diverse group of service members.

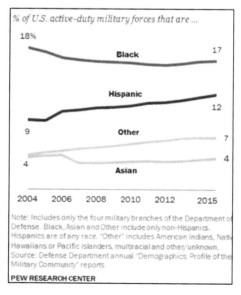

Figure 1.2. Profile of military communities

Fact 3: Women play an ever-increasing role in the military.

According a Pew Research Center study, the percentage of women in military service is now at 16 percent and growing.[7] While this percentage varies across the services, there are now more women serving in the armed forces than ever before. Nearly one in three of the roughly 1.8 million female veterans served in our military since 9/11—by far the largest cohort of female veterans. Because of the asymmetrical nature of the wars in Iraq and Afghanistan and shifts in DoD policy, we've seen a new generation of female veterans who have combat experience serving in roles and occupational specialties once reserved for their male counterparts. Serving side-by-side, men and women are colocated on bases throughout forward-deployed areas, and, according to most accounts, have remained singularly focused on the mission. Steven Meyers, author of *Women at Arms: Living and Fighting Alongside Men, and Fitting In*, writes that while some had reservations as to how these policy changes would affect morale and combat readiness, much of this change has occurred without issue: "The wars in Iraq and Afghanistan 'have cultivated a new generation of women with a warrior's ethos—and combat experience—that for millennia was almost exclusively the preserve of men. This change has occurred without the disruption of discipline and unit cohesion that some feared would unfold.'"[8]

What does this mean for hiring managers and businesses? First, you will continue to see an ever-increasing number of female veterans who've served their country in exactly the same manner their male counterparts have served. Second, and perhaps equally important, significantly fewer male veterans served in "gender isolation," whether they were deployed to active combat or served here in the United States. Gender equality in the workplace is an essential element of any successful business, and for today's veterans, these shifts in policy and inclusive practices foster this principle long before they transition to the civilian workforce.

Fact 4: More veterans are college-educated now than ever before, with rates surpassing those of civilians.

There was a time, not that long ago, when there were two distinct, divergent paths: the path for those who went to college and the path for those who

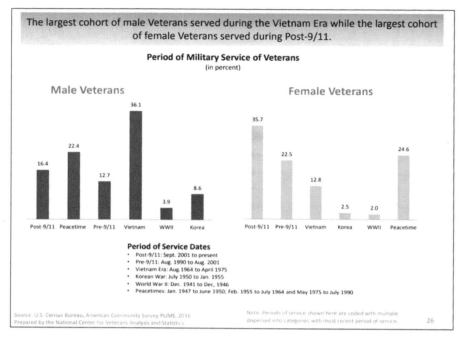

Figure 1.3. Period of service of veterans
Source: National Center for Veterans Analysis and Statistics, Profile of Veterans 2015: Data from the American Community Survey (Washington, DC: US Department of Veterans Affairs 2016), https://www.va.gov/vetdata/docs/SpecialReports/Profile_of_Veterans_2016.pdf.

joined the military—and never did the two meet.[9] Times have certainly changed. Because of a highly competitive military recruiting market and the implementation of the Post-9/11 GI Bill, we've seen a dramatic shift and significant increase in the level of education our service members have achieved before, during, and immediately following their time in service. While military officers have habitually outpaced their nonveteran counterparts in both bachelor's and advanced degrees, now the overall cohort of both officers and enlisted service members are on par with and, in certain demographics (female veterans), surpass their nonveteran counterparts. If you look at only post-9/11 veterans (enlisted and officer), there are more with some college, bachelor's degrees, and advanced degrees than there are nonveterans in the same cohort. The bottom line is that whether your candidate served for four years as an enlisted Marine or is an Air Force officer who retired after twenty years, veterans are likely to have a much higher

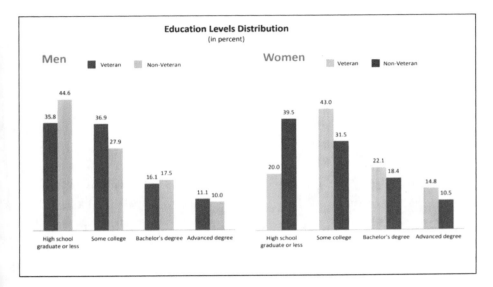

Figure 1.4. Veteran education levels
Source: National Center for Veterans Analysis and Statistics, Profile of Veterans 2015: Data from the American Community Survey (Washington, DC: US Department of Veterans Affairs 2016), https://www.va.gov/vetdata/docs/SpecialReports/Profile_of_Veterans_2016.pdf.

level of education than in years past. Even if you have a candidate who hasn't achieved a college degree, it's very likely that they have some college, and with the Post-9/11 GI Bill, they are more than likely looking to finish that degree in conjunction with their transition from military service.

Fact 5: Veterans are agile and don't require hierarchy to thrive.

Hiring managers within "flat" organizations may assume that veteran candidates would not be right for their organizations based on the assumption that veterans require very specific structure and guidance to thrive. In fact, veterans have had trouble breaking through in specific industries (tech companies, startups) because of the assumption that these organizations function outside of the veteran's cultural comfort zone. The fact is that most veterans operated in very fluid and asymmetric environments, where accomplishing the mission required both autonomy and agility. Whether it's as part of a small team in remote Afghanistan, or as part of a larger team here in the United States, service members thrive when given an objective—not a specific laundry list of tasks. The "why" of the mission is just as important as the "how" of the mission—if not more so. With the right resources and training, veterans are both agile and autonomous in operating as part of a team or leading one.

Fact 6: Nearly four in ten service members are "warrior citizens" (Reserve and National Guard members).

The Reserve and National Guard components make up 38 percent of the overall military, serving in communities across the country (see Table 1.1). While many have served alongside their active duty counterparts in the conflicts in Afghanistan and Iraq, typical Reserve and National Guard service members traditionally serve in uniform while simultaneously holding down jobs in their communities. These Reserve and National Guard members—historically labeled "warrior citizens"—are teachers, doctors, lawyers, students, and employees of all shapes and sizes, balancing the dual responsibilities of service to their country and obligation to the organizations in their communities. Many don't necessarily serve in the same role in uniform that they do in their civilian jobs. They do, however, call upon many of the leadership and professional skills they've fostered during their time in uniform.

Balancing and managing these two roles and cultures is not without its challenges. Reserve and National Guard units serve in isolated pockets, at times far removed from the resources and support of military instillations. Psychologically, the prospect of postdeployment reintegration is daunting as well. While their active duty counterparts return to military communities that wholeheartedly embrace their return, Reserve and National Guard members return to their civilian communities and occupations with less fanfare and a sense that they are playing catch-up as they reassume their civilian roles. The warrior citizen's ability to adapt and adjust to these circumstances clearly demonstrates their agility and resilience and has served as the model for active duty members as they transition from the military. In many ways, this cohort is a microcosm of how veterans in general can accept the challenges of transitioning. It's often said that there is no greater challenge than the commitment of a Reservist or National Guard member. Nevertheless, tens of thousands of them thrive every day in their civilian careers, bringing the best of who they are in uniform to their workplace, no matter the job.

Table 1.1. Manpower by service component

TABLE 2 Manpower by Service Component IN THOUSANDS	Active	National Guard	Reserve	Reserve Component (percent)
Army	490.0	350.2	202.0	53%
Navy	323.6	-	47.3	13%
Air Force	310.9	105.0	67.1	36%
Marines	184.1	-	39.2	18%
Total Force	**1,308.6**	**455.2**	**355.6**	**38%**

Source: U.S. Department of Defense, Office of the Assistant Secretary of Defense for Readiness and Force Management, Total Force Planning and Requirements Directorate, *Defense Manpower Requirements Report, Fiscal Year 2015*, June 2014, p. 2, Table 1-1, http://prhome.defense.gov/Portals/52/Documents/RFM/TFPRQ/docs/F15%20DMRR.pdf (accessed August 14, 2015).

Source: Total Force Planning Requirements Directorate, Defense Manpower Requirements Report, Fiscal Year 2015 (Washington, DC: Office of the Assistant Secretary of Defense for Readiness and Force Management, June 2014), 2, Table 1-1, http://prhome.defense.gov/portals/52/documents/RFM/TFPRQ/docs/fl5%20DMRR.pdf.

Fact 7: Behind most veterans is a family, and families serve too.

There's an old saying in the US Marine Corps (and the Army as well) that if the Marines wanted you to have a family, they would have issued you one. Times and attitudes certainly have changed. In fact, while marriage rates within the civilian community continue to decrease, today's veterans continue to embrace the institution—at least until they get divorced.

Of all men who are veterans, 80 percent are either married or divorced, compared to 58 percent of men who are not veterans. More than 70 percent women who are veterans are either married or divorced, compared to 60 percent of their nonveteran counterparts.[10] This is significant because veterans are more likely to have experienced specific life stages (such as having a family) than their nonveteran counterparts, which certainly shapes the benefits and work environments that these veterans are looking for. There's a saying that every veteran with a family truly appreciates: military families serve too.

Children of veterans have experienced multiple moves, various schools, and continuous change from an early age. Additionally, many spouses place their own careers on the backburner to support their significant other's military career. While veterans are very used to and willing to commit to long hours, significant travel, and whatever it takes to get the mission done, these family considerations may play a significant role in their willingness to do so. At the end of what may have been a very challenging operational cycle, many veterans are looking for opportunities to support the stability of their families and achieve some semblance of a work-life balance that places the needs of their families on par with their postmilitary careers.

Fact 8: Serving in uniform was the first choice of many options.

The narrative of reinventing oneself through military service has been the hallmark of many movies and TV shows, and even the focal point of many military recruiting campaigns. This narrative may lead many Americans to presume that the decision to join the military is born of necessity rather than choice. The reality of today's all-volunteer force and the thousands of men and women who join its ranks every year, however, is that the clear majority do so as the first choice of many opportunities that they may have. Given the range of options and opportunities in front of these young men and women the question remains: Why do they choose military service? A 2011 Pew Research Center study found that the top reason recruits join the military is directly tied to the very principle of service itself.[11]

Nearly 90 percent of recruits say the primary reason they joined the military was to serve. Additionally, 75 percent joined for the educational benefits, which are a primary factor in the ever-increasing level of education veterans have as they transition back to civilian life. Just over half joined to gain a job skill or training. What's telling, however, is that fewer and fewer recruits (less than one-third) joined the military because they faced challenges finding civilian employment. Service members have always joined to serve their country—that's certainly not a new phenomenon. What's changed over recent decades is that highly qualified young men and women are joining the military's ranks as a first choice over several other opportunities.

 **LEARNING POINT**

Military Phrases to Help You Understand Military Culture

While many professions and institutions have their share of acronyms, mottos, and catch phrases, when it comes to sheer volume, the military is in a class all its own. From official acronyms such as PMCS (Preventative Maintenance Checks and Services) to the not-so-official ones such as ROAD (Retired on Active Duty), each of the branches has its own unique slang, and there are some universal sayings that capture the common ethos between all the services. While the phrases themselves may be unique to the military, the principles they represent are not.

1. **"Good initiative, poor judgment."** This phrase applies when somebody steps up to solve a problem but doesn't necessarily apply the best or well-thought-out solutions. Generally, this action shows good initiative because the problem might have been above the pay grade of person trying to solve it and they took the initiative nonetheless. In military circles, the act of taking charge and making things happen is seen as a positive, even if permission was not fully granted and the result not fully achieved.

   How it translates to the civilian workplace: While it is conventional, the military is some-times less hierarchical than the civilian workplace, so taking initiative without permission can certainly create challenges. While veterans may be used to the premise that taking charge is paramount they may need to temper that initiative and conform to established protocols.

2. **"No pride in ownership."** The basic principle behind this phrase is that ideas, products, and solutions can only be improved if you are willing to set aside ownership and egos and allow the group to take what you have created and make it better. Military leaders serve for a very finite period; it's the units they lead that are lasting. So, who owns it is less important than how it's implemented, as initial ideas rarely resemble the end product, and the person who came up with the initial concept might very well be long gone.

   How it translates to the civilian workplace: With less potential turnover and the realities of merit-based bonuses and evaluations, it's not quite as easy to say, "Take my idea and make it your own." Veteran employees can find themselves at odds with a culture that requires them to take credit for success when they are focused on the singular goal of accomplishing the mission.

3. **"Who else needs to know?"** Who needs this information, and who needs to take part in the process of making the decision? These are the most important questions you ask both yourself and those around you. Information is as powerful as any weapon in military, and serving as part of a collective group that's entrusted with this information and making decisions is truly rewarding.

   How it translates to the civilian workplace: When in positions of leadership, veterans will look to inform a robust team. When they are not serving in a leadership role, simply being a part of the decision process is as important as any title or position. For most veterans, there's nothing worse than the slow and certain death of being excluded from meetings, group huddles, and brainstorming sessions. If you're a supervisor and you think you're doing your veteran employee a favor saving them from another meeting, think again, because in the military culture they came from, being in the loop is all that matters.

4. **"You can delegate authority but not responsibility."** Anyone who's served in a leadership role in the military, regardless of the branch, type, or size of the unit, knows that responsi-bility lies squarely on their shoulders. Leaders must, however, decentralize their efforts and give both autonomy and authority to their subordinate leaders as well. When things go well, praise is widely distributed throughout the unit. When things don't go well and the mission is not completed, responsibility falls squarely on the shoulders of the leader. That's, as they say, why leaders get paid the big bucks.

How it translates to the civilian workplace: Veterans will look to their leaders and supervisors, anticipating that they will empower them with autonomy while simultaneously providing them with top-cover when they need it. When in positions of leadership, veterans will entrust their direct reports with the authority and resources they need to succeed, but if for whatever unforeseen reason things go wrong, they will readily assume responsibility because it's what has been ingrained in them from their time in uniform.

5. **"Got your six!"** This phrase is all about loyalty. While each of the services has its own mottos and values, perhaps the one with the most universal appeal is loyalty. Having someone's "six" means that you have their back, no matter what, both in times of combat and metaphorically in the garrison back home. No matter the time of day, circumstances, or cost, having someone's six is sacrosanct.

How it translates to the civilian workplace: While there are a few service-related professions that share this mentality (first responders, etc.), it's unlikely that most veterans who transition to the civilian workforce will recapture this sentiment in their postmilitary careers. That reality is probably one of the bigger assimilation challenges veterans face. Trust, commitment, and loyalty are not forged overnight and seldom occur in the confines of today's workplace.

Today's veteran is a diverse, educated, family-focused, and skills-trained individual who's capable of achieving remarkable things within your workforce. Now that you have a better understanding of the cultural makeup and mind-set of this diverse group, you can go through the next chapters of this book with the knowledge that both veterans and employers must be willing to demystify the cultural barriers between us.

ENDNOTES

1. Arnie Stapleton, "Retirement Not on Peyton Manning's Radar," Associated Press, June 22, 2014, https://pro32.ap.org/article/retirement-not-peyton-mannings-radar.
2. Department of Defense, *2015 Demographics: Profile of the Military Community*, http://download.militaryonesource.mil/12038/MOS/Reports/2015-Demographics-Report.pdf.
3. Logan Nye, "The Top 10 Militaries of the World in 2017," *Military.com*, August 4, 2017, https://www.military.com/undertheradar/2017/08/top-10-militaries-world-2017.
4. Sara Kintzle, Janice M. Rasheed, and Carl A. Castro, *The State of the American Veteran: The Chicagoland Veterans Study* (Chicago: Loyola University Chicago, 2016), http://cir.usc.edu/wp-content/uploads/2016/04/CIR_ChicagoReport_double.pdf.
5. Department of Defense, *2015 Demographics*, v.
6. Department of Defense, 8.

7. Kristen Bialik, "The Changing Face of America's Veteran Population," *Pew Research Center*, November 10, 2017, http://www.pewresearch.org/fact-tank/2017/11/10/the-changing-face-of-americas-veteran-population/.

8. Steven L. Meyers, "Women at Arms: Living and Fighting Alongside Men, and Fitting In," *New York Times*, August 16, 2009, https://nyti.ms/2kp2Tx0.

9. National Center for Veterans Analysis and Statistics, *Profile of Veterans 2015: Data from the American Community Survey* (Washington, DC: US Department of Veterans Affairs 2016), https://www.va.gov/vetdata/docs/SpecialReports/Profile_of_Veterans_2016.pdf.

10. National Center for Veterans Analysis, 8.

11. Rich Morin, "The Difficult Transition from Military to Civilian Life," *Pew Research Center*, December 8, 2011, http://www.pewsocialtrends.org/2011/12/08/the-difficult-transition-from-military-to-civilian-life/.

CHAPTER 2

The Business Case for Hiring Veterans

Hard work is a buzz term that we regularly use when describing military veterans. But when we dig deeper and go beyond the simple platitude, we find a real business case for hiring veterans. Veterans do not waste their day playing with their phones or going through social media. Throughout every moment of the work day, veterans are going at full speed to complete every task that is presented to them, because that is what they were trained to do. This level of determination and commitment is what every employer is desperate to find in a candidate, and they can always find it in a military veteran.

—Jack Fanous, Founder and CEO of JobPath

In 2016, SHRM reported that more than two-thirds of surveyed organizations hiring full-time staff were having a difficult time recruiting for job openings.[1] Veterans often possess the experience, capabilities, attitude, and desire for these open positions, but are overlooked because potential employers do not understand how to connect with these veterans.

This same SHRM report also found that 84 percent of HR professionals reported applied-skills shortages in job applicants over the last year. The most commonly reported missing applied skills were

- Critical thinking and problem-solving (45 percent),
- Professionalism and work ethic (43 percent),
- Leadership (35 percent),
- Written communications (29 percent), and
- Teamwork and collaboration (28 percent).

As you will see, veterans excel at each of these skills, but many managers and senior leaders are not fully aware of the business case for hiring veterans and military spouses.

As a general matter, veterans are entering the workforce with a wide variety of skills and abilities and varying amounts of time in the military. They have also all benefited from some of the most advanced training in the world, having learned skills and values such as leadership, mission accomplishment, teamwork, and integrity. They have all learned how to be responsible for others, whether for a few at the lowest levels of responsibility or up to hundreds or thousands of others at a time. They have been entrusted to make critical decisions and find creative solutions to unforeseen obstacles, often in the most austere environments.

 **LEARNING POINT**

Since Memorial Day 2013, Walmart has hired more than 194,000 veterans, and more than 28,000 have been promoted to roles of greater responsibility. Veterans can explore career options with the company at www.walmartcareerswithamission.com.

This training starts at the very beginning of their time in the military. Civilians may think that boot camp is simply a torturous period designed to weed out those who may not succeed in the military, but that is far from the truth. It is during this initial basic training that new recruits start to learn the valuable skills of teamwork, leadership, and discipline that will be the backbone of their experience in the military. All service members share this core skill set, and they continue to develop it as they are promoted through the ranks, where they embrace more responsibility and attend a wider variety of schools and training. This only crystallizes more when serving in challenging operational environments that require incredible initiative and fortitude.

BREAKOUT BOX

Who Is a Veteran?

38 U.S.C. § 101 defines a veteran as "a person who served in the active military, naval, or air service, and who was discharged or released therefrom under conditions other than dishonorable."[2] For our purposes, a veteran is defined as anyone who served on active duty in any job capacity while a member of the US Army, Navy, Air Force, Marines, or Coast Guard active components, or of the US National Guard or Reserves, and was not discharged dishonorably.

When we talk about one of today's veterans, we are talking about someone who signed a blank check to our country saying that they were prepared to pay whatever price necessary to ensure our way of life here at home. Some veterans have never deployed, while others may have deployed many times. Some veterans might have been trained in the toughest possible environments, but are now looking for careers that takes advantage of their other skills and abilities. Also, when I talk about our veterans, I include in that group military spouses and caregivers, who are a critical part of any veteran-hiring program.

You want operational experience and someone you can trust? You want someone encouraged to take the initiative, but who also fully believes in the value of teamwork? You want someone who believes in merit-based promotion and has been entrusted to make critical decisions in the blink of an eye? Look no further.

Today's veterans are coming out of the military with an incredible array of skills and abilities. Many of them worked in tech-related fields, and just about everybody has served in some sort of leadership capacity. Each veteran was an important part of a team that had to work long hours to accomplish the mission and meet hard deadlines. These veterans will show up for work on time, take the initiative when appropriate, and will not quit until the job is done.

"QUOTABLE"

"The technology skills obtained in the service are transferable to the civilian sector. With some assistance in education, employment, and entrepreneurship, many veterans are well-suited to jobs in the tech ecosystem."

–Katherine Webster, Founder of VetsinTech

BREAKOUT BOX

Hiring Veterans for Leadership and Not a Specific Skill Set

At Greencastle Associates Consulting, we have been hiring veterans exclusively for twenty years within the project management field. As veterans and business owners, we know the value that a veteran brings to our organization. Leadership, emotional intelligence, mission-first attitude, expertise in problem-solving—all skills that are hard to teach in a seminar or college. The military training our employees have completed allows us to work on extremely difficult, confusing, and often ambiguous projects that our clients are trying to undertake.

We don't hire veterans because they are experts in energy or telecommunications. We hire veterans because they are self-starters and leaders. We teach them the industry skills they need to succeed. But by leveraging their inherent skills for "getting things done," any organization can benefit by hiring a veteran.

—Joe Crandall, Partner at Greencastle Associates Consulting

Often, companies hire veterans out of a sense of patriotism or social responsibility, or for the public relations value of doing so. But veterans are not looking for pity or tokenism. A far more compelling reason is that hiring veterans can positively affect your bottom line and benefit your company in meaningful ways. In fact, a number of recent industry studies and academic reports support the business case for hiring veterans.

As detailed in a report from the Center for a New American Security (CNAS), veterans have strong leadership and teamwork skills; they are largely reliable, trustworthy, dependable, and drug-free; they bring discipline and safe processes to the workplace; and they have the right expertise for companies. Additionally, employers praised veterans' effectiveness, resiliency, loyalty, and ability to make decisions in dynamic circumstances.[3] What these veterans bring to the marketplace will help your company, whether it is small, medium, or large.

"QUOTABLE"

"Most of the men and women of today's all-volunteer force joined the military to challenge themselves and to serve others. The majority of veterans want to take on new challenges and continue to serve as a valued member of a team. America's business owners and hiring managers would certainly benefit from adaptive, hardworking employees who are able to anticipate change, multitask and work well under pressure. In short, there is a strong business case for hiring US military veterans."

—William B. Caldwell IV and Crispin J. Burke in *America's Veterans: A Sound Investment*[4]

These companies mentioned multiple reasons to hire veterans, and more than three-fourths of them provided three or more reasons.

BREAKOUT BOX

Top Reasons Companies Hire Veterans, According to Employing America's Veterans[5]

- Veterans have leadership and teamwork skills that companies value.
- Veterans' character makes them good employees.
- Veterans are disciplined, follow processes well, and operate safely.
- Veterans have expertise that companies seek.
- Veterans adapt and perform well in dynamic environments.
- Veterans are effective employees.
- Hiring veterans is the "right thing to do."
- Other veterans in the organization have been successful.
- Veterans are resilient.
- Veterans are loyal to their organizations.
- Hiring veterans carries public relations benefits.

Veterans are not embraced by just a small number of industries; their backgrounds and training have helped them thrive in industries as diverse as healthcare, financial services, IT, construction, hotel and restaurant management, and advanced manufacturing. Tracey Shoemaker, director of talent acquisition at CarMax, says, "We are actively recruiting men and women with military backgrounds because they share our core values of integrity, respect, and honesty, and naturally make a great fit." Other companies' efforts are listed below:

- First Data, a major financial services firm, has increased the percentage of veteran and military-spouse new hires by more than 10 percent in two years, and has a dedicated talent acquisition team focusing on recruiting veterans, National Guard members, Reservists, and military spouses.
- In 2013, Starbucks committed to hiring at least 10,000 veterans and military spouses by 2018. In March 2017, they announced that they had met their goal 18 months early and expanded their goal to 25,000 by 2025.
- Amazon currently employs more than 10,000 veterans and military spouses, and has pledged to hire 25,000 veterans and military spouses by 2021, and to train 10,000 more in cloud computing skills through AWS Educate.
- Microsoft hosts Microsoft Software and Systems Academy (MSSA), an intense eighteen-week training course that provides aspiring veterans and transitioning service members with the career skills required for today's growing technology industry. More than 280 companies have hired MSSA graduates. The program has a 92 percent employment rate.
- Since 2013, Hilton has hired more than 10,000 veterans and military spouses and has committed to hiring an additional 20,000 by the end of 2020.
- In 2016 alone, the Hospital Corporation of America (HCA) hired over 5,400 military veterans and 1,100 military spouses.

The list goes on and on!

Academic studies also support corporations that decide to hire veterans because they are good for business.

"QUOTABLE"

"Specifically, academic research from the fields of business, psychology, sociology, and decision-making strongly links characteristics that are generally representative of military veterans to enhanced performance and organizational advantage in the context of a competitive and dynamic business environment. In other words, the academic research supports a robust, specific, and compelling business case for hiring individuals with military background and experience."

—Institute for Veterans and Military Families (Syracuse University),
The Business Case for Hiring a Veteran: Beyond the Clichés[6]

Specifically, the Institute for Veterans and Military Families (IVMF) at Syracuse University issued a brief in 2012 that surveyed relevant academic research and compiled a detailed list of attributes that are critical in the business world and shared by many veterans. Some of those attributes are included in the following list, which is reproduced faithfully but trimmed for length:[7]

1. **Veterans Assume High Levels of Trust:** The ability to trust coworkers and superiors has been consistently highlighted in organizational behavior literature as a significant predictor of high-performing teams, organizational cohesion and morale, and effective governance systems. Research indicates that military service engenders a strong propensity toward an inherent trust and faith in coworkers, and also a strong propensity toward trust in organizational leadership.

2. **Veterans Are Adept at Skills Transfer Across Contexts/Tasks:** The ability to recognize and act on opportunities to transfer skills learned in a specific context, to a disparate context, represents a valuable organizational resource. Several studies focused on skills transfer have highlighted that military service members and veterans are particularly skilled in this ability.

3. **Veterans Have [and Leverage] Advanced Technical Training:** Military experience, on average, exposes individuals to highly advanced technology and technology training at a rate that is accelerated relative to nonmilitary, age group peers. Research validates the suggestion that this accelerated exposure to high-technology contributes to an enhanced ability to link technology-based solutions to organizational challenges, and also the transfer of technological skills to disparate work-tasks.

4. **Veterans Are Comfortable/Adept in Discontinuous Environments:** The contemporary business environment is dynamic and uncertain, and research consistently highlights the organizational advantage conferred to firms that are able to act quickly and decisively in the face of uncertainty and change. Cognitive and decision-making research has demonstrated that the military experience is positively correlated to the ability to accurately evaluate a dynamic decision environment, and subsequently act in the face of uncertainty.

5. **Veterans Exhibit Advanced Team-Building Skills:** Several studies have compared military service-members and veterans to nonveterans in the context of team-building skills and efficacy. Findings from that research illustrate that veterans are more adept with regard to: (1) organizing and defining team goals and mission; (2) defining team member roles and responsibilities; and (3) developing a plan for action. Further, research also suggests that veterans exhibit an inherent and enduring belief that they can efficiently and effectively integrate and contribute to a new or existing team.

EMPIRICAL EVIDENCE TO SUPPORT THE BUSINESS CASE FOR HIRING VETERANS

As a matter of course, organizations still struggle to find high-quality talent. A 2012 CEB (now Gartner) Corporate Leadership Council study determined that traditional recruiting pools are not paying off. [8] Among more than two hundred surveyed companies, there exists a 16 percent turnover rate among all employees, and a 23 percent turnover rate among new hires. However, they found that the turnover rate for veterans is only 13 percent. They also determined that, on average, veterans perform at higher levels than nonveterans. Together, these trends result in better business outcomes and cost savings for the corporations.

The low rate of turnover by itself is a significant factor in the business case for hiring veterans. The high attrition cost (up to eighteen months' salary for each manager or professional who leaves and up to six months' pay for each hourly employee) can add up quickly. Thus, the difference of just a few percentage points in the turnover rate between veterans and nonveterans should resonate with you. On top of this, with the lower turnover rate associated with hiring veterans, you will see reduced recruitment and training costs as well as fewer inefficiencies during training for replacement hires.

"QUOTABLE"

"CarMax is proud to honor and support our nation's veterans and those who are currently serving our country. Veterans, active duty military, and military families bring significant value to the success of CarMax and our continued growth for the future."

—Bill Nash, CEO of CarMax

Further, as reported by IVMF at Syracuse University, the attrition rate for veteran employees at GE is 7 percent lower than for nonveteran employees. Similarly, TriWest reports that absenteeism from work is lower among military employees. Both of these findings equate to significant cost savings and increased productivity from veteran employees.[9]

BREAKOUT BOX

Veterans Are Trained to Be Trainable

Many companies focus on the leadership qualities of veterans as the key to what makes them great employees. However, my experience has shown that leadership is only one of the things that veterans learn from their training. They were trained how to follow orders and work together as a team. They were trained how to handle complex machinery far advanced from anything they dealt with prior to their service. They were trained not only how to fight, but how to provide support to civilians and care to those who need it most. They were trained to move quickly from one area to another to perform different tasks, and to do so without skipping a beat. More than anything, they were, as one veteran put it to me years ago, trained to be trainable.

—Jack Fanous, CEO and Founder of JobPath

FIVE MYTHS (AND FACTS) ABOUT HIRING VETERANS

Simply said, it makes good business sense to hire veterans. Companies that already do so uniformly speak positively about this strategy, and the veterans often turn into leaders at those companies. Their loyalty, teamwork, initiative, respect, and leadership truly enable them to bring great value to the private sector. That being said, there still exist a handful of myths related to veterans and whether they can thrive after their time in the military.

Myth 1: Military skills don't translate into the civilian workforce.

Fact: It is well documented that veterans bring extensive leadership experience, mission focus, teamwork, and initiative to the corporate environment. Besides these and other "soft" skills, however, many service members receive security clearances for the work they do, and those clearances often remain active for two years after they leave the military. Hiring a veteran with an active clearance can save employers tens of thousands of dollars and six to twelve months in background checks. Veterans also bring with them detailed work histories and specialized training in a plethora of fields. In fact, military jobs are categorized into more than seven thousand occupational specialty codes, and a significant majority of them directly correlate to positions in the private sector. Often, jobs in the military are identical to those in the civilian sector, only more demanding.

Myth 2: All veterans served in combat.

Fact: While it is true that we have had significant numbers of troops deployed to combat since the terrorist attacks of September 11, 2001, that was not always the case. There are significant numbers of veterans in the workforce who left the military before 9/11 and never deployed, and there are also plenty of veterans from the post-9/11 generation who have never deployed. It is reported that about 80 percent of the jobs in the military are noncombat occupations, and those include roles found in the finance, logistics, administration, broadcasting, human resources, healthcare, and engineering sectors (see Figure 2.1).

Myth 3: All veterans have PTSD and it makes them unemployable.

Fact: Due in large part to military movies and stories in our media, many think that all veterans have PTSD. However, the numbers do not bear this out. Studies conclude that 10–20 percent of post-9/11 combat veterans have PTSD, which equates to approximately five hundred thousand people. Compare that number to the 8 percent of civilians in America who will

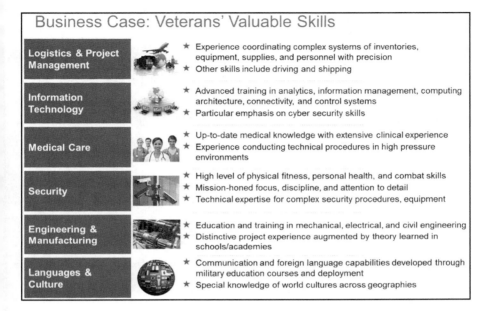

Figure 2.1. Veterans' valuable skills
Source: Institute for Veterans and Military Families, *Hiring Veterans*, 12.

experience PTSD throughout their life (often from car accidents, violent assaults, rape, natural disasters, and growing up in traumatic environments), which is approximately twenty-six million people. You are probably already used to working with, for, or around somebody with PTSD, but just do not know it. Many veterans with PTSD, like the authors of this book, have gone through counseling for it, and are excited to be part of our nation's workforce. We know what our triggers are and the appropriate responses, and how to manage a productive workload at the same time.

Myth 4: Veterans can only follow orders.

Fact: While service members certainly learn and adhere to the value of strictly following orders while in boot camp and officer candidate school, every veteran has had experience leading other people. With promotions come greater responsibility and more opportunities for initiative and creative problem-solving. The military prides itself on its leaders providing their intent, and then, without micromanaging, pushing the responsibility to accomplish the mission down to lower levels. This is especially true in a deployed environment where there are far too many variables for a commander to control, and even the most junior members make many decisions every day. Veterans are taught to accomplish the mission and get the job done, and that often involves an independent thought process.

Myth 5: National Guard and Reserve employees have unpredictable schedules.

Fact: The typical training schedule for those who continue to serve our country includes one weekend per month and two weeks in the summer. That training does not just pop up, and the details will usually be made available months in advance. This is also true in the case of a scheduled deployment. Members of the National Guard and Reserve do occasionally get called up to active duty with no notice in the case of natural disasters or emergency military deployments. However, these are opportunities for your employees to serve their community (and yours) when they are needed most, and should be understood.

Ultimately, any company can implement an effective and impactful veteran-hiring program once it puts its mind to it. As you can see from the following case study provided by Panasonic, the opportunity to do so might be right in front of you. As Panasonic realized, hiring veterans not only solved a unique employment pain point for them, but also created a pipeline for many future opportunities.

· · · · · · · · · · ·
CASE STUDY

Building a Better Workforce in Nevada: Panasonic Hires Veterans

It was late 2014 when Panasonic Corporation of North America announced the creation of Panasonic Energy of North America (Panasonic Energy), a new company dedicated to manufacturing lithium-ion battery cells for electric vehicles (EVs) in Sparks, Nevada. Although new, the company projected high growth and a long buildout schedule, anticipating continuous hiring over a period of several years. The hiring strategy fell right in line with the needs of Panasonic's manufacturing requirements, which call for hires who are analytical, compliance-focused, and team–oriented—exactly the qualities veterans bring to a team.

Panasonic Energy's talent acquisition team moved quickly to fill open positions in the new factory, but began to encounter challenges with the available work pool. Led by US Air Force veteran Kris McLean and several other service veteran recruiters, the team worked to make connections between Panasonic Energy and the large local community of US military veterans and active duty service members. The recruitment team found that the individuals in this group exhibited the skills and experience Panasonic was looking for and were well-trained leaders with a strong work ethic and goal-oriented work style. The company quickly realized how much talent was available and started coming up with new ideas to expand veteran recruitment.

Gaps and Challenges in the Available Workforce

Sparks and neighboring Reno, Nevada, are largely dependent on a seasonal tourist economy. Much of the available workforce is accustomed to short-term work in the entertainment or hospitality industry at places like ski resorts or casinos. There are also jobs available in mining, but few of these provide advancement opportunities.

Panasonic faced a shortage of highly skilled workers who could meet the requirements of the available jobs. Although the company could have looked to have internal candidates relocate to the area, it preferred to find local talent looking to develop themselves into leadership roles. Panasonic works hard to retain new hires in the long term, and the corporate culture has a focus on giving back to the community around its offices. There was a lot of discussion about whether locals would be more interested in staying on long-term and if they would be more interested in giving back to local communities, so the recruitment team had to decide: do we import talent or can we find the talent by searching smarter in Sparks and Reno? They chose the latter.

As the team increased their interactions with the local military community, they uncovered a veteran population with exactly the skills they were looking for and seized the opportunity to match job seekers exiting military service at local bases with job openings at Tesla's Gigafactory. Thanks to Sparks's proximity to bases where many new hires had once served, these employees remained engaged and embedded in the military community. This feature of the factory's location created a recruitment opportunity and offered a built-in word-of-mouth networking strategy: hires who loved their new careers encouraged others to apply as they transitioned out of the military. Encouragement quickly grew into talent acquisition programs and a strong funnel of desirable incoming talent.

Becoming a Destination

Panasonic had found a goal: to become a well-known destination for exiting vets in all branches of the service and a recommended option for employment. As the recruitment team continued hiring vets, the local military bases began to reach out to Panasonic and a real partnership developed delivering mutual benefits through the military's transition assistance program (TAP). TAP now recommends Panasonic as an ideal destination for service members moving back into civilian life and seeking civilian employment.

Panasonic Energy's recruitment team truly understands what it is like to transition from service to civilian life and understand how a veteran's résumé translates into open positions. This awareness has allowed the team to create hiring practices and interviewing techniques that level the playing field between civilian candidates and military candidates seeking managerial or office positions. This awareness also helps Panasonic showcase the variety of opportunities available in the ways that most effectively appeal to military candidates.

Today, veterans can seek diverse opportunities with Panasonic, from machine operation to finance and procurement positions. Every skill set is represented and desired.

—Linda Woodruff, VP Human Capital and Motivation,
Human Resources, Panasonic Corporation of North America

ENDNOTES

1. Roy Maurer, "This Is Why Finding Talent Is Getting Tougher in 2016," Society for Human Resource Management, June 20, 2016, https://www.shrm.org/hr-today/news/hr-news/pages/recruiting-gets-harder-in-2016.aspx.
2. Veteran's Benefits, 38 U.S.C. § 101 (2006).
3. Margaret C. Harrell and Nancy Berglass, *Employing America's Veterans: Perspectives from Businesses* (Washington, DC: Center for New American Security, 2012), https://www.

cnas.org/publications/reports/employing-americas-veterans-perspectives-from
-businesses.

4. William B. Caldwell and Crispin J. Burke, *America's Veterans: A Sound Investment* (Washington, DC: Center for New American Security, 2013), 5, https://www.cnas.org/publications/reports/americas-veterans-a-sound-investment.

5. Harrell and Berglass, *Employing America's Veterans*, 15–20.

6. Institute for Veterans and Military Families, *The Business Case for Hiring a Veteran: Beyond the Clichés* (Syracuse: Syracuse University, 2012), https://ivmf.syracuse.edu/wp-content/uploads/2016/06/The-Business-Case-for-Hiring-a-Veteran-3-6-12.pdf.

7. Institute for Veterans and Military Families, 1.

8. CEB Corporate Leadership Council, "The Business Case for Hiring Veterans," presentation, 6, https://www.cebglobal.com/human-resources/forms/military-hiring.html.

9. Institute for Veterans and Military Families, *Guide to Leading Policies, Practices and Resources: Supporting the Employment of Veterans and Military Families* (Syracuse: Syracuse University, 2016), 56, https://ivmf.syracuse.edu/wp-content/uploads/2016/07/guidetoleadingpractices1.pdf.

CHAPTER 3

Sourcing Military Talent

To be a great company, you need to hire great people! Knight Point Systems is always searching for exceptional talent. We firmly believe our success is a direct result of the people we hire. We love to hire leaders, overachievers, and people who are self-driven. All branches of the military are represented at KPS and many of our managers are retired officers and noncommissioned officers. KPS is well aware of the dependability, determination, leadership, and discipline that veteran-hires bring to an organization. KPS actively recruits veterans through our relationships with state workforce agencies, by attending military job fairs throughout the year, and by partnering with organizations like the Washington Redskins and the West Point Society of DC.

—Bob Eisiminger, CEO of Knight Point Systems

SOURCING MILITARY TALENT

You are familiar with the business case for hiring veterans and military spouses, and your organization is committed to doing just that. Inevitably, the next couple of questions are then, "Where do I find the veterans? Is there one website where I can connect with the ones I am looking for?" Unfortunately, just like with the other types of job seekers you are searching for, there is no one-stop shop that will answer all your needs. That being said, there are a wide variety of resources for you to use in connecting with hardworking veterans, and they typically fall into several different categories.

Naturally, federal, state, and local government entities and agencies have a variety of programs to help employers and job-seeking veterans. There are also quite a number of nonprofit and at-cost resources available to you as well. To make things easier, in this book we will simply classify the selected resources as governmental, nongovernmental, and veterans service organizations. Please keep in mind that while we are showcasing a number of the more well-known organizations, this is not an exhaustive list.

BREAKOUT BOX

Sourcing Military Talent

Veterans are provided with many avenues to seek employment. It's incumbent on the employer to take full advantage of intercepting these service members and veterans at various steps in their transition experience. Partnering with the transition offices well in advance of the member's separation is a proven method. Exhibiting at job fairs on base is another great opportunity to meet members who are getting closer to the big day. Working with state and federal veteran employment representatives is also a way to catch those members who may be undecided on what industry they want to explore. Finally, keep up the messaging on social media. Someone reading it may not separate from the military for years, but there's a good chance they'll remember you when the time comes to begin a new chapter.

—Chris Davidson, Warrior Integration Program Manager at BAE Systems

---

When filling your pipeline with veteran recruits, you will have the opportunity to choose between resources. Of course, a more robust program will seek to access more than one of these resources at the same time.

As with any aspect of your business, you will need to devise a strategy around your military hiring program. How you find and attract veteran candidates includes many different pieces, and prioritizing your efforts requires that you are aware of your best options. Before you spend your precious time and money, you will need to dedicate concentrated effort on program objectives, metrics, and deliverables.

BREAKOUT BOX

Five Essential Steps in Executing a Successful Military Hiring Strategy

1. Establish SMART goals (specific, measurable, attainable, realistic, and timely).

2. Seek and secure support from leadership at the highest level of the organization; this is the most critical step. Refine strategy as necessary.

3. Identify and establish an internal core team of passionate, crossfunctional, and multileveled veterans and civilians to execute the strategy; recommend at least one veteran as senior advisor.

4. Schedule a kickoff meeting to align and outline program objectives and deliverables.

5. Assign team roles as necessary and establish a recurring meeting schedule.

—Dave Strachan, Chief of Staff, 7-Eleven, Inc.

 LEARNING POINT

Veteran recruiting begins with developing an outreach network that establishes points of contact across the military and veterans support community. Transitioning active duty service members, National Guard members, and members of the Reserves are best reached via military base, Reserves, and state National Guard Transition Assistance Programs (TAPs), wounded warrior transition programs, and related job boards and social media. Veterans are best reached via federal and state veterans employment organizations, student veteran organizations, and nonprofits specializing in veteran employment.

—Gary Patton, Vice President of Military and Veterans Affairs at CACI International Inc.

Government Resources

You will certainly want to utilize existing government resources in your employee search. They are free of charge, and some have grown to be quite innovative over the last five years. Here are a few to start with.

The Department of Veterans Affairs (VA) used to spearhead a program that employers could access to find veterans and transitioning service members looking for employment. That program no longer exists, but the VA has partnered with the Department of Labor to create a website that helps veterans looking for jobs, and helps employers find veterans looking for new careers (www.veterans.gov). On this site you can also find good information about various laws related to hiring veterans with disabilities.

The Department of Labor's Veterans' Employment and Training Services (VETS) program has the mission of preparing America's veterans, service members, and military spouses for meaningful careers, providing them with employment resources and expertise, protecting their employment rights, and promoting their employment opportunities. To find the regional VETS office closest to you, follow this link, which will help you identify a specific point of contact in that office and their contact information: https://www.dol.gov/vets/aboutvets/regionaloffices/map.htm. The VETS website is designed to help employers with a number of tasks, including finding qualified transitioning service members and veterans, and providing information regarding veterans' employment rights, apprenticeship programs, and their upcoming HIRE Vets Medallion Program recognizing employers who recruit, employ, and retain veterans.

The Department of Labor's Career One Stop employment tool includes a section specifically designed for employers who want to hire veterans. You can find this resource at www.careeronestop.org/vets. There, you can post your job openings on your state job bank. You can also find a link to help you contact a Local Veterans Employment Representative (LVER) at an American Job Center, as well as find American Job Centers near you. These LVERs aim to help veterans find work by identifying job and training opportunities, ensuring that veterans get priority in job listings from federal contractors, promoting federally funded job and training programs, and more. These representatives will be able to help you identify qualified veterans.

Similarly, Disabled Veterans' Outreach Program (DVOP) specialists develop job and training opportunities for veterans, with special emphasis on veterans with service-connected disabilities. The Department of Labor provides grant funds to each state's employment service to maintain DVOP specialist positions in the state. DVOP specialists may be stationed at regional offices and medical or veterans' outreach centers of the VA, state or county veterans' service offices, Job Training Partnership Act program offices, community-based organizations, and military installations. DVOP specialists work with employers, veterans' organizations, the VA, Department of Defense, and community-based organizations to link veterans with appropriate jobs and training opportunities. You can learn more about the LVER and DVOP programs at https://benefits.va.gov/VOW/docs/LVER_DVOP _Factsheet.pdf.

Although it no longer has a standalone program to help employers find veterans, the VA does have a robust vocational rehabilitation program. It is called VR&E, which stands for Vocational Rehabilitation and Education. What should interest you most about this opportunity is that through their on-the-job training program, they subsidize veterans' salaries so that employers pay an apprentice-level wage while training veterans. As the veteran progresses, the employer pays a larger portion of the veteran's salary, until the training program is completed and the employer is paying the full salary. VR&E can also provide specialized tools, equipment, and workplace modifications to eligible veterans, allowing them to perform their duties. These valuable services help veterans without additional cost to employers. Finally, through the Special Employer Incentive program, employers may receive an incentive to hire veterans facing extraordinary obstacles to employment, which includes reimbursement of as much as 50 percent of the veteran's salary for up to six months. You can learn more about this program at www.benefits.va.gov/ VOCREHAB/employers.

Employers and job seekers who are located near military bases should take advantage of the resources located in the TAP offices. Each military branch has its own version. For instance, if you are near an Army base you would contact the Army Career and Alumni Program, or ACAP. The staff in the ACAP offices plan and coordinate hiring events or job fairs, and also offer career counseling, job hunting skills, and many more services to help transitioning service members and their spouses find employment. They are often looking to bring in more employers who are interested in training, hiring, or connecting the veterans to career opportunities.

LEARNING POINT

If your business is near a military installation, consider sending recruiters to the TAP office, which aids veterans with their transition into the civilian workplace. Each installation's TAP office offers a wide range of services, including preseparation counseling, employment workshops and benefits briefings, verification of military experience and training, and individual assistance and referral. Also, be sure to reach out to family service centers (they're also called family support centers, family readiness groups, and other names). These groups are networks of programs, services, people, and agencies that work to support veterans and their families across a range of issues.

—Hiring Our Heroes Employer Roadmap, Transition Assistance Program Offices

Although this last governmental organization does not relate to finding potential employees, there are times when your veteran-hires will need some sort of accommodation. The great news is that many of these accommodations do not cost anything, and if there is a cost, it is typically below $500. A great resource for all things related to accommodations, including one-on-one consultations, product vendors, and ADA (Americans with Disabilities Act) compliance assistance is the Job Accommodation Network. It is typically referred to as JAN, and the website is www.askjan.org. From there, just click on the button for private employers.

Nongovernmental Resources

The US Chamber of Commerce Foundation offers a variety of programs for veterans and employers under the Hiring Our Heroes initiative. Hiring Our Heroes, also called HOH, launched in 2011 as a nationwide initiative to help veterans, transitioning service members, and military spouses find meaningful employment opportunities. In just over five years, HOH has held more than one thousand job fairs across the country, and twenty-eight thousand veterans and military spouses have obtained jobs through HOH events. Employers can participate in their programs at no cost, which includes listing your available job positions, participating in job fairs, and accessing their database of veteran résumés. You can learn more about this database of veteran résumés at www.resumeengine.org. Also, HOH's Employer Roadmap has been very helpful to a number of companies with varying levels of expertise in their veteran-hiring programs (https://www.vetemployerroadmap.org/). You can find more at www.hiringourheroes.org.

LEARNING POINT

[USAA's] Military Talent Management team attends meetings at the Warrior and Family Support Center at Ft. Sam Houston, Texas, to brief transitioning injured service members and their families regarding job searches and preparing for civilian careers. That team also has continued to increase its outreach through military blogs and a presence on social networking sites such as LinkedIn and Facebook, which helps to reach millennial job seekers. The company also advertises job openings in a wide range of military-related publications, to include job-related veteran publications, local military newspapers, websites, and job fair brochures.

—Hiring Our Heroes Employer Roadmap, Branding

The Veterans Job Mission began in 2011 as a coalition of 11 leading companies committed to hiring 100,000 Veterans by 2020. Since then, the coalition has grown to include more than 230 private-sector companies that represent virtually every industry in the US economy. The Veteran Jobs Mission coalition originally was called the 100,000 Jobs Mission and is sometimes still referred to by that name, although it has now collectively hired more than 360,000 veterans. Building on this momentum and reflecting the significant contributions veterans have made to the companies that have hired them, the Veteran Jobs Mission has raised its goal to hiring 1 million US military veterans. Beyond their ongoing search for top military talent, Veteran Jobs Mission members are increasing their focus on veteran retention and career development in the private sector, and they often share best practices with each other. You can read more about them at www.veteranjobsmission.com.

BREAKOUT BOX

Ernst & Young and the Veteran Job Mission

Five years ago, Ernst & Young joined the Veteran Jobs Mission, a coalition of 230 companies committed to employing one million veterans nationwide. Coalition members share performance and retention strategies geared specifically toward veterans. We gain access to tools and resources that help veteran employees better adapt to work situations, and we learn how to build our commitment to veterans into company-wide programs that motivate and engage our entire workforce. Since joining the coalition, we have hired more than nine hundred veterans for roles across all service lines and sectors in more than fifty cities. We hire across all levels from entry and senior level to experienced manager, senior managers, and PPED levels. Just last year, we reaffirmed our commitment to hiring and retaining veterans when we signed the Employer Support of the Guard and Reserve (ESGR) statement of support.

—Joseph M. McHugh, Northeast Leader of Complex Program Management
at Ernst & Young LLP

Hire Heroes USA provides a number of services to transitioning service members, veterans, and military spouses, including personalized career coaching, job search assistance, tailored résumés, and interview preparation. They help approximately one hundred veterans and spouses secure employment each week. They offer companies job posting and recruiter's packages that allow employers to post jobs on their job board and search their résumé database. These are not free, but can be purchased at different price points. You can find more information about them at www.hireheroesusa.org.

Corporate America Supports You, or CASY (pronounced Kay-See), provides a number of services to veterans seeking employment. Also, for a fee, employers can place unlimited job postings on CASY's job boards. Their recruitment experts will mine their résumé database to source veteran candidates who are a good fit for your jobs. They will also market your jobs, with an emphasis on social and digital marketing techniques. CASY works with over 1,000 corporations, 1,900 small and midsized businesses, and 185 trade associations with their direct placement assistance program. They recently celebrated over 20,000 veteran-hires since 2010. You can read more about them at www.casy.msccn.org.

Military.com was created in 1999 to revolutionize the way the thirty million Americans with military affinity stay connected and informed. Today, Military.com is a division of Monster Worldwide. At Military.com you can find a wide variety of resources to help your veteran-hiring program, ranging from guidance on tax credits for hiring veterans, access to job fairs and employer events, and a job board where you can post the specific positions you have available. Find more at www.military.com/hiring-veterans.

• • • • • • • • • • •
CASE STUDY

JobPath: A Powerful Platform for
Employers and Job seekers

What Is JobPath

JobPath is the leading tool for veterans transitioning from the military to civil life by providing online job training linked to real job opportunities. Established in 2013 by nationally renowned leaders in the veteran employment community, JobPath gives highly trainable veterans the platform they need to grow their skills and work in any position, and offers them a powerful résumé generator, a military skills translator, social mentoring, and a job board with over three hundred thousand open positions at companies nationwide.

Through this free website for veterans, JobPath gives users the opportunity to search for employment and take critical business courses online to develop the skills they need to complete their next employment task. From Basic Bookkeeping and Microsoft Office to dozens of important soft skills courses, JobPath's training library comprises two hundred diverse and intricate courses that veterans can utilize to become better candidates. In addition, companies can develop their own customized online courses within the site to get veterans trained for specific jobs they are looking to fill. Over the years, members of the military and veteran community have adopted these tools to bridge the gap between employers who want to hire veterans and the veterans who previously did not qualify for certain positions. With tens of thousands of veterans already enrolled and twenty-four thousand more joining every month, JobPath has quickly become a leader for current and former military members looking for work.

Who Is Using JobPath

FedEx, Verizon, and Panasonic are just three of the 950 employers who have posted with JobPath. These employers have posted well over three hundred thousand jobs on the site, with more companies signing up daily to be a part of the only job hunting, training, and mentoring system in the United States. Moreover, the success of JobPath is due to the committed relationships in the military and civilian community, as well as the scalable technology JobPath makes available to a diverse group of organizations and their members.

Our growth over the past few years is a testament to our philosophy that veterans are more than simply "leaders." They have proven through their time in service that they can adapt to any environment, any task, and any situation they are put in. And through JobPath, employers are learning the true, complete value of a military veteran's training.

—Jack Fanous, CEO and Founder of JobPath

• • • • • • • • • • •

SPECIAL OFFER FOR EMPLOYERS—Use this link for a free month of JobPath services: www.yourjobpath.com/shrmdiscount.

Veteran Service Organizations

Beyond the parameters of social responsibility, collaborating with veteran organizations can certainly help your company succeed with its veteran-hiring program. An array of military veteran organizations exists to help America's employers connect with transitioning service members, veterans, and military spouses who want civilian jobs. Some of these groups find, assess, and if necessary, train candidates for open positions. Partnering with these groups can expand your recruiting efforts and provide your company with a pipeline of qualified candidates who meet your hiring needs—millions of veterans and their family members belong to these organizations. After 9/11, over forty thousand nonprofit organizations sprung up across our country to provide different services for our veterans and their families. While that is a good thing, it can make things difficult for you when trying to figure out whom you should connect with.

BREAKOUT BOX

Connect with Groups That Might Help You

Establishing relationships with any of these following groups (and others) can help you connect with a wide variety of veterans and military spouses. Further, these organizations may post your jobs on their sites, and can help share your messages on social media.

- Association of the United States Army (AUSA), www.ausa.org
- Association of the United States Navy (AUSN), www.ausn.org

- National Guard Association of the United States (NGAUS), www.ngaus.org
- Veterans of Foreign Wars (VFW), www.vfw.org
- Air Force Association (AFA), www.afa.org
- The American Legion, www.legion.org
- Coast Guard Association (CGA), www.cgauxa.org/auxa/
- American Veterans (AMVETS), www.amvets.org
- Disabled American Veterans (DAV), www.dav.org
- Military Officers Association of America (MOAA), www.moaa.org
- Military Order of the Purple Heart (MOPH), www.purpleheart.org
- Wounded Warrior Project (WWP), www.woundedwarriorproject.org
- Non Commissioned Officers Association (NCOA), www.ncoausa.org
- National Military Family Association (NMFA), www.militaryfamily.org
- Navy League of the United States (Navy League), www.navyleague.org
- Marine Corps League, www.mclnational.org
- Paralyzed Veterans of America (PVA), www.pva.org
- Reserve Officers Association of the US (ROA), www.roa.org
- United Services Organization (USO), www.uso.org
- Vietnam Veterans of America (VVA), www.vva.org
- US Naval Academy Alumni Association (USNAAA), www.usna.com

Job Fairs

Job fairs are quite common now, and because so many organizations host them, there are hundreds, if not thousands, of military career fairs held around the country every year. Attending them can certainly be a good use of your time, and they are often free or inexpensive. However, without proper planning and coordination, they will provide you very little return on investment. Your representatives should have a good understanding of the type of military experience that fits well with your open positions, and you should have enough personnel at your booth to talk with several different job seekers at the same time.

Whether you have a mature veteran-hiring program or are new to the game, you should definitely include job fairs as part of your strategy for finding appropriate veterans and military spouses. For two years I ran the Wounded Veteran and Caregiver Program at the US Chamber of Commerce Foundation, and as part of that program we hosted specialized job fairs just for the men and women in our demographic. I had heard of many of the employers who attended, though not all, but I noticed that even a small, relatively unknown company could make a significant impact with the job seekers if they had a solid strategy driving their efforts at the career fair.

"QUOTABLE"

"At CarMax we're making it as easy as possible for our recruiters to reach out to the candidates they meet at job fairs. The store manager and recruiter use a tablet to capture candidate contact information, positions of interest, and locations of interest. This is especially important because some candidates we meet aren't transitioning out of the service for several months or even a year or more. We can stay in touch as these high-quality candidates transition from military service to the civilian work world."

—Jack McCarthy, Senior Recruiter for Military Hires at CarMax

As part of your strategy for the day of the job fair, here are a few tips to keep in mind. These tips are designed to make your interactions with job seekers as impactful as possible, to make a strong impression, and to use your time most wisely.

- **Decide beforehand if you are accepting résumés.** The job seekers are often advised to bring copies of their résumés to give out to interested employers, but a number of employers now insist on purely online applications. Be prepared to explain why you are not accepting hard copies (e.g., Equal Employment Opportunity Commission concerns), but do discuss what positions you have open, how to apply, and any other recommendations you may have.
- **Wear a name tag.** The job seekers across from you will meet many other people that day, and even something this simple will make their conversation with you a little bit easier.

- **Know what jobs you have available.** By speaking authoritatively about what openings you have, you demonstrate clarity and organization, which the veterans will appreciate. Also, because they may not have much time to speak with you, being prepared will expedite your conversations.
- **Include a veteran from your organization.** While there are certainly some civilians who have incredible knowledge about the military, it is typically easier for veteran job seekers to connect with another veteran. There is something to be said for being able to "speak the language" of the job seekers, not only in quickly understanding their skill sets, but also in making them more comfortable.
- **Engage the job seekers.** You will be far more approachable if you are standing the entire time. Be friendly as they walk near your table (but not too aggressive!). You are assessing these veterans just as much as they are assessing you, and the quicker you can establish some sort of connection, the better. They may have no idea what you offer, and therefore will be hesitant to approach you without seeing a friendly face.

BREAKOUT BOX

Be Ready to Hire!

La Quinta Inns & Suites (based in Irving, Texas) says: Be ready to hire! If possible, conduct interviews at the hiring fairs. Contact the organizer of the event ahead of time to see if there will be an area you can use for interviews. This will allow you to have a personal conversation about the candidate's experience and interests. Then you can tell them about your organization and why you value service members and their families. Ideally, have veteran and/or military spouse employees attend the fair to participate in the recruiting efforts.

—Hiring Our Heroes Employer Roadmap, Job Fairs

Hosting Your Own Events

A number of companies and organizations host their own events to show-case their corporate culture to veterans and provide significant opportunities for one-on-one interaction. Some companies, such as Ernst & Young, peri-odically host résumé-writing workshops on Saturdays (so that the event does not interfere with veterans' weekly schedules) in partnership with some of their clients. This allows numerous companies to provide expert assistance to the veterans and military spouses, and provides an environment where it is easy for veterans to network with friendly faces and supporters from several companies at one time.

· · · · · · · · · · ·
CASE STUDY

The Cosmopolitan of Las Vegas

I've always been a firm believer that you should only participate in objectives that align with who you are as an organization. So, if you want to be a champion for a veteran-hiring initiative, you must truly feel it deep in your soul and believe in it with every breath that you take.

At The Cosmopolitan of Las Vegas, we believe that as part of our Supporting Our Veterans initiative, it is important that we assist as many veterans, military spouses, and caregivers as possible. It is equally important that every action we take, every event we host, and every communication we send is a direct reflection of our edgy brand and what we stand for as an organization. We design our events so that our guests feel comfortable and can present themselves authentically and with positive energy.

The Mixer: Cocktails Anyone?

Early on, we opted for less formal methods to engage with veterans. Who says that you must sit stiffly across from one another sweating and shaking with nerves? Instead, one of our favorite events is our Military Career Mixer. These events are hosted in one of our brilliant, breathtaking penthouse suites. We treat these men and women with respect and over-the-top service. From the ridiculous view and specialty mocktail beverages to the roaring applause that they receive as they enter, they know they are in for a unique experience. While the visual stimulation is a boost of confidence for sure, the intentional format of these events has value beyond the wow factor for both the veterans and the hiring leaders. All attendees introduce themselves to the group, are encouraged to speak to everyone in attendance, and are then allowed to enjoy themselves as they engage in open dialogue with other veterans and hiring leaders from all of our operational divisions. The feedback we received coupled by the increased hiring confirms that we have successfully aligned our efforts with our brand, and had a lot of fun at the same time.

The Benefits

- Veterans are at ease. They are less focused on the discomfort and uneasiness of a typical interview.
- Communication is a two-way street. Open dialogue in a fun, engaging environment allows both parties to gain more insight.
- Candidates report a boost in their self-esteem and higher level of confidence in presenting themselves to a nonmilitary organization.
- Candidates gain a solid understanding of the organizational culture and divisional leadership styles and can make educated decisions about overall fit. We recognize that we are not for everyone. Therefore, we present ourselves in a true manner and let the candidates decide for themselves.
- Résumés come to life as they are presented by the person who owns the accomplishments.

The Career Fair: It Takes a Village

As a single luxury resort, the number of career opportunities we offer is far from equal to the number of exceptional veteran candidates that we meet. We truly believe that if we can help veterans secure employment with *any* organization, it is a success that we celebrate. The need to help veterans secure employment is one that has greater success if companies pull together versus compete individually.

To demonstrate how companies can come together as a community to support these brave men and women, we made the decision to host a career fair covering all associated costs. We invited our top competition, other diverse industries both locally and regionally based, and veteran organizations that offer support and resources to this amazing group and their families.

In 2017, we hosted the second event of this kind with over three hundred attendees. Of course, our events are true to our brand and over-the-top (we love to throw a good party) with gorgeous décor, specialty treats, and even showgirls.

The Benefits

- Veterans have a one-stop shop that allows them to meet with a variety of organizations and explore a variety of career opportunities.
- The community successfully comes together.
- Organizations without their own formal veteran-hiring initiative can witness the candidate quality firsthand.
- The number of hires across the city and across industry types is greatly increased.
- Organizational relationships are developed for continued partnership opportunities.

We recognize that every organization is different and believe that each veteran-hiring initiative should be as well. One size doesn't fit all. The key is to be committed, passionate, and engaged. All actions should be a direct reflection of your brand. Show how committed you are by your actions. After all, they speak louder than words.

—Lori Calderon, Director of Talent for The Cosmopolitan of Las Vegas

Social Media

It should be no surprise to you that many veterans find out about job opportunities through their various social media platforms. Consistently pushing out valuable information about your organization, how you are military friendly and military ready, and why you value veterans and military spouses is an easy way for you to connect with veterans who are likely already following you. While there is not one specific platform that works particularly better with veterans, your social media activities should be part of your overall efforts to brand yourself as military friendly and military ready.

BREAKOUT BOX

Why and How Employers Should Use Social Media

LinkedIn's mission is to connect the world's professionals to make them more productive and successful. It's wise to have a point of contact on your company's LinkedIn page who is dedicated to recruiting veterans and their spouses. When veterans ping your page, it streamlines the connection for both you and them.

Because Facebook connects friends and family members, its focus is less on the career and more on the personal side of life. That said, you can showcase your company's family-friendly policies, plus photos and short write-ups about your military support activities and community volunteerism and activism among your employees. Think of Facebook as a place where people get to know the human side of your operation. Proactively show them why you care—and how you care for them.

As much as Twitter is used for advertising a company's products, it deserves a second look for your recruiting outreach efforts. A designated military recruiter can follow groups like the Military Officers Association of America and the National Military Family, to name a couple. Engage in conversations with them and their Twitter followers in real time. You'll see a ripple effect by doing so, because those who follow those groups will notice your engagement and interest. That, in turn, could lead to conversations about job openings, the potential you offer for career advancement, your support for military families and how people should send their résumés for your consideration. Just like face-to-face conversations, one thing leads to another. This is doubly true on Twitter, which makes it possible for those interactions to take place swiftly and easily.

Scrapbooking on the web may not be your company's thing, but if you're not on Pinterest, you're missing out on an opportunity to reach military families and job candidates on a visual and emotional level. Pinterest allows you to create photo boards, which are like collages on the Internet. Like Facebook, the dynamic of Pinterest is that you get to showcase your company's outreach efforts, your philosophy about hiring veterans and spouses, and your corporate culture. Pinterest is less about direct recruiting and more about painting a portrait of your company's environment. You also connect with military families by "repinning" photos of theirs to your own Pinterest site.

—Hiring Our Heroes Employer Roadmap, Social Media

College and University Campuses

For decades, companies across virtually every industry have participated in some sort of college recruiting effort. With the explosion of veterans utilizing the Post-9/11 GI Bill and pursuing college degrees, you are missing the boat if you do not focus to some degree on connecting with this motivated population. Also, you should be aware that veterans can transfer these impressive educational benefits to their spouses and children, so a number of military spouses you may want to consider are on these same campuses.

Two premier student-veterans organizations deserve special attention, although they certainly are not the only groups out there. The Student Veterans of America (SVA) is a coalition of student-veterans groups on college campuses worldwide. Chapters often coordinate campus activities and provide professional networking opportunities. To learn more about them, and to join the other companies who are already part of the Student Veteran Success Corps, follow this link: http://studentveterans.org/30-partners-sponsors/122-student-veteran-success-corps.

FourBlock was started by Mike Abrams, a Marine officer, and its mission is to help transitioning enlisted service members now in college begin new, meaningful careers at our nation's top companies. FourBlock is also providing a platform across fifteen cities nationally for corporate executives to give back to their communities through teaching and sustained mentorship of veterans. Read more about them at www.fourblock.org.

Career Skills Programs/Fellowships/Internships

All three of these types of events are quite similar, but different enough to describe each one separately. What they do have in common is that they provide opportunities for organizations to work with transitioning service members and observe if they are a good fit for each other. There is no cost to the employer, who can see how well the service members work within their particular corporate culture. It provides the service members with real-world corporate experience, often working on projects they have expressed an interest in. These opportunities provide them private-sector material for their résumés, allow them to network in professional circles with managers and supervisors they normally would not meet, and allow them to determine if they want to work with that particular company after leaving the military.

 **LEARNING POINT**

A career skills program is a vocational and technical program developed for military personnel who are nearing the end of their military careers and are transitioning to civilian life. The program focuses on the practical application of learned skills that are intended to lead to employment in a specific career or technical trade. For more information, visit https://www.army.mil/standto/archive_2015-07-02.

BREAKOUT BOX

How to Create a Career Skills Program (CSP)

- Consider the jobs your organization needs to fill as well as available training installations in your area.
- Connect with the Army's Soldier for Life Program and the regional career skills program coordinator in your area.
- Review the Department of Labor requirements for internships.
- Draft a memorandum of agreement (MOA) for your regional CSP coordinator and the installation management command headquarters.
- Allow the installation management command to review and approve your MOA.
- Once approved, begin your organization's internal CSP.

To learn more, visit www.psycharmor.org.

The most developed example of a corporate fellowship program for veterans is probably that hosted by HOH at the US Chamber of Commerce Foundation. They have hosted more than twenty fellowship cohorts in eleven locations since 2015, and nearly five hundred Fellows have graduated from the program. HOH has worked with over 125 companies nationally to host Fellows, and the national average for salaries for graduates of the program is $70,000. It is a twelve-week program, held three times per year at various military installations around the country. Each class hosts fifteen to thirty active duty service members (and military spouses in select locations) who gain experience working in the private sector and attend weekly educational sessions. To participate, companies must have the ability to train Fellows four days per week for twelve weeks, they must offer hands-on training, and they must be willing to interview Fellows for management or professional-level positions or willing to refer Fellows for jobs elsewhere in their network upon completion of the program. Companies and service members interested in learning more about this program should go to www.hiringourheroes.org/fellowships.

Many companies already have internship programs for college students or other particular demographics, and there is no reason not to offer the same opportunities to veterans. PenFed Credit Union, for example, brings in a wide variety of people for their internship programs, and typically includes 10 percent veterans in the group. Other companies have started implementing internship programs solely for veterans. Not only does this expose the corporations to as many veterans as possible, but it benefits the veterans as well. Teamwork is part of veterans' DNA, and we are very used to working around each other—when your veteran interns have other veterans to talk to and compare notes with, it is naturally much more appealing to them.

· · · · · · · · · · ·
CASE STUDY

CBS Veteran Internship Program

In 2013, our team sat down to determine where we could have the biggest impact for veterans looking for employment. We don't have a high volume of jobs to fill and experience is important for many available positions. With this in mind, we decided to focus on providing quality internships that would create a pipeline of talent with real-world experience. Now, our Veteran Internship Program is a key part of the veteran initiatives at CBS Corporation.

Internships have been a part of CBS culture for decades and are in the company's DNA. What better way, we thought, to change the lives of veterans, while working along the grain of our corporate culture. We recognize that the skills developed in the military—leadership, problem-solving, teamwork, and attention to detail, for example—are the same qualities essential to our success as a company. The CBS Veterans Network team went from department to department, meeting with leaders and discussing the unique experience and skills veterans will bring to our workforce. We were able to find roles that were both suitable and challenging.

The summer of 2017 was our fourth year running, and we had interns in our major offices in Los Angeles, San Francisco, and New York, as well as our stations in markets like Boston and Detroit. Each summer, veterans across the US from a variety of universities and colleges take roles in marketing, business, accounting, production, and others. Working in these positions, they join CBS managers and executives for a summer of learning and engagement. We are proud that some stay on at CBS with full-time employment, and those who don't stay on leave with valuable skills and the necessary experience to start a successful career. For more information, visit www. cbscorporation.com/careers.

—Josh Brackett, Head of Veterans Initiatives, CBS

FOR THE VETERAN IN CAREER TRANSITION

You, as a veteran or military-spouse job seeker, are often just as confused as employers, trying to figure out which companies are hiring, how to connect with them, and how best to present yourself. Although you may feel nervous about this stage of the process, keep in mind that you are very much in demand and an equal player at the table. And just as companies put a lot of effort in their public image and determining the best fits for their openings, you should also ensure that you are positioning yourself as well as possible and learning as much about the employers as you can. As detailed in the chapter about the business case for a military hiring program, veterans bring incredible skills and attributes to the marketplace, but we are often our own worst critics, so spending time now to set yourself up for success is critical to a healthy transition and a new career. In fact, it is never too early to start preparing, and if you are still on active duty, it is a great idea to start at least six months before you transition out.

BREAKOUT BOX

The Benefits of Preparing Six Months before Leaving the Military

Through a detailed survey conducted in 2016, Hiring Our Heroes found that respondents who started their job search at least six months prior to leaving active duty were twice as likely (25 percent vs. 12 percent) to have a job before leaving active duty compared with those who started less than six months before transitioning. Those who started early were also twice as likely to report never being unemployed and being financially better off.

—Hiring Our Heroes[1]

💡 LEARNING POINT

When considering employment opportunities, don't put *all* your energies into one employer. Think about other fields and employers that are comparable to your interests and explore those. Always have a plan B and C.

—Robert Schwartz, Senior Program Manager of Helmets to Hardhats

Keep in mind that simply because you worked in one particular field does not mean you automatically need to continue in that same area. Many industries now offer free training to veterans for necessary certifications that often cost hundreds or thousands of dollars, and you should take advantage of them if they will help your career development. Of course, if you enjoyed what you did in the military and can continue doing so in a civilian capacity, that is a great scenario for you!

"QUOTABLE"

"We found at Microsoft that many transitioning service members need encouragement and a structure path to their next career. Our Microsoft Software and Systems Academy has convinced many service members with no prior IT experience that a foundational education and training program can set them up for a successful tech career."

—Joe Wallis, Career Transition and Talent Acquisition Professional
for Microsoft Military Affairs

If you are currently transitioning out of the military, you should first explore what is available to you on your base. The TAP office is typically a good starting point; there you can learn about companies that are currently looking for military veterans. Often, you can also sign up for classes to help you with your résumé and cover letter. Even if your TAP office does not provide those services or cannot help you with interviewing or job searches, there are many nonprofit organizations that do, and your TAP office may have a list of them. Take the time to introduce yourself to the people working there and explore what they have to offer. All of this is probably new to you, but these offices have a lot of experience and there is no reason to reinvent the wheel.

That being said, before you can make the most out of your visit to the TAP office and at every other aspect of your job search, you must take the time to answer a few critical questions that will guide the next phase of your life:

- Where do you want to live?
- What type of work do you want to do?
- What are the quality of life considerations that are most important to you?
- Is this a good time for you to go to school?
- How do the needs of your family (if applicable) factor into all of this?

The earlier you can answer these questions, the sooner you can truly start your transition from a position of strength. You won't inadvertently waste time looking at options that do not fit into your long-term plans.

 LEARNING POINT

The military is a team sport, and none of us served alone. We also don't transition alone. Whether you are married, single, or divorced, our friends and families have loved and supported us throughout our military careers. Include those who supported you, especially your spouse and children, in planning this journey.

—Brian Anderson, Director of Career Transition and Member Services for the Military Officers Association of America (MOAA)

BREAKOUT BOX

Prior Preparation

Embarking on your next career requires preparation; the sooner you start, the better. Whether you are single or have a family, you want your transition to be as smooth as possible. The first question is, Where will you be returning to? Some veterans have multiple options, so figuring this out early on is important. Doing this will allow you to research the employment opportunities in the area. Once you've identified where your interests lie, you can then research any application procedures that need to be completed or additional paperwork that may be required. This is also a good time to build a relationship with possible employers before you get home. Communicating your timeline and availability goes a long way.

—Robert Schwartz, Senior Program Manager at Helmets to Hardhats

Monthly Transition Budget Worksheet—Practical Exercise

Housing
    Rent or mortgage   _____
    Heating/electricity   _____
    Cable/telephone   _____
    Maintenance   _____
    Subtotal   _____

Food
    Groceries   _____
    Restaurants   _____
    Miscellaneous   _____
    Subtotal   _____

Transportation
    Car payment   _____
    Gas/maintenance   _____
    Public transportation   _____
    Subtotal   _____

Insurance
    Medical/dental   _____
    Auto   _____
    Personal/life   _____
    Renter's   _____
    Home   _____
    Subtotal   _____

Medical
    Doctor/dentist   _____
    Prescriptions   _____
    Subtotal   _____

Debt
    Credit cards   _____
    Loans   _____
    Other   _____
    Subtotal   _____

Clothing
    Work/job search   _____
    Family/personal   _____
    Subtotal   _____

Childcare
    Daycare/babysitters   _____
    School expenses/fees   _____
    Allowances   _____
    Subtotal   _____

Personal
    Haircuts/cosmetics   _____
    Laundry/dry cleaning   _____
    Subtotal   _____

Taxes
    Property tax   _____
    Income tax   _____
    State/local tax   _____
    Subtotal   _____

Miscellaneous
    Education   _____
    Savings   _____
    Retirement   _____
    Other   _____
    Subtotal   _____

Monthly expenses total   _____
Monthly income   _____
Current savings   _____

Source: Wounded Warriors Project

Obviously, financial considerations are a big part of this decision-making process; therefore it is vital for you to spend some time on a monthly budget to help you understand how much you need to earn. As you leave the military, you will be exposed to a lot of new costs that were previously absorbed by the military (e.g., healthcare, gym memberships, childcare, more expensive grocery stores, etc.). Feel free to use the sample monthly budget form on the previous page to help you get a firm handle on your expenses.

 LEARNING POINT

Don't forget that the military will pay for your last permanent change of station (PCS) move as you exit the military, and you can use that to go anywhere you want. You are not limited to your home of record, and you can save yourself a lot of money if you decide where you want to live before you move back home.

Networking

It is not unusual for veterans to feel a little squeamish about networking and having to talk about themselves. The conventional wisdom is that while we were in the military, we never had to network because we were assigned to our bases and billets without any real input. While that is somewhat true, it does not paint the full picture: we were networking in many ways without realizing it.

BREAKOUT BOX

Need-to-Know Facts about Networking and Preparing for Your Job Search

- Approximately three hundred applications are submitted for every advertised job, and roughly 70–80 percent of all jobs are never advertised. Instead, they are filled by people who were recommended to the company.

- Applying to an advertised job gives you a 1:50 shot of getting an interview (*if* you're a qualified candidate).

- Recruiters and headhunters account for about 10 percent of all jobs filled, so don't put all your hopes into one opportunity—keep your options open at all times.

- The majority of all job seekers spend most or all their time applying for jobs online rather than networking.

- The average résumé receives only six to ten seconds of attention.

- Networking remains the most effective way to find a job. It is a skill most people do not have, but it can be easily learned.

- Use key words in your résumé that apply to the job description.

- Finding a job is a full-time job, and you must treat it that way.

- Keeping your unemployment status to yourself is a recipe for disaster.

- Your attitude, positive or negative, will impact your ability to get a job one way or the other.

—Wounded Warrior Project[2]

When we think of networking, many of us probably think of a job fair or a crowded room full of people shaking hands and discussing their accomplishments. But networking is far more than that. It includes conversations with family members about contacts they may have, following up on conversations started by potential employers through social media, going with a friend to a business breakfast hosted by your local chamber of commerce, or any other number of scenarios. At its core, networking is about connecting with people who may be in a position to help you, or who could benefit from your help. You may not even have an immediate goal or see a worthwhile advantage from meeting some of these other people, but you never know when that connection will come in handy. As you explore LinkedIn, for example, you will understand the power of accessing the networks of your friends and colleagues.

 **LEARNING POINT**

Position yourself on LinkedIn, using your headline and your summary statement to highlight your strengths, skills, and results. Ensure your résumé, LinkedIn profile, biography, and business cards reinforce your brand. Some practitioners, including LinkedIn corporate representatives, are recommending first person voice for LinkedIn summary paragraphs.

—Brian Anderson, Director of Career Transition and Member Services for the Military Officers Association of America (MOAA)

The truth is that you have already done plenty of networking while serving in the military. By simply submitting your "dream sheet" of your preferred duty stations, you were showing others where you wanted to work. Although this was probably a mandatory part of the process, you were still influencing those who could make a difference in your professional life. And how many of you sat down with your career planners, face to face, and explained to them where you wanted to go, what you wanted to do there, and why? When you make a personal connection with someone, you are much more likely to influence that person's decision. As you progressed through the ranks, you certainly had opportunities to talk with those more senior to you about their recommendations for you, or any assistance they could provide within their personal circles. This is all networking and we are surrounded by it every day. The sooner you feel comfortable embracing the idea of networking, the more irons you will have in the fire.

"QUOTABLE"

"Networking is the process of purposely developing relationships with others. It is the most critical element of a successful transition plan. The more you develop, expand, and maintain your network, the easier and more successful your transition."

—Brian Anderson, Director of Career Transition and Member Services
for the Military Officers Association of America (MOAA)

BREAKOUT BOX

People often underestimate the power of networking when conducting job search strategies. Strong networkers realize that networking is similar to a full-time job, and it's not just something you can wing. Networking includes skills that create the power of influence and create opportunities that connect with different cultures, different age demographics, special interest groups, and political networks. In addition to connecting with these groups, strong networkers focus on consistent follow-up, making connections within connections and building strong alliances.

—Wounded Warrior Project[3]

Like so much else in life, successful and impactful networking requires follow-up. For instance, I recently attended a benefit gala as a guest of a major corporation and had the chance to sit next to an influential person from that corporation during the dinner. I knew that without any follow-up afterward she would very quickly forget about me, so I sent her a thank-you note on my personalized letterhead. Not only will she probably remember that handwritten note, but she may even look up the URL for my website at the bottom of that card and learn a little bit more about my business. Because we are all bombarded with new information, introductions, and connections all the time, you simply have no choice but to follow up.

Another aspect of networking to consider is that it is not just about connecting with people who are in a position to help you. The simple act of talking with a wide group of friends and associates about what they are doing, what worked for them, programs they are aware of, or anything else that ties into your goals is not only a form of networking but often the best source of information for you. Unfortunately, details about the best programs or opportunities may never reach you if you don't constantly have feelers out, simply because of the deep river of information that we swim in every day. Many of the veteran benefits, nonprofit resources, and corporate partners I have come across over the years have merely been through fortuitous conversations I had with others who had once been in my position and were sharing what they had learned. For instance, how many Purple Heart recipients are aware of the nonprofit organization started by two Marines called Vacations for Veterans that provides one-week vacation homes for Purple Heart recipients from the wars in Iraq and Afghanistan? This probably will not help with a job search, but it is a nice benefit to be aware of! I heard about it from another wounded warrior in the hospital through a random conversation, and now I tell as many others about this resource as I can. We live in a nation of people and organizations that want to support their veterans, but you have to stay motivated to ensure you connect with the right ones over time.

BREAKOUT BOX

List of Organizations You May Want to Connect with Regarding Your Transition

1. If you are a Purple Heart recipient from the wars in Iraq or Afghanistan and want to learn more about free one-week vacation rentals, or if you would like to donate your vacation home or timeshare for one week to Purple Heart recipients, please visit Vacations for Veterans at www.vacationsforveterans.org.

2. Helmets to Hardhats is a national, nonprofit program that connects National Guard, Reserve, veterans, and transitioning active duty military service members with skilled training and

quality career opportunities in the construction industry. Once you've created your account you can search for apprenticeships by trade, location, or both. The first step in the career hunt is to register on the site: www.helmetstohardhats.org.

3. VetsinTech supports current and returning veterans with reintegration services, and connects them with a wide variety of tech-based companies and resources. VIT is committed to bringing together tech-specific programs and opportunities for veterans interested in education, entrepreneurship, and employment. See www.vetsintech.co for more information.

4. Troops to Teachers was established in 1994 to assist veterans in their goal of becoming teachers. Sponsored by the Department of Defense, the program provides veterans with training to become certified, learn where the jobs are, how to network, how to market themselves, and how to enhance their candidacy. Counseling services are also provided. Since inception, over twenty thousand veterans have been placed in full-time teaching positions. See www.proudtoserveagain.com for more information.

5. The American Red Cross is dedicated to the mission of providing relief and hope to communities around the world and offers confidential services to all veterans and their families by connecting them with local, state and national resources through their network of chapters in communities across the US and offices on military installations worldwide. See http://www.redcross.org/about-us/careers/military-occupational-specialty-translator for more information.

BREAKOUT BOX

The Benefits of Following Through

Through Cisco's Corporate Affairs website, the Vets Program office gets three to four emails each week asking about Cisco's veterans programs and employment opportunities at the company. We respond to each email, providing information about our veterans programs and telling them about other resources available to veterans. For example, because we're an IT company and most of these types of inquiries relate to IT education and careers, we tell them about vet programs such as Onward to Opportunity, Veterans Career Training Program, Amazon's AWS Educate, USO Metro, NPower, and VetsinTech. In my six years of experience in the veterans field, I have learned that too often veterans don't know where to look for the learning resources available to them, often for free, and they get so frustrated with their searches that they give up looking.

—Michael Veysey, Director of Veterans Programs at Cisco Systems

---

There are coalitions of corporations and organizations, such as Philadelphia Salutes, Vetlanta, and America's Warrior Partnership (read more about AWP in the chapter on community collaboration) that have periodic meetings to discuss the events that the individual members are holding, and to highlight significant veteran events coming up in their community. If you know some-one who works for one of the member companies and attends their events, ask if you can tag along one time. I attended one recently and met at least a dozen people who were interested in helping me in some capacity. Of course, because we are always thinking about networking, I collected busi-ness cards from each of them (and gave mine in exchange), wrote a note on each one to remind myself where we met, and then connected with them on LinkedIn later that evening!

Internships

Earlier in this chapter we provided a few ideas about implementing intern-ships to employers to help them find highly qualified veterans and mili-tary spouses, but you should also be looking for these opportunities from your end. Many internships are paid positions, and they provide an excellent opportunity to learn more about the host organization and determine if they would be a good fit for you. BP is an example of a company that hires veterans for a wide variety of positions, and one way they do that is through their internship program.

· · · · · · · · · · · ·
CASE STUDY

BP's Veteran Internship Program

The skillset that veterans bring to the table directly aligns with BP's core values of safety, respect, excellence, courage, and one team, meaning that historically BP has been able to hire veterans into a wide range of positions.

As a company with over eighty thousand employees based in over eighty locations across the globe, BP naturally has a wide spectrum of diversity across its workforce. Spanning so many parts of the world, BP wants its team to represent the societies in which it operates.

Military Placement Program (MPP)

BP decided to develop a military placement program designed specifically for newly separated veterans with little to no corporate experience. The program is a one-year paid internship that gives veterans an opportunity to train with BP's integrated supply and training business personnel.

Veterans are trained in various areas, including commercial, finance, and operations. They are placed with mentors who work closely with them to help them acclimate to their new environment. After six months in the program they are eligible to apply for any open position within the company. So far, BP has successfully placed all its interns into full-time positions.

The Benefits

- The program helps veterans develop skills and knowledge that position them for a permanent role within BP and enable them to apply for roles in the wider job market.
- Veterans build relationships and network with people throughout the company while interning, an opportunity you would not have as an external candidate.
- Interns gain a solid understanding of the business and culture of the company. They can make an educated decision about overall fit.
- Candidates are eligible to turn their experience into a full-time position.

—Pree Newton, Resourcing Specialist at BP

Job Fairs

For job seekers attending job fairs, it can certainly feel overwhelming at first. You are often in a large area with sometimes hundreds of employer booths, and you may have never even heard of some of those companies. Even if you are familiar with them, you may not be aware of all the opportunities they offer that fit into your wheelhouse. For example, you may walk past a booth for a car dealership without giving it a second thought because you were not a mechanic in the military, but perhaps they have openings for IT, marketing, administrative support, or management.

Going to job fairs, however, provides you the opportunity to learn about options at many different companies, forces you to practice talking with potential employers, and allows you to connect with a live representative directly. Even if they cannot hire you on the spot (most cannot), they can

probably provide you with helpful advice on their particular hiring practices, or they can tell you what you should do if you are not quite ready
for a position with them. Job fairs are certainly not for everyone, but if you
have not attended any yet, give them an honest chance before you make up
your mind.

BREAKOUT BOX

List of Organizations That Host Hiring Fairs

- Hiring Our Heroes (www.hiringourheroes.org)
- Corporate Gray (www.corporategray.com)
- Recruit Military (www.recruitmilitary.com)
- Vet Jobs (www.vetjobs.com)
- Service Academy Career Conference (www.sacc-jobfair.com)
- Hire Veterans (www.hireveterans.com)
- Orion International (www.orioninternational.com)
- Lucas Group (www.lucasgroup.com)
- NCOA Career Expos (www.ncoacareerexpos.org)
- Cleared Jobs (www.clearedjobs.net)

Companies that host job fairs and other similar events often advertise
them through social media, so keep that in mind when deciding whom to
follow and on what platform. It is far better to know about an upcoming
event and have the option to attend or not than to find out about the event
after it already transpired and wish you could have attended.

Social Media

It is just as important for job seekers to utilize various social media platforms
to attract and connect with potential employers as it is for employers. More
and more veterans are making personal connections to corporate recruiters and HR professionals on LinkedIn, Twitter, and Facebook, as well as
other platforms. Just like you should talk with existing employees you may
already know at companies you are interested in, you should also follow

those organizations on social media so you can learn more about them, find out about upcoming events and opportunities, and identify more deeply with what they stand for and what you have in common with them.

Of course, you have to understand that as part of these relationships you are creating, those employers will probably research you as well. It is critical for you to brand yourself in a positive way that will appeal to potential recruiters. See the tips in the following Breakout Box to ensure you position yourself as well as possible.

BREAKOUT BOX

Goodwill's Online Tips

Many online tools are available for users to connect and learn about each other; the ability to network on social media opens hundreds of thousands of possible doors to job leads. The following tips can help veterans as they use social media:

- Create and maintain a civilian email account formatted for a professional presence similar to the email format used while in the military: Example (firstname.lastname@email.com).

- Make sure your profile on every platform (Facebook, LinkedIn, Instagram, Twitter, etc.) has a professional photograph of you. Business casual attire is strongly advised.

- Post your relevant work experience, education, and skills, and never post anything inaccurate about your professional brand. For example, do not falsify your education or your years of experience.

- Abstain from posting your political or religious views online, since these posts will become part of your brand too.

- Maintain your profile on the private or friends-only setting. This will prevent unwanted solicitation and ensure that only those you know will be able to see your posts.

- Post that you are searching for a job opportunity on the platform you see fit and discover how people in your network might know someone and open a new door.

- Stay on top of new training programs, career opportunities, job fairs, and hiring events by following employers, schools, and organizations that promote them. For example, the University Veteran Site, Goodwill Career Centers, the Veteran Employment Centers, and so on.

—Jezreel Ramirez, Employer and Community Relations Partner for US Military Services
at the Goodwill of Central and Northern Arizona

Keep in mind that whether you are choosing to attend a job fair, pursue an internship, apply for a particular position, or any number of other steps required for a healthy transition, the importance of proper planning cannot be overstated. There are a number of free tools out there to help you with your planning, and a number of nonprofit organizations that specialize in this. The following case study from Ken Falke really drives home the point about being prepared, and you can use the graphic he provides here to help you set your priorities.

· · · · · · · · · · ·
CASE STUDY

Clarity Toward Retirement

I can't tell you how many of my peers made the mistake of not gaining clarity in their transition process. I have heard, hundreds of times, "I spent twenty to thirty years in the service and I told my spouse, when we retire, I'll do whatever you want to do (thanks for following me around during my career)." This leads to a move back to small-town USA, followed by the purchase of a "retirement" house, a new car or two, and a few weeks off to decompress from military service. Then the terminal leave paycheck stops, the savings start to get depleted, and the job hunt turns into a nightmare. "Home" isn't what it used to be. The jobs have all dried up, and so has the savings account. Using the tool below will allow you to gain the clarity needed before making these major life decisions. As my dad always said, "Don't spend more than you make!"

My hope is for folks to establish clarity before jumping into a job search. I tell them to answer these questions independently and then to compare and have a compromise session to see what's best for the family. Once they have this clarity, then they can job search. My next advice is networking. Most of our enlisted folks don't really have great networks and I really focus on the importance of creating an "individual brand" and then meeting as many folks in their area of interest as they can.

—Ken Falke, Chairman, Boulder Crest Retreat for Military and Veteran Wellness
· · · · · · · · · · ·

CONCLUSION

Acknowledge that it typically takes some time to get your affairs in order and mentally prepare yourself for the transition out of the military by determining (in consultation with your family or others close to you) where you want to go next and why (see Figure 3.1). Transitioning service members should start all of this at least six months before they leave the military. This also includes planning your budget and saving as much money as possible so you don't have to make any decisions out of desperation. Even your haircuts are going to cost more than you are used to and you will find that every little thing adds up.

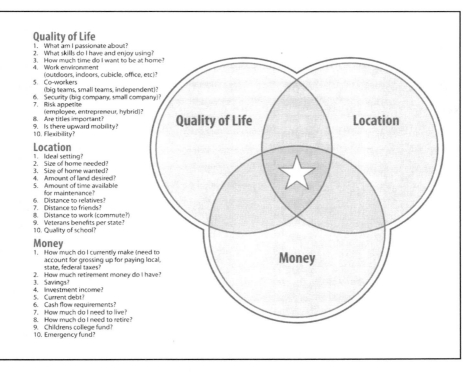

Figure 3.1. Guide to determining priorities for finding your ideal career

---

BREAKOUT BOX

Warriors Ethos

Warriors Ethos (WE) is a 501(c)(3) nonprofit dedicated to providing transition support to service members who are separating from the military and veterans looking for that next journey in the civilian world. WE follows a three-step process: engagement, education, and placement. WE works with each service member or veteran to provide the necessary tools and resources specific to their own unique transition, whether it be career advice, résumé counseling, training, mentorship, or placement. In turn, to ensure the best opportunity for success, WE also works closely with businesses and corporations to understand their needs and provide information and help that they might need when hiring from the talented veteran population. Whether an employer or veteran, learn more about how you can get involved with Warriors Ethos here: www.warriorsethos.org/.

You should also ensure that you are connecting with some of the organizations detailed in this chapter to help you prepare your résumé and upload it to the right platforms so a wide variety of employers can find it. And of course, make sure that you thoroughly document any medical issues before you leave active duty, have a complete copy of your medical record, and if appropriate, start your VA paperwork so that, if you will be paid a monthly compensation from them, it will kick in as soon as possible after you separate.

ENDNOTES

1. Hiring Our Heroes, *Veterans in the Workplace: Understanding the Challenges and Creating Long-Term Opportunities for Veteran Employees* (Washington, DC: Chamber of Commerce Foundation, 2016), https://www.uschamberfoundation.org/sites/default/files/Veterans%20in%20the%20Workplace_0.pdf.
2. Wounded Warrior Project, *Warriors to Work Planning Guide*, 6.
3. Wounded Warrior Project, 49.

CHAPTER 4

Reading and Understanding Military Résumés

Educate your entire sourcing and recruiting team to read military résumés and translate skills so they can be advocates for veteran candidates.

—Carl Vickers, Global Veteran Strategy Lead
at PeopleScout

READING AND UNDERSTANDING MILITARY RÉSUMÉS

One of the biggest challenges faced by veterans transitioning to the private sector is effectively communicating the value of their experience and training to a recruiter or hiring manager. Résumés are not used in the military, and therefore transitioning service members and veterans typically have little experience preparing them. Typically, junior personnel (enlisted and officers alike) are promoted after a designated period of time in their particular billet. Later promotions are based on annual performance evaluations, awards, completion of mandatory training and schools, and other criteria. Thus, they are often new to the idea of describing to employers what they did in the military, especially in a way that someone unfamiliar with the military will understand.

Also, corporate recruiters typically do not understand the technical jargon often included in military job descriptions. While a number of resources exist to assist transitioning service members with translating their military experience into language more familiar to hiring managers, the résumé remains a friction point for both parties. We hope to alleviate some of those challenges in this chapter. To fully make progress here, both parties need to learn how to communicate well with each other.

BREAKOUT BOX

Tips for Reviewing Veteran Résumés

1. **Recognize the language barrier.** Military nomenclature is often very different than civilian terminology, but the skills required in the military are often the same.

2. **Identify a "translator."** Source a veteran or active military service member who can help you understand the military lingo and terminology.

3. **Ask for an explanation.** If you don't understand a term or acronym, ask the applicant to explain.

4. **Be open.** Remember that many transitioning veterans have no experience crafting or reading résumés.

5. **Provide feedback.** If you can, help veterans improve their résumés or presentations by providing feedback in a supportive way.

—Larissa Hanpeter, Director of Human Resources at ARServices

A best practice used by hiring managers regarding military résumés is to spend a little bit more time than you would normally spend on a civilian résumé. While you may typically quickly scan the text looking for industry-specific buzzwords or particular jobs, you very well may not find those from your applicants coming from the military. Remember, while highly qualified, military applicants are not necessarily making a lateral transfer into your positions, so their résumés may not contain the exact same verbiage you are looking for. Further, while thousands of jobs in the military have direct civilian counterparts, veterans may not describe those jobs the same way you are used to. Though it is common for recruiters to spend as little as six seconds per résumé, it is probably a good idea to spend a little more with your veteran or military spouse candidates.

"QUOTABLE"

"The most important thing to know when looking to hire more veterans is that their skills may be a great fit for your business, but their résumés may not show it. Many jobs done in the military are situation specific, but the abilities to excel under pressure, learn fast, and analyze complex problems are just a few of the highly transferrable skills you could be missing out on if you're ruling candidates out because of missing 'required' skills or experiences."

—Linda Woodruff, VP of Human Capital and Motivation for Human Resources
at Panasonic Corporation of North America

Ideally, your organization will have a veteran working in the HR department who can quickly answer questions related to the military. Additionally, one of the benefits of an engaged veteran employee resource group is that you can reach out to those members to field your questions. But of course, it is far more efficient if the hiring managers and recruiters themselves have enough basic knowledge to determine if a résumé warrants a second look.

Each industry has its own acronyms. Members of the military use thousands of acronyms, often to make big concepts easy to communicate. While veterans are often encouraged to not use these acronyms in their résumés, they may still creep in there, so we will just discuss the most basic here. Some basic acronyms you will probably see on the résumés relate to the service member's or veteran's branch of service. USA is the United States Army, and they are Soldiers. USMC is the United States Marine Corps, and they are

Marines. USAF is the United States Air Force, and they are Airmen. USN is the United States Navy, and they are Sailors. USCG is the United States Coast Guard, and they are Coast Guardsmen or simply coasties.

LEARNING POINT

There are thousands of widely used acronyms in the military and recruiters often run across them on résumés. Read the *DOD Dictionary of Military and Associated Terms* for more information.[1]

You might see the acronym "MOS" in a résumé or other military documents from those who served in the Army or Marine Corps. "MOS" is an abbreviation for Military Occupational Specialty, which indicates the service member or veteran's job specialty. The Navy uses the Navy Enlisted Classification (NEC) System, and the Air Force uses the Air Force Specialty Codes (AFSC). Essentially, each of these codes quickly indicates the industry field or specific job a person did while in the military, and he or she may actually list several occupation codes. Examples include infantry, judge advocate (attorney), medic, public affairs, and admin. Service members are frequently counseled against including their actual occupation codes on their résumés. Instead, they are told to use the corresponding job title, but civilian recruiters for specific industries often take the time to understand both.

LEARNING POINT

Employers should not judge applicants solely by their job title. Military job titles often do not seem to correlate with civilian job titles only because of the particular way the military classifies occupational job titles.

An important component to the successful employment of a veteran is having a strong military skills translator that is easy for both veterans and companies to use. With a powerful military skills translator, veterans can quickly take their military occupation and translate it into easy-to-understand language for employers. The translator can also help employers by enabling them to understand the skills, expertise, training, and related business areas that align with the thousands of military occupations. Ultimately, this helps employers find candidates for their open positions based on what service members did while they were performing in the toughest work environment in the world.

LEARNING POINT

JobPath hosts a powerful military translator that serves several functions. In addition to the capabilities listed above, it identifies whether a veteran's particular MOS qualifies for special certifications based on that military career. It also tracks a candidate's security clearance eligibility based on his or her military occupation. This is an incredible asset to employers who require security clearances because it can often cost tens of thousands of dollars to reactivate or obtain new clearances. For more information, see https://yourjobpath.com/enterprise.

BREAKOUT BOX

Security Clearance and Certifications

Many positions in the federal sector require a security clearance. Specifically in the federal information systems industry, many positions require certifications compliant with DoD Directive 8570.1 for Information Assurance Technicians (IAT) and Information Assurance Managers (IAM). These clearances and certifications should be prominently positioned on the veteran's résumé. By doing so, the veteran job applicant is greatly assisting job screeners and recruiters in determining qualified job candidates.

—Gary Patton, Vice President of Military and Veterans Affairs at CACI International Inc.

Military Schools

Veterans are often encouraged to include on their résumés the schools they attended and courses they completed while in the military. Remember, the Department of Defense spends a great deal of time and resources to develop and implement these courses, and they are quite impactful—feel free to ask about them in an interview. As a general matter, there are a handful of different schools or courses you should be aware of, and here we describe a few of them that are common across the services.

The first enlisted leadership school is designed for E-4s, typically at the rank of corporal (US Army), petty officer (USN), or senior Airman (USAF). Even in this description it is difficult not to use an acronym! An E-4 refers to the fourth rank of an enlisted service member. Once someone is promoted to E-4, they become a noncommissioned officer, or NCO. This is the first significant leadership rank in the enlisted ranks. The school is called the Corporals Course in the Marine Corps, the Airman Leadership Course in the USAF, and the Basic Leader Course in the US Army. If you see this on a résumé, that means the applicant has received formal training on the skills necessary to lead other people, including the core values and mind-set necessary for effective leadership. Keep in mind that the Department of Defense allocates significant training resources very early in the careers of service members, which is why they often have training that you will not see reflected on the résumés of their civilian counterparts.

For more senior enlisted personnel, you may see that they completed the Senior Non-Commissioned Officer Academy from the USAF or the First Sergeants Course in the US Army or Marine Corps. This fast-paced course provides E-7s and E-8s the training necessary to lead larger groups of troops, and it also focuses on training management, unit administration, communication skills, discipline, and unit morale. Of course, there are other courses and schools, but these are the ones that you are most likely to see on the résumés of enlisted applicants.

LEARNING POINT

For a detailed explanation of many military training courses and the skills learned there, download the free ebook from RAND titled *What Veterans Bring to Civilian Workplaces*.[2]

For your officer applicants, you will see that virtually all of them attended some form of formal schooling. Depending on the individual service, the more junior officers will have attended the Basic School, the Expeditionary Warfare School, the Squadron Officers Course, the Basic Officer Leaders Course, or the Division Officer Leadership Course. At each of these schools they learn the basic building blocks to effectively lead and develop junior troops, communicate with different audiences and make tactical decisions. Some midlevel officers may also list completion of their service's command and staff college on their résumés. These schools focus on developing what are known as "field grade officers," with an emphasis on successfully operating in a joint environment, which means working with other branches of the military. Classes typically include numerous individual and group problem-solving exercises, organizational operations, and senior-level management skills.

Military Job Titles

Of course, chances are that you will not recognize the typical job titles in the military. But there are some billets, or leadership positions, that you will consistently see, so we are going to discuss a few of those now.

 **LEARNING POINT**

Many of the skills that a service member develops while on active duty are relevant to the civilian workforce, but the proprietary nomenclature used by the military may differ. It may be necessary to probe a bit deeper on veteran résumés to learn more about the skills and how it relates to your open positions.

—Larissa Hanpeter, Director of Human Resources at ARServices

On the enlisted side, you may see that they started out as a fireteam leader. A fireteam consists of four or fewer members, and the role of each fireteam leader is to ensure that the team operates as a cohesive unit. This is the first step in learning small unit leadership.

Two or three fireteams make up a squad, led by a squad leader, which is another common billet. Squad leaders are responsible for nine to thirteen troops, and this designation should stand out to you if you see it on a résumé. Like midlevel managers in the private sector, squad leaders are responsible for training their teams, ensuring their administrative issues are quickly resolved, and maintaining discipline and morale.

You will also probably see that some of your applicants were platoon sergeants, which are similar to squad leaders but typically responsible for thirty troops. Platoon sergeants are often the main conduit between the junior officers and the other troops. They are responsible for training the junior troops in every aspect of their jobs and are the eyes and ears of the platoon. They need to know what is going on with everyone underneath them, both professionally and personally, so that they can help resolve whatever problems bubble up. These young leaders inspire those around them, discipline when necessary, and make sure the officers are aware of especially good work that is being done.

The officer leadership billet typically starts with the platoon commander. A platoon commander is normally in charge of thirty to fifty troops and is personally responsible for several million dollars of equipment. They are often responsible for developing their own plans for accomplishing missions, delegating work appropriately, and spot-checking. They write operation orders; conduct mission briefs; and plan, resource, execute, and assess training. They are responsible for the morale in their platoon and set the tone every day. They are also responsible for the professional development of their troops, which includes ensuring they are in good physical condition and up to date on all their required training.

Company commanders have those same responsibilities and more, because they are typically in charge of 140–200 people. Company commanders are usually captains, and enjoy a significant amount of responsibility. They are typically hand-selected for these positions from a senior leadership team.

So, now you know a little bit more about some typical aspects of a service member's career path, including schools they attended, positions they held, and how their skill sets are often similar to what you look for in leaders in the private sector. That being said, here are a few more considerations when you are reviewing a military résumé. We know you often don't have much time for this, and while the language may be different than that on the résumés from your civilian applicants, there are some key factors you should keep an eye out for.

One, focus on soft skills. You already know most veterans have a strong work ethic and leadership skills. You will see examples of these in their résumés, and who wouldn't want someone in their organization who has already learned extensive leadership skills from our military? It is not realistic to expect your veteran applicants to have the same experience or talking points as their civilian counterparts coming to you from a rival company, but that is not why you are interviewing them in the first place. Also, keep in mind that most service members have served in some sort of leadership capacity, whether it is indicated on their résumé or not, and it is a fair question to ask about their leadership experience.

"QUOTABLE"

"Hiring and honoring veterans and military spouses allows us all to benefit from their leadership, experience, and sense of service."

—Herrick Ross, Staffing Program Manager of Global Talent Acquisition for Starbucks

 LEARNING POINT

Veterans often do not include enough management experience in their résumés to highlight the amount of people they were responsible for managing and leading or the amount of financial controls they assumed. For example, if a noncommissioned officer is responsible for a team of four or twelve service members, he or she is also responsible for their overall performance and for the expensive equipment the team utilizes.

—James Rodriguez, Founder and Principal of the Rodriguez Group and Former Deputy Assistant Secretary of Defense for the Office of Warrior Care Policy

Two, take note of achievements and awards. You may not know off the top of your head what a Navy Achievement Medal or Purple Heart Medal means, but quickly referencing that information is easy to do. Understanding the significance of each award will give you a fuller and richer picture of the veteran applicant. A list and description of military awards can be found at https://en.wikipedia.org/wiki/Awards_and_decorations_of_the_United_States_Armed_Forces.

Three, be mindful of the typical length of time at one billet or job. In the military, service members are normally transferred to a new base or a new assignment every two to three years. So while this may indicate job-hopping on a civilian résumé, that is not the case in the military. Keep in mind the extra skills it takes to move to an entirely different office, typically on a different base, and continue to meet the mission and do well on a regular basis.

VETERAN AND MILITARY SPOUSE RESOURCE CENTER

Just as it is often challenging for civilian employers to understand military résumés, veterans often struggle with writing résumés that succinctly capture their skills and achievements in language that is easy to read for those unfamiliar with the military way of life. Common questions include: What do civilian employers really care about and what should I include? How far back should I go? Is there one template that is the best? This section offers some broad guidance for those preparing résumés and includes a sampling of resources. Remember, there are tens of thousands of nonprofit organizations across America that exist solely to help the veteran community, so do not be afraid to search in your local area to connect with them—many either offer employment-related services or have contacts with other groups that do.

LEARNING POINT

Veterans should display total inclusive time of service in their résumé. Service professionals with as many as twenty years in the military often account for only half or fewer years in their résumés. As a result, a civilian hiring manager reviewing the résumé may not fully comprehend the true scope of leadership experience and skills acquired over their career and the veteran subsequently runs the risk of being eliminated from consideration.

—Tyrone Tobias, Manager, Field Talent and Veteran-Hiring Initiatives, 7-Eleven, Inc.

Just like with other aspects of finding a great career after the military, there are a wide variety of organizations willing to help with writing your résumé. If you are still on active duty or in the National Guard or Reserve, you should start with the TAP center. Virtually every major military base has one of these offices (although they may have a slightly different name), and they offer a variety of basic services related to your transition out of the military, including preparing a résumé. They will likely also review your résumé for you and provide constructive guidance on improving it.

Another free government resource is the Department of Labor American Job Centers. These are located all across the country, offer priority service to veterans and family members, and provide one-on-one assistance with résumés. Learn more about them at https://www.careeronestop.org/Veterans/JobSearch/Resumes/resumes-and-applications.aspx.

BREAKOUT BOX

Free Resources for Résumé Writing

There are a number of organizations that help veterans and military spouses with their résumés at no cost. Here is a short list to help you get started.

- JobPath (https://yourjobpath.com/auth/signup)
- Hiring Our Heroes (https://resumeengine.org/)
- Hire Our Heroes (https://hireourheroes.org/veterans/build-a-resume/)
- US Department of Labor (https://www.careeronestop.org/Veterans/JobSearch/Resumes/resumes-and-applications.aspx)
- US Department of Defense (https://www.realwarriors.net/veterans/treatment/resumehelp.php)
- Disabled American Veterans (https://www.dav.org/wp-content/uploads/Resume_Writing_Tips.pdf)
- Call of Duty Endowment (http://www.callofdutyendowment.org/veteran_support)
- Hire Heroes USA (https://www.hireheroesusa.org/tools-resources/)
- Corporate America Supports You (CASY; https://casy.us/jobs-for-veterans)
- HirePurpose (www.hirepurpose.com)

The bottom line is that writing a résumé is a necessary part of your career search, and the earlier you start on it, the better. Keep in mind that just like when you are figuring out what you want to do after the military, you should dedicate some time in a quiet space where you can work on this document. It typically is not something that you can easily create off the top of your head. To that end, print out copies of your fitness evaluations or other supporting material you may already have in your service record book to help you detail the work you did and accomplishments you achieved while serving.

CASE STUDY

From Army Logistician to School District Fleet Manager

When I first met Adam at a Transition GPS class, he insisted his résumé was "done." He had it written in the correct format (chronological), checked all the spelling and grammar, and managed to squeeze his fifteen-year career in the Army onto one and a half pages. After looking it over, I realized Adam was far from done.

The reason Adam attended my course on personal branding for a successful civilian career is because he'd been sending out forty résumés to employers each week for six months. The results were dismal: he rarely received any responses, interviews, or even rejection letters. Instead, he felt he was emailing and mailing his résumé into an employment black hole.

A conversation with Adam revealed several things:

1. Adam was emotionally tied to his MOS in the Army—logistician.
2. He was not targeting employers who hired former military individuals.
3. Adam was not clear about who he wanted to work for or the kind of work he wanted to do.
4. He could not clearly explain why he would be of value to these employers.
5. Adam had no clear differentiation strategy through which to market himself.

Adam had a lot of work to do to get his résumé ready to send again. Working together, here are the steps we took:

1. We reviewed what Adam's service in the Army meant to him. Some key questions we discussed were:
   a. What motivated him to enlist? How did the military meet his personal goals and values? *This was challenging because his values and the military's values became so closely aligned.*
   b. What highlights or successes did he experience during his service that he is most proud of? Why? *This was a tough one for Adam because he is reluctant to take credit for successes without giving credit to those he served alongside.*
   c. What work did he do that he most enjoyed? Why? *Building from the work he enjoyed most allowed us to identify his skills, strengths, and interest for postmilitary work.*
   d. What does it take to be successful as a logistician in the Army? *His answers gave Adam a sense of further accomplishments and skills he possessed.*
2. Next, we talked about Adam as an individual:
   a. How does he want to be remembered in his legacy? *This was a tough question for Adam, but an important one to understand his vision for his life out of uniform.*

b. What is he passionate about? *In his reply, Adam talked about liking to see things organized, on time, and efficient. He is passionate about processes, systems, and effectiveness in all he does.*

3. Then, we discussed the kind of people Adam enjoys working with:

   a. His target audience, we decided, would be people who valued efficiency and timeliness.

   b. He likes to work with people of similar values and strengths.

   c. He prefers being part of a bigger organization, not a small company.

What these questions provided was a foundation to build his brand, value proposition, and (then) résumé. During the process, Adam learned a great deal about the kinds of logistics work he would not want to do and the companies he would not enjoy working with. This was valuable information!

Adam also gleaned insight into the companies, industries, and types of work he would enjoy doing, where his skills and successes would be valued, and where his military service would be appreciated. Ultimately, we revised his résumé to target school transportation districts, specifically for the role of fleet manager or something similar. Adam is currently working as a fleet manager and loves his job! Not only does it leverage his background and tap into his passion and strengths, but it also aligns with his core value of ensuring safety for all. He takes pride in safely delivering children to and from school every day. Oh, and he loves his new job title now.

—Lida Citroën, CEO of LIDA360

Cover Letter

A résumé is not the only document you need to create to help you secure that job interview. While you certainly should tailor your résumé to the requirements for each particular job you are seeking, it is still difficult to achieve a personal connection through a résumé. That is why you should spend time not only creating the template for an impactful cover letter to accompany your résumé, but also tailoring each individual cover letter to connect with that particular employer.

LEARNING POINT

Your cover letter should focus on the energy, enthusiasm, and results you will bring to the position. Explain why you're applying for the job, what makes you unique among the many applicants for the position, and how you will add immediate value to achieve specific results, which generally involve making money or saving money.

—Brian Anderson, Director of Career Transition and Member Services
for the Military Officers Association of America (MOAA)

BREAKOUT BOX

Why Write a Cover Letter?

A cover letter is an introduction to an employer that highlights your experience, key accomplishments, and level of responsibility directly in line with the job you are applying for. Additionally, it adds credibility and a laser focus to your résumé. In today's job market, many employers will not look at a résumé that is not accompanied by a cover letter. Cover letters allow job applicants and candidates to tell the employer exactly why hiring them, instead of numerous other candidates, is the best decision. Additionally, having the opportunity to articulate your strongest qualities, value, and passion will have a great impact and leave a lasting impression. Regardless of how well a résumé reads, it has limited value to employers if they cannot make the connection to the work you're looking for and why you're best qualified.

The cover letter also serves as a complement to a résumé and can be utilized to explain details your résumé does not address. For example, if you (a) have employment gaps because you went to school or you were deployed, (b) changed career or industry focus, or (c) decided to relocate and conduct a long-distance search, a cover letter can easily explain these circumstances in a positive way because it is more personal and addressed specifically to the hiring manager.

Remember you want to be an attractive candidate to potential employers and not another average Joe. By understanding your value, you will build confidence in your ability to deliver your strongest qualities, value, and passion, both verbally and in writing.

—Wounded Warrior Project[3]

Elevator Pitches and Networking

Although perhaps not as important as your résumé and cover letter, job seekers are often advised to have their elevator pitch down. This idea refers to the thirty or sixty seconds—however long you may share an elevator with somebody—you have to concisely and clearly convey your business proposition. This is just as relevant for budding entrepreneurs as it is for job seekers, because you never know who is going to help you move to the next step.

You may already be going to official networking events. As discussed in the chapter on sourcing military veterans, these can take the shape of job fairs, career exploration events, such as those hosted by FourBlock (www.fourblock.org), or industry-specific workshops organized by Veterans on Wall Street (www.veteransonwallstreet.com) or other similar groups. There are also many informal events, such as monthly gatherings hosted by veteran service organizations, periodic corporate events, résumé workshops hosted by Ernst & Young or other organizations with some of their corporate partners that bring together veterans and potential employers, and outdoor recreational activities with numerous nonprofit organizations where you often have the chance to meet some of the corporate sponsors.

By periodically attending these types of formal and informal networking events, not only will you expand your professional group of contacts, but you will be networking in some shape or form. To make the most of those opportunities, it is a good idea to have your personal elevator pitch in place so that you can quickly explain the opportunities you are looking for in an impactful way. You should also find a moment to practice this and give yourself ample time to explore what you truly want to talk about.

 **LEARNING POINT**

For more information about networking, be sure to read the "For the Veteran in Career Transition" section in Chapter 3.

Just to be perfectly clear about networking, it is not something that many veterans are typically comfortable with, but you really do have to embrace it. While we come from a background that frowns on bragging about our accomplishments, after you leave the military you must be able to talk comfortably about what you bring to the table. Of course, this does not mean immediately explaining how great you are to every person you meet; it means understanding what different employers are looking for and explaining how you meet their needs based on your past performance. Keep in mind that many people find jobs based purely on personal relationships and from letting others know what they are looking for through a variety of networking activities.

 LEARNING POINT

Doing is the new résumé: 67 percent of jobs are never posted on a job board, so that requires going out and networking, asking about business challenges and opportunities, and plugging in to be a part of the solution. Show up and find ways to add value, and if you prove to be capable, a good team player, and valuable, a job is sure to follow.

—Todd Connor, CEO of Bunker Labs

BREAKOUT BOX

Putting Together Your Elevator Speech Is Actually Pretty Easy!

Make sure you know your audience, since it is best to target your speech to the employer or industry needs. Start by putting together a bullet outline of your speech. Consider what you have to offer and what you want others to know about you. What are your key strengths? What problems are solved by the utilization of your skill set? How can you be a valuable asset to a potential employer? Take each bullet and expand it into a sentence, then review what you've written to ensure it flows. Cut out any unnecessary words—don't trap listeners in a long-winded tale about your entire life history. You'll have ample opportunity to hone your delivery by using it at career and networking events, informational interviews, and even the grocery store. Introduce yourself with your speech using your name, what you are looking for, your most recent position and major responsibilities, and a brief description of your proudest accomplishment. Keep it in a conversational tone, and remember to stay within about a minute in duration. Then smile and be yourself!

—Brian Anderson, Director of Career Transition and Member Services, MOAA

CASE STUDY

Top 10 Résumé Mistakes (and Solutions)

1. Using so much military jargon that an HR professional cannot determine where you would best fit with the company.

Solution: Describe the skills you gained in the military in a transferable manner; don't focus on one aspect of your position but rather on the responsibilities and accomplishments as a whole that is not specific to the military.

2. Including multiple phone numbers.

   Solution: Include only your primary phone number, and make sure you have an answering machine or voicemail set up along with a courteous professional greeting. Avoid using slang or songs in your greeting.

3. Leaving off your email address.

   Solution: Always include your email address. This is the second most popular way (after the telephone) the vast majority of employers and recruiters correspond. Always use a professional, civilian email address.

4. Including a picture on the résumé.

   Solution: Leave off all pictures. In the United States, this information could be considered discriminatory and should always be left off.

5. Adding personal information about yourself (e.g., married with two children ages seven and nine).

   Solution: Leave this off altogether. You do not want to allow the hiring manager to make assumptions they are not allowed by law to make. For example, the HR professional may feel you will not travel because of your family.

6. Including any information that would specifically lead a reasonable person to know from a résumé your race, color, or religious affiliation.

   Solution: Leave off all information regarding any group or award that specifically reveals your race, color, or religious background. Knowing this background is a hot potato for an employer and will cause them to immediately eliminate the résumé from consideration.

7. Résumé is longer than three pages.

   Solution: The longest any résumé should be is two pages. Remember: The purpose of a résumé is to tell a brief career history—emphasis on brief. Many people feel they will look better to an employer if they have a longer résumé. The reality is that the reverse is true. A curriculum vitae, which is used in countries outside the United States and Canada, should be longer, but not a résumé. It is alright to have multiple résumés that highlight different jobs—it will all depend on the targeted career objective.

8.   Using the word "I" anywhere in the résumé.

   Solution: A résumé is written in the third person.

9.   Using elaborate or nonstandard fonts.

   Solution: Use a standard font. The closer the font is to one that is used in a book, the better. Both people and optical character readers (OCRs) can read the standard fonts such as Times New Roman or Courier. Remember, the purpose of sending a résumé to an employer is to have it read. The top three industry fonts are Times Roman, Garamond, and Arial.

10.   Having a résumé that does not match the person.

   Solution: People are brought in for interviews based on their résumé. If the person who shows up to the interview does not match the résumé, then the organization feels misled.

—Wounded Warrior Project[4]

. . . .

ENDNOTES

1.   Chairman of the Joint Chiefs of Staff, *DOD Dictionary of Military and Associated Terms* (Washington, DC: The Joint Staff, February 2018), http://www.jcs.mil/Portals/36/Documents/Doctrine/pubs/dictionary.pdf.

2.   Tracy C. McCausland et al., *What Veterans Bring to Civilian Workplaces* (Santa Monica: RAND Publications, 2017), https://www.rand.org/pubs/tools/TL160z1-1.html.

3.   Wounded Warrior Project, *Warriors to Work Planning Guide*, 38.

4.   Wounded Warrior Project, 30.

CHAPTER 5

Interviewing Veterans

US veterans are some of the most personable and fun-loving people you'll ever meet, but can sometimes seem stoic or rigid during an interview. Hiring managers can begin interviews with an icebreaker to help loosen things up. We've found acknowledgment of their service to the country and a genuine display of gratitude is a great way to start.

—Dave Strachan, Chief of Staff, 7–Eleven, Inc.

MAKING YOUR VETERAN INTERVIEWEE FEEL COMFORTABLE

The interview is a critical part of your hiring process, and it is very important that both you and the veteran across from you feel comfortable. The good news is, there are some relatively easy steps that you can take to make that veteran feel more at home.

 LEARNING POINT

From the beginning of the interview or phone conversation, encourage the candidates to tell their stories. During an introduction, the interviewers might set a clear example and establish a more comfortable tone by briefly telling their own professional background in story form.

—Todd Dombrowski, Director of Revenue Management for Pricing Strategy at MillerCoors

There are a few easy steps you can take to make job seekers a little more comfortable when they walk into your office. Because you want them to relax and set a conversational tone, start by offering them a bottle of water. Right off the bat, the job seeker will probably revert to their military training and call you "Sir" or "Ma'am." Explain to them that you certainly appreciate their military courtesy, but that they should just refer to you by your first name.

Many of you have some experience yourselves with the military or have family members or close friends who have served. Make sure to take this opportunity to share this experience. It will make veterans feel a lot better knowing you have some familiarity with their background. Remember, a large majority of veterans are concerned that civilians do not understand them, so any bridges you can quickly build with the job seekers across from you will help them stay relaxed throughout the interview. Ultimately, this helps you have a good conversation with them and identify if they are a good fit. If you don't have any personal experience with the military, you may quickly discuss why your company values veterans and how many veterans you have already hired.

 LEARNING POINT

When possible, hiring managers without prior military service should consider inviting a veteran within the organization to sit in during the interview. The veteran candidate, as well as

the hiring manager, may feel more at ease with a "translator" present, significantly reducing anxiety and allowing the dialogue to flow more freely.

—Dave Strachan, Chief of Staff, 7-Eleven, Inc.

Also, take the time to talk about your time with the company, and provide the structure for the interview. This way, the job seeker understands what you do on a daily basis and understands the way ahead for the interview. Veterans are familiar with how many military briefings go, but because this interview will follow a different format, your guidance here will be helpful.

"QUOTABLE"

"Veterans, for the most part, do not speak about their accomplishments. Asking questions that allow veterans to open up about their achievements is critical to getting the most out of them. Taking the time to listen and truly be interested in who they are will go a long way in building trust and respect."

—Jerry Flanagan, CEO and Founder of JDog Junk Removal

Finally, it is a good idea to start the interview with some simple questions about the military that the veteran can answer easily to help them feel more at ease. Ask them why they joined the military, and how they picked the particular branch they joined. Ask them about their overall experience in the military. Ask why they decided to leave the military. Ask about some of the values they appreciated in the military. Now they will certainly feel a lot more comfortable than when they first walked into your office.

 LEARNING POINT

Many service members join the military right out of high school or college, so if they are coming to you straight from the service, they probably have never sat through an interview like this before.

BREAKOUT BOX

Making Your Veteran Interviewee Feel Comfortable

1. Ask them to call you by your first name.

2. Talk about any connections you may have to the military.

3. Discuss the reasons your company likes to hire veterans.

4. Provide the structure for the interview.

5. Start with softball questions to make them feel more at ease.

UNDERSTANDING THE VETERAN ACROSS FROM YOU

It is important for you to understand a few things about the veteran's experience and comfort level with interviews. This will help you view things from the veteran's perspective. Right now we are going to focus on four points that apply in a general sense to many veterans.

The first is that in the military, you never have to interview for a job. You take a whole battery of tests when you first join to make sure you are eligible, but during your time in the military there is a higher ranking officer called a career planner who decides what position would be the best for you, based first on the needs of the service and then what is a good fit for you. Often, if a service member has to come in to an office like yours and have a one-on-one conversation like this, it is because something bad has happened. So, the veterans are probably very nervous when they come to see you.

Second, the veteran probably will not have the typical stories that other applicants bring from other corporations, but will have a set of skills and values that should be explored. Civilian candidates for your positions will probably come to you from companies similar to your own, often making lateral moves of some sort, and therefore can provide examples of work they have done that correlate nicely with what you are looking for. For example, if you are looking for a program manager, someone who has already worked with your competitor as a program manager knows exactly what you are looking for. But a veteran may very well have performed those duties in the military without realizing it, and won't necessarily know what to stress during the interview.

 LEARNING POINT

Our military spends a lot of time and money teaching leadership, teamwork, and confidence to our troops. Make sure you ask about these soft skills, because you can teach the industry-specific skills.

Third, veterans are taught from day one the value of the team over themselves, and thus it is unnatural for them to openly discuss their accomplishments. In the private sector you understand that part of networking is not just identifying how you can help somebody, but also highlighting some of your personal accomplishments; that thought process is not one that veterans typically share. Because teamwork is so critical to success in the military, and in combat can be the difference between life and death, their first instinct is not to talk about themselves. This, however, is counterproductive in an interview.

And finally, veterans often take their skill sets for granted. Many veterans are used to talking and hanging out with other veterans or service members, and therefore it does not occur to them that the skill sets they have picked up and honed in the military do not exist everywhere else. They are often unaware that the capabilities they have developed in the military are actually extremely beneficial in the private sector. Therefore, they may not be as forward about highlighting these talents as their civilian counterparts may be.

Just understanding this general background information will help you create a more comfortable interview environment, because it will help you shape your questions and give you further insight regarding how the veteran across from you answers your questions.

BREAKOUT BOX

Understanding the Veteran across from You

1. This very well may be the veteran's first official job interview.

2. These veterans may not be as conversant with industry language as their civilian counterparts, and their work examples may be different than what you are used to.

3. Teamwork is critical in the military, often with life-or-death repercussions. Therefore, these veterans may be more inclined to talk about what their teams did than their own individual accomplishments.

4. Veterans often take their unique skill sets for granted.

PEELING BACK THE ONION

For the reasons mentioned above, you may have to ask several follow-up questions to pull out the material you are really looking for. Service members are often taught to simply answer exactly what they have been asked and only offer explanatory details upon further prompting. For example, if you asked a veteran what she did during her deployment, she may say, "I drove a truck." That does not necessarily sound very impressive unless you peel back the onion with further questions and find out that she led a team of four while she was there, drove that truck during many combat missions and was personally responsible for maintaining it, and received an award for her time there. She probably takes for granted the leadership and logistical skills that go into "just" driving a truck in Iraq, and may not spell those out for you.

 LEARNING POINT

Service members are taught not to brag. Feel free to ask follow-up questions to get the information you are really looking for.

BREAKOUT BOX

Questions You Should Ask to Learn More about the Veteran in Your Office

1. What formal schooling or courses did you take while in the military?

2. Did you ever hold any "B" billets (assignments outside primary specialty)?

3. What did you like about your favorite duty station?

4. What was your favorite rank and why?

5. Did anything surprise you about the military after you joined?

BREAKOUT BOX

A Hiring Manager's Guide to Interviewing Veterans

1. **Learn the language.** Military experience on a résumé doesn't always translate clearly into an average civilian job description. For a better interview with a veteran candidate, learn a bit of the language and structure of the military for a broader view of how experience and responsibilities may translate into corporate roles.

2. **Get what's behind the résumé.** From training to combat, teamwork is central to all in the military. This background can make veterans ideal employees, but not always ideal job

candidates, as they may be reluctant to highlight individual accomplishments and instead speak more of team-oriented achievements in an interview. By asking deeper questions on a candidate's experience and talents, hiring managers invite a candidate to share more insight into their personal background and expertise.

3. **Go beyond military experience.** No candidate can be defined by a particular aspect of their background, no matter how important it may be. While critical to connecting a candidate's military experience to possible corporate roles, their potential should not be limited to their military service. Instead, that should be the beginning of a meaningful conversation on their complete background. Conversation that goes into other interests may also provide opportunity for veteran candidates who worry about being pigeonholed for positions by being evaluated solely on their military experience.

—Patricia A. Lee, Senior Vice President of HR and
Chief Diversity Officer for Wyndham Worldwide

WHAT TO ASK DURING THE INTERVIEW

As in any other interview, once you have developed a little connection, you can move on to asking substantive questions to figure out if your veteran job seeker will be a good fit for your company. We already identified that because their job in the military might not have lined up exactly with the civilian job they are applying for, you have to determine if they have the basic skills to provide good value to you. After you ask the following questions, you should be listening for can-do attitudes, initiative, going above and beyond, and awards or recognitions they may have received. Notice that the questions don't focus on skills they may have learned at a private company, but the answers will help you determine if the job seeker will fit well within your corporate culture and be valuable to you. You can always teach the specifics of your industry company, but typically you cannot teach attitude and work ethic.

- **Tell me three things about this job that are important to you professionally.**

  This is a good way to identify if they have really thought about what this job would mean to them, and you will have further insight into where they want to go professionally.

- **What do you want to find, achieve, or accomplish in this next role?**
  Many veterans are great leaders, and here they may identify for you how they see their growth path with your business. They may also use this as an opportunity to explain how they envision translating what they learned in the military to benefit your organization.

- **Describe your ideal team environment or corporate culture.**
  Listen for similarities to your team and culture to ensure a good match if you do hire them. If there is not much of a match here, the likelihood that this will result in a long-time employment relationship is probably low compared to a veteran who is closely aligned to what the company offers them professionally.

- **I understand that veterans have a very strong focus on missions. What do you do in the planning stage of a mission to ensure success?**
  This will help you understand how the veteran will approach challenges in the workplace.

- **What characteristics or attributes do you see as similar between the position you are applying for and your job in the military?**
  This gives veterans an opportunity to talk about why their background is relevant to the particular position, which you may not have been aware of from reading their résumé. This helps veterans talk about something they are familiar with, and helps you understand a job history you may not be familiar with.

- **As a leader, how do you create an environment of success for your team?**
  Virtually every veteran has served in some sort of leadership capacity, and this a great way to find out how they can bring that to your team. Also, teamwork is critical for the success of any organization, and this provides an excellent opportunity for veterans to show you how they would lead small teams well.

Of course, you will likely want to ask more questions than this during your interview. This list will provide a good base for you to understand a lot more about the veteran across the table from you, and these questions can serve as a good guide for you to use when crafting your own questions.

LEARNING POINT

High-performing organizations often value many of the same skills embraced and nurtured by our military. It is worth your time to find out how veterans can apply what they have learned to your office.

BREAKOUT BOX

Sample List of Further Questions

1. I noticed on your résumé that you have received a number of military decorations. Please talk to me about those.

2. What is the largest number of people you have led? What were some challenges you faced with that and how did you resolve those challenges?

3. Effective communication is important to us, and I know that is also true in the military. Tell me about some effective communication techniques and practices you have experienced or used during your time in the military.

4. I know it is important in the military for you to take care of each other, and you often have leaders around you helping you make the right decisions. Do you have any thoughts about how that attitude can be implemented in the private sector?

5. During your time in the military, you must have had a chance to observe many different aspects of leadership. What are some of the things you have learned about leadership that you bring with you today?

QUESTIONS *NOT* TO ASK IN AN INTERVIEW

Of course, the job seekers who come and interview with you are probably nervous. But the truth is, you are probably a little nervous too as you initiate the interview. It makes sense that if you are not well versed in the ways of the military and are a unsure about what is fact and what is just a stereotype of military life, this can be a somewhat nerve-wracking.

It is up to you to ask the right questions and avoid asking the wrong ones. Not only is this an issue of making sure you conduct an impactful interview, but you also have to be careful to not ask any questions that are precluded by law. Needless to say, it is always a great idea to consult with your organization's attorneys to make sure your typical questions are consistent with the laws surrounding job interviews. That being said, there are only a few areas you should avoid that are particular to veterans:

1. **What type of discharge did you get from the military?**

   As you may already know, service members can receive several different characterizations of their service when they leave the military. However, except for some very limited situations typically related to federal contractors, this is a question you cannot ask. That being said, you can of course ask all sorts of questions about what the veteran learned in the military and how it applies to the position they are interviewing for.

2. **Will you be deployed anytime soon?**

   Or a related question: Will you miss much work because of your military service? You may have noticed from the résumé that the applicant in front of you is in the Reserves or National Guard, but you are strictly precluded from asking about any sort of future deployments. It is against the law to discriminate against someone in the Reserves or the National Guard, and this question is typically interpreted as discriminatory in nature.

3. **Anything related to potential combat injuries.**

   Under the Americans with Disabilities Act, it is illegal to ask applicants questions about disabilities. Similarly, it is illegal to ask veterans questions about PTSD, TBIs, whether or not they are seeking mental health treatment, or if they were injured in combat. Of course, you can ask them about their training and education and whether they can perform the minimum requirements for the job.

☀ LEARNING POINT

Never ask a veteran if they killed somebody. It may sound obvious to you, but this is a question often posed to veterans.

Those are the four main areas to stay away from. Of course, you should always prepare your questions for the interview in advance and take the time to carefully read over the candidate's résumé before the interview. It is also important for you to ask the same questions to every candidate; that way you can ensure that you are comparing apples to apples.

Now go and enjoy that impactful interview!

VETERAN AND MILITARY SPOUSE RESOURCE CENTER

A common expression many veterans will be familiar with from our time in the military is the six *P*s. It stands for Proper Planning Prevents Piss-Poor Performance, which may sound a little harsh. Every aspect of a successful transition requires proper planning, and the interview piece is no different. When you are unprepared, interviews can be very humbling experiences. However, when you take the time to prepare by following the advice below, you will find that interviews are something to truly look forward to because they allow you the opportunity to shine and explain all the attributes you have to offer.

There are three basic steps you want to take before any interview. One of the biggest mistakes you can make is to assume that you can wing it and not put in the time before the interview to prepare and be on top of your game when you walk into that critical meeting.

1. **Research the company.** Talk to other veterans who work there, scroll through the company's website, and read their press releases. Knowledge is power, and understanding their corporate culture is important for your interview.
2. **Review your résumé.** The HR professional across from you will likely ask you questions based directly on your résumé, so you need to know what is on there! This is a good chance to consider how those positions you held relate to the one you are seeking now.
3. **Rehearse answers to commonly asked interview questions.** Talk to friends of yours who have already made the transition to the private sector specifically about questions they answered in the interview. Literally practice saying your answers out loud until you are comfortable addressing a number of different topics.

BREAKOUT BOX

Commonly Asked Interview Questions

1. Tell me about yourself.

2. What do you know about our company?

3. What value do you believe can bring to our company?

4. What salary are you seeking?

5. What is your leadership style?

6. How will your military experience benefit us?

7. Tell me about a challenging situation you faced in the past and how you resolved it.

8. Describe your ideal team situation/corporate culture.

9. What is the significance of some of your military decorations?

10. Give me both a good and a bad example of leadership styles you saw in the military and what you learned from them.

If you think about it, this first interview is not so different from some of the meetings you may have already had in the military, especially when you first check in to a unit. Of course, that meeting is often more formal and may not be as in-depth as your corporate interview, but the idea is the same. You have the chance to make a great first impression, identify your work history and what you can add to the new team, and perhaps even ask a few questions about what will be expected of you.

 LEARNING POINT

Veterans are highly sought after by many top employers, and they should be. However, being called in to interview doesn't guarantee a job offer. Avoid beginning the interview with inquiries about salary, vacation, and other "What can you do for me?" type questions when the potential employer is most concerned with your ability to perform in the role.

—Tyrone Tobias, Manager, Field Talent and Veteran-hiring Initiatives, 7-Eleven, Inc.

Just like in the military, follow a few basic rules to start off on the right foot. As we often say, If you are on time, then you are late! Make sure you arrive ten to fifteen minutes early for your interview and allow plenty of time for unexpected traffic and parking issues. If it looks like you will be late, make sure to contact the interviewer at the earliest opportunity. Of course, as part of making a strong first impression, dress the part, give a good handshake, maintain eye contact, and be confident. These are lessons we all learned early in boot camp or officer candidate school, and the private sector appreciates these practices also.

It probably goes without saying that you should silence your cell phone or completely turn it off before you walk into the building and under no circumstances should you look at it during the interview. Finally, speak in a conversational tone, answer any questions in complete sentences, and use language that civilian employers can understand (no acronyms!).

 LEARNING POINT

To prepare for an interview, create a career narrative. Ideally, this should move beyond the standard thirty-second elevator speech or commercial and express your professional statement of purpose. Who are you professionally; what do you do well; how have you added value in the past; what do you want to do next and why? Practice this narrative and get comfortable delivering segments of your career narrative on the fly.

—Brian Anderson, Director of Career Transition and Member Services for MOAA

BREAKOUT BOX

How Do I Answer Their Questions?

Use the STARS format:

1. **Situation**: Describe the context within which you performed a job or faced a challenge at work.

2. **Task**: Describe your responsibility in that situation.

3. **Action**: Describe how you completed the task or endeavored to meet the challenge. Focus on what you did, rather than what your team, boss, or coworker did.

4. **Result**: Finally, explain the outcomes or results generated by the action taken.

5. **Skills**: Skills you used to be successful, including both hard skills (technical) and soft skills (leadership, teaching, etc.).

—Chad Storlie, Founder of Combat to Corporate

Many people fail to follow up after their interviews and this can be a critical mistake. Following up demonstrates that you are proactive and interested in the position. Ensure that you either call the interviewer later in the week or send a thank-you note over email or through the traditional postal system. Thank them for their time and reinforce that you are very interested in the position.

 **LEARNING POINT**

It is an imperative to promptly send a thank-you note, even if you do not think the interview went well or you have doubts about the culture of the company. A well-written thank-you note will preserve future options with the employer.

· · · · · · · · · · ·
CASE STUDY

Five Sample Thank-You Notes: Use, Customize, and Improve

1. Thank you for the opportunity to discuss the _____ role with [the company]. I believe my [A] and [B] skills, combined with significant [C] and [D] experience, would be an asset to your team. I look forward to future discussions to learn how I can contribute to your organization's goals. Sincerely,

2. I very much enjoyed our conversation yesterday about the _____ opportunity on your team. After our time together, I'm even more enthusiastic about how my experience can make a measurable impact on your department's deliverables, and I hope to hear from you in the near future. Best regards,

3. It was a pleasure meeting you yesterday to learn about the _____ position with [the company]. I am very interested in learning more and continuing our conversation. I feel my background is a strong fit for your team. Thank you for the opportunity to meet, and I look forward to hearing from you. Very truly yours,

4. I truly appreciate the time you shared yesterday to talk about the _____ role in your department. Your insights about the position were very helpful, and I hope to have the opportunity to further continue our dialogue and learn more about a career with [the company]. Thanks and regards,

5. Thank you for our interview this week; the time and insight you shared were very much appreciated. After our meeting, I've become even more enthusiastic about

the _____ opportunity with your company, and I know that my experience and industry background would allow me to quickly make a contribution to your team. I look forward to future discussions with [the company]. Kind regards,

—Wounded Warrior Project[1]

Like every other aspect of your career search, make it a priority to reach out to others and benefit from their experience when preparing for your interviews. In most areas around the country, with a little digging you can find a nonprofit organization or corporate entity that will provide these services to you. Remember, many HR departments that focus on hiring veterans have at least one veteran working in that department and they periodically will take extra steps to make sure our nation's veterans are properly prepared for networking, writing résumés, and interviewing. In the final case study for this chapter, you can learn about what BP did to support female veterans. With a little research, you can probably find similar opportunities in your community no matter your demographic.

CASE STUDY

Female Veteran Interview Skills and Training Program

At BP, we believe that in an ongoing effort to support our veterans, it is important not only that we provide them with employment opportunities, but also that we train them in the areas of interviewing and résumé writing in preparation for employment opportunities.

After introducing the Military Placement Program (MPP), we saw a low number of female applicants for the program compared to male applicants. We decided to create an initiative that would (1) broaden our reach within the veteran talent pool for women, (2) bring greater gender balance in the applicants for MPP and other career opportunities at BP, and (3) equip female candidates with the right skills to be fully prepared for interviewing to improve their candidacy in hiring decisions.

We partnered with veteran service organizations in the community that had a focus on female veterans. BP presented a two-hour résumé writing and interview skills workshop. The session covered basic résumé writing tips (types, style, format, and purpose), personal branding advice, and interview dos and don'ts from a recruiter or hiring manager's perspective, suitable for candidates pursuing full-time careers in any industry.

The Benefits

- Veterans were able to ask questions directly to the experts involved in the recruitment process.
- Female veterans were able to comfortably relate to the recruiting team as the team shared real-life examples and career stories.
- Veterans were able to personally connect with BP professionals via LinkedIn, building their network.
- Attracting, hiring, retaining, and developing a diverse workforce is critical to the future success of BP's business, and increasing the proportion of ex-military employees within its workforce is key to this.

—Pree Newton, Resourcing Specialist, BP

ENDNOTE

1. Wounded Warrior Project, *Warriors to Work Planning Guide*, 67.

CHAPTER 6

Creating a Military–Friendly and Military–Ready Work Environment

Veteran employment is a micro-market with fewer candidates, higher demand, and more competition for top talent. A shift from being veteran "friendly" to actively attracting and pursuing veterans will be required as the market tightens and competition to hire gets steeper.

—Karin Childress-Wiley, military spouse and
CEO of Authentic Veteran Solutions

We have already discussed some important aspects of attracting veterans to your business and hiring them. You have learned some great sources for military talent, as well as how to read a military résumé and interview veterans. But of course, that is only part of the equation. You must also be able to identify who your veteran-employees are (both existing and incoming) and how to create a working environment that inspires them and makes them feel valuable to you.

VETERAN SELF-IDENTIFICATION

Virtually every organization with a veteran-hiring initiative struggles to ensure that all of their veteran-employees actually self-identify as veterans. There are a number of reasons why they may not. Some simply may not want to be labeled a veteran. Some may not consider themselves veterans because they did not serve for twenty years (this is a common misperception among those who confuse "veteran" with "retiree"). Some may not have had a positive experience while serving in the military and simply prefer to move on. Some may think you want to track them for negative reasons. Some veterans are concerned that corporations will assume they have PTSD if they identify as veterans.

But in order to measure both the effectiveness of your veteran-hiring initiative's ability to attract, develop, and retain veterans and the impact veterans make within your organization, it is important that you know which employees are veterans and where they work. After all, how can you demonstrate the value of hiring veterans if you are not gathering any sort of metrics on them?

Failure to track and measure veterans' performance within the firm may lead to a poor understanding and lack of recognition of veteran-employee contributions. When you are able to track your veterans, you can affirmatively and authoritatively identify how many have been promoted compared to their civilian counterparts, how they are progressing in general, and how their retention rates compare with other employees. We know that veterans bring incredible skills and abilities to your workplace, but you will not be able to adequately share that information with your colleagues and chain of command if you do not have an accurate understanding of who your veterans are.

"QUOTABLE"

"In order to measure both the effectiveness of a program's ability to attract, develop, and retain veterans and the impact veterans make within the organization it is important that an organization know which employees are veterans and where they work."

—Institute for Veterans and Military Families[1]

It is critical for you to educate veteran and military families in your workplace about the benefits of tracking. Assure them that when you take efforts to identify your veterans, it is ultimately for their benefit, and to ensure support from upper management so that your organization can hire more veterans.

 LEARNING POINT

Many companies include a generic question about military service, such as "Are you a military veteran?" at the bottom of an employee application. And often, those questions go unanswered for the reasons listed above. However, a more thoughtful question designed to inspire a response would be, "At ABC Company, we truly value military service and prioritize hiring veterans and military spouses. Please indicate here if you served in the military (including the National Guard or Reserve)."

BREAKOUT BOX

Five Tactics Used by Corporations with Mature Veteran-Hiring Programs to Encourage Veteran Self-Identification

1. Host social events and cocktail hours just for veterans to recognize and honor their service. This encourages your veteran-employees to attend the events and gives them an opportunity, especially if you have computers available, to physically update the employee database and self-identify.

2. Leverage the veteran-employee resource group and ask the members to reach out to other veteran-employees who have not yet self-identified.

3. If you have one, utilize your internal social media site and create a great military or veteran group. You can invite current veteran-employees to join and share information through the platform. The veterans could provide short articles about how their military experience has

benefited them at your organization, and this could also be posted in your internal newsletter (if applicable).

4. Create a veteran wall at your headquarters profiling your veteran-employees with their pictures and details about their service to our country. This positive recognition can help reduce concerns about identifying as veterans.

5. Develop a challenge coin modeled after coins in the military. In many cases the CEO gives out the coins to recognize and honor veterans company-wide. This incentivizes veterans to self-identify because these coins are associated with hard work and well-deserved recognition.

Ultimately, tracking your veteran-employees should be identified as a top human resources concern. Naturally, employees are critical to your organization's well-being. To get a true statistical picture of whether veteran retention is an issue, you first need an accurate number of how many of your employees are veterans.

After identifying who your veterans are, it is important to assess what happens once your new veteran-hires show up for work, specifically what steps you should take to create a military-friendly onboarding process and work environment. Ultimately, creating an inviting and impactful environment for your veteran-employees will go a long way toward their extended retention, providing ever-increasing value for you. Later in this chapter we will discuss why veterans typically leave their first jobs out of the military. A lot of that has to do with corporations not empowering them with the levels of responsibility they are used to, and not providing the culture of inclusivity and teamwork to which they are accustomed.

As a quick review, more than 2.5 million Americans have served our country in the military since the terrorist attacks of 2001.[2] Also, due to sequestration and the drawdown of our military, the military currently discharges approximately a quarter of a million service members annually and that number is likely to remain at the same level over the next three to five years.[3] At the same time, according to the Bush Institute, 84 percent of veterans say the American public has "little awareness" of the challenges facing those who wear or have worn the nation's uniform, and 71 percent of Americans say they do not understand the problems faced by those who have served since 9/11.[4] So, across our country we certainly have what is called a civ-mil divide, but there are a number of steps you can take to create a military-friendly work environment at your organization. A thoughtful onboarding process is critical if you want to attract and retain veterans, and the veteran orientation is the first part of that.

BREAKOUT BOX

Describing the Civ-Mil Divide

The civil-military divide is characterized by a widening geographic, demographic, cultural, and social gap between the nation and those who serve in the all-volunteer military. Currently, only 1.1 percent of the population serves in the active duty or reserve components of the US military, or as Department of Defense civilians. Similarly, just 7 percent of the nation's population are veterans—approximately 22 million out of 320 million. These proportions reflect a number of demographic phenomena, including the fading away of the large World War II, Cold War, and Vietnam War cohorts, the end of conscription, and the growth of the US population relative to the size of the military. These trends are likely to continue, creating a broader and deeper divide between American society and those who serve in the military.

—Center for a New American Security (CNAS)[5]

Before we even address steps you should take to directly welcome your new veteran-hires aboard and to set them up for success, one important piece has to already be in place: you need to have a corporate champion who is an executive-level leader within your company who is a supporter of and spokesperson for veteran employment. Virtually all firms that have successfully implemented veteran-focused programs have also identified executive-level champions responsible for those initiatives. So, what exactly is a corporate champion and why are they important?

CORPORATE CHAMPION

The veteran employment champion will lead your efforts in a highly visible and critical area: serving as the point of contact both internally and externally for your veteran-hiring program. Remember, your executives often have robust networks outside of your organization and can leverage contacts within your industry or supply chain to encourage other organizations to join your veteran initiative.

Visible and proactive commitment from your leadership is critical. The importance of recruiting and onboarding veterans needs to be conveyed not only to the veterans you are hiring, but to two other groups as well:

- **Overall staff.** Helping them understand that recruiting and supporting veterans is a priority and good for business will foster an atmosphere of acceptance and respect among all of your employees.
- **Customers and business partners.** Letting them know of your commitment to recruiting and successfully onboarding veterans may encourage them to do the same, and they will likely appreciate the fact that you have instituted this program.

BREAKOUT BOX

Involvement of a Corporate Champion

U.S. Bank celebrates, honors, and engages veteran-employees and employees with family in the military. Through the Proud to Serve Business Resource Group (BRG), employees are connected with opportunities to develop personally and professionally, give back to the community, and support the business strategy.

The driving force behind BRGs is employees—and U.S. Bank's executive management team leads by example. President, Chairman, and CEO Andy Cecere leads BRG efforts across the company. John Elmore (vice chairman of community banking and branch delivery) and Mike Ott (president of private wealth management and USAF veteran) serve as executive sponsors of the Proud to Serve BRG.

U.S. Bank leaders honor veterans' contributions in many ways:

- Leaders who are also veterans personally welcome veteran-employees.
- The entire company is invited to attend an annual Veterans Day event that honors employee veterans and military family members.
- Deployed employees are personally contacted by Cecere and other senior leaders.
- Proud to Serve BRG's vision and strategy is informed by an advisory council of veterans.

There are a number of potential programmatic benefits for your organization when an executive oversees a particular program:

- Executive-level engagement promotes robust assessment and the development of metrics designed to evaluate progress.
- Reporting progress at the executive level promotes opportunities to address institutional barriers and enhance opportunities for veterans.
- Programmatic successes connected to executive-level engagement are likely to be visible inside and outside the organization.
- The commitment of resources to enable recruitment, hiring, retention, and advancement is more likely given executive-level engagement.

"QUOTABLE"

"With executive sponsorship at the highest levels of our organization, our veterans network is able to spread the word about the value of hiring and retaining veterans in the workplace. Members attend networking events, career fairs, and panel discussions specifically directed toward veterans. This helps our veterans connect with one another, our clients, and the larger veteran communities across the United States."

—Joseph M. McHugh, Northeast Leader of Complex Program Management at Ernst & Young LLP

Often, corporate champions for veteran-hiring initiatives served in the military themselves, but that does not necessarily have to be the case. What is required is that the champion fully supports veterans and military spouses, understands the values they bring to the workplace, and is willing to provide the leadership necessary to make your program a success.

VETERAN ORIENTATION

Make Them Feel Welcome

In the military, service members often have "sponsors" when they first check in to a new duty station, and that person shows them the ropes related to their job and introduces them to other people in the shop. Therefore, your new military veterans will probably feel more comfortable if you welcome them on their first day and introduce them to key personnel within your organization as soon as they arrive. It will be easier for them to interact with these employees later if they have already been introduced.

LEARNING POINT

At CarMax, we recognize and show support for our military associates by providing them with a commemorative pin to wear on their uniforms and honor their military service.

—Bill Nash, CEO of CarMax

If you have a veteran-employee resource group (VERG) or similar group at your organization (see the section later in this chapter specifically about VERGs), it is a great idea to introduce your veteran-hire to the ERG leadership as soon as possible. These men and women will be great resources for your new hire and the sooner they know each other, the better. The first day can be challenging for any new employee, so introducing this veteran to other veterans right off the bat can alleviate some of that stress.

CASE STUDY

AGS and Creating a Team

The Tribe

We throw a lot of aphorisms around at AGS—"Be like water," "It takes a village," "It's just hard work," and "Hope is *not* a plan." This helps us reinforce certain behaviors that emphasize the importance of a team approach to doing business. To become a stronger tribe, we need to be like water and know that flexibility is key. We understand that we can't take on the world ourselves, but if the village takes on the task, we can tackle anything. In a fast-paced, growing environment, we are all required to work hard. The reinforcement that no matter what we do together, it's just hard work gets us through some long days and nights together. Last but not least, the basis of our tribal thinking is the idea that as a team, we don't hope—we plan, we communicate, and we execute.

How This Helps Our Veterans

Veterans are part of one of the largest teams, tribes, or fraternities on earth and are comfortable with social activities and events that promote community and public recognition. Be it a town hall, a company-sponsored social event, or even employee-led events, the culture encourages an environment where employees feel more like family than a group of individuals who look out for their own needs. At AGS, we believe that the flock, the tribe, and the family spirit lends well to most employees, but especially those who experienced the close-knit nature of military life. Once again, the more we can create a community that is informative, comfortable, safe, and supportive, the better chance we have of attracting and retaining quality veterans.

—David Lopez, President and CEO of AGS

• • • • • • • • • • • •

 LEARNING POINT

Having a robust orientation on day one will make your veteran feel welcome and demonstrate that you care about their presence and contribution.

If you provide mentors for your new hires, it is very beneficial to introduce the veteran to their mentor on the first day in case they have early questions. The mentor should be sure to discuss how work expectations differ in the military from what they encounter in the private sector and at your particular company.

 LEARNING POINT

Mentorship is often taken quite seriously in the military, so veterans are often used to warmer welcomes than we may typically see in the private sector. On their first day, it might be a great idea to get the whole department together (if possible) for lunch or have at least two other team members take the new hire to lunch. If you have a VERG, make sure to include them.

Of course, your new hires should definitely meet with their first-line supervisors and any other members of the leadership team as appropriate on their first day. Veterans typically are used to checking in with their leadership right away in the military, so this should be a familiar process for them. Also, having frequent check-ins will allow managers to assess what the new hire has learned in their first few weeks, and will help gauge whether or not they need assistance in any areas.

BREAKOUT BOX

Integrating Veterans Right Off the Bat

When integrating veterans into a new work environment, it's important to recognize that the first impression of the employer is as important as the first impression of the veteran-employee. While getting oriented into the new workplace, the veteran should know who their immediate leader is who their mentor or advisor might be (if possible), and what success in this environment looks like for them. Having a network of other veterans, new employees, and mentors can ensure an easier transition for the veteran and better potential outcomes for retention.

— Victor LaGroon, Director of the Office of Veterans Affairs for the City of Chicago

---

Provide a Roadmap for Success

While in the military, service members are taught very early on what it takes to succeed at their rank and what they need to do to be promoted. They know what courses they need to complete, what kind of scores they need on their physical fitness tests, and how they will be graded against their peers. Therefore, right from the start, make sure your veteran–hires understand how your company works; its policies, and its procedures. This will help them fit in easily and quickly and immediately contribute to the company. Chances are, they will have a lot to process when they start at your organization, and this type of information will make them feel a lot more comfortable.

BREAKOUT BOX

Why Provide a Roadmap for Success?

It is very important to assist with veterans' transitions by providing a roadmap for success within your organization. Veterans are accustomed to being part of a team, and their new roles may require them to be self-sufficient and work as individual contributors. This new environment may cause a sense of isolation, but having another veteran-employee meet with the new hire regularly will make the transition easier. And, getting involved in employee resource groups, especially veteran-focused groups will allow the veteran to be part of a new team.

—James Rodriguez, Founder and Principal of The Rodriguez Group

---

You probably hired this veteran because you value their military service and recognize that the skills they learned in the military will help you and your company succeed. Therefore, emphasize how their military background makes them a great fit for the company and the job you hired them to do. Veterans often state that while in the military they enjoyed being part of something much larger than themselves, and this is likely to help provide that same feeling.

Also, provide a vision for the future and help the veterans understand where they fit within your organization. It is important for you to remember that your hierarchy or corporate organization may be quite different than what they are used to. By communicating that you are willing to invest time and money in order for them to achieve mutual goals, you greatly increase the likelihood of a successful onboarding process.

 LEARNING POINT

One of the reasons that veterans leave their civilian jobs is that they do not feel they have much of a purpose there—tying their background in with how they can provide great value to your organization can help alleviate that issue.

Communicate Expectations

When the veteran's new manager first meets with them, it is important that they effectively communicate expectations. Remember, this might be the first civilian job your new employee has held since joining the military. It is likely that some of the metrics you use to define and measure success at your company are different than those in the military, so time spent here is certainly time well spent.

"QUOTABLE"

"Understanding the military life cycle is critical to retaining veteran talent. The military has a distinct career trajectory with job rotations every two to three years. The lack of clarity on growth opportunity in a civilian role can be problematic for a veteran and cause him or her to look for opportunities elsewhere. Transparency around growth and development can help bridge the divide between civilian and military culture."

—Kate Migliaro, Director of Diversity and Veterans Initiatives at Apollo Global Management

Set clear expectations with the veterans about their role and contribution. Because veterans come from an environment where orders and instructions are often written down, it is helpful to provide them with a written plan or job description detailing objectives, related tasks, and the most appropriate points of contact.

 LEARNING POINT

The military is mission driven, as are most companies. Discuss the company or department's mission and vision with them early on. Missions are familiar to them and will make them feel more at ease.

 LEARNING POINT

While a lateral hire may have a very good sense of how your company fits into the larger industry, it is often helpful to explain to your new veteran-hire how your organization is viewed internally and externally, and its business challenges and opportunities.

BREAKOUT BOX

Five Keys to a Robust Veteran Orientation

1. Have somebody ready to meet them on their first day and introduce them to their team and chain of command.

2. Take them to lunch on their first day and include members of the VERG if possible.

3. The first-line manager should spend dedicated time with the new hire on their first day and also check in periodically over the first few weeks.

4. Emphasize how their military background will help them succeed with you.

5. Be clear about what it takes to succeed at your organization and how they can do so.

Including Military Families

Over half of active duty and Reservist military members are married and taking care of the family is important in the military. Even those who are not married are often included in family events around holidays. The military understands that a strong family unit at home increases the productivity and well-being of their troops. Therefore, it is likely that your new veteran–employee comes from a background that stresses the importance of family.

While this same focus does not always exist in the private sector, there are steps you can take to make your veteran feel more at home. For instance, if your organization provides volunteer work, you can select a nonprofit organization focused on military families as one of the groups you will support. While you are not helping the veteran directly, it sends a loud message that you support military families. Of course, this can tie into your branding efforts to be more military friendly. And if any of your employees deploy with the National Guard or the Reserves, you can periodically check in with their family to see if they need assistance of some sort.

BREAKOUT BOX

Four Ways Your Organization Can Support Military Families

1. Invite the family members of your deployed employees to corporate social events.

2. When you prepare care packages for your deployed employees, ask their families for advice on what to give and if they want to participate.

3. If your deployed employee is married, that spouse is probably doing the work for two during that deployment. Periodically ask what your organization can do to help.

4. Volunteer time or donate money to local military organizations that support military families.

BREAKOUT BOX

List of Ten Organizations That Support Military Families

1. Armed Services YMCA (www.asymca.org)

2. Blue Star Families (www.bluestarfam.org)

3. National Guard Family Program (www.jointservicessupport.org/FP/)

4. Operation Homefront (www.operationhomefront.net)

5. United Service Organizations (USO; www.uso.org)

6. Wounded Warrior Project (www.woundedwarriorproject.org)

7. Navy Marine Corps Relief Society (www.nmcrs.org)

8. National Military Family Association (www.militaryfamily.org)

9. MOAA Military Family Initiative (www.moaa.org/foundation)

10. Quality of Life Foundation (www.qolfoundation.org)

MILITARY BRANDING

Most transitioning service members have been part of the military longer than any other job and identify deeply with the military lifestyle. They are full of talent, but are often uncertain of what steps to take when leaving the military and joining the private sector. Naturally, they wonder whom they can trust, where they should start, and whom they should talk to.

These men and women are looking for organizations that clearly value their military service and understand the value that our veterans bring to the marketplace. That is why it is so important for you to successfully brand your company as military ready or military friendly. There is no simple solution for this, and it requires a concerted, coordinated effort across your entire organization. But because hiring top military talent is important to you, your efforts here will pay off exponentially.

For starters, put yourself in the shoes of the veterans who visit your website to learn more about you and to determine if you would be a good fit for them:

- What content and visuals on your website tell a visitor that military talent is welcomed and valued in your workplace?
- Does your homepage include links to a separate page devoted to content specifically for the military job seeker?
- Do you list benefits programs and employee resource groups and activities on your website that signal ongoing engagement after hire?

 **LEARNING POINT**

Ultimately, you need to be able to answer yes to the question, "If you were in the shoes of a transitioning service member, veteran, or military spouse, would you get the sense that you are welcomed at this company?"

Demonstrating your appreciation to veterans in your offices is an easy and fun way to brand yourself as military friendly and military ready. Plus, many of your employees will likely appreciate the opportunity to participate in events that celebrate our nation's military.

BREAKOUT BOX

Branding Your Organization

Make sure your website and all your recruiting materials clearly state that your company supports the hiring of veterans, including those with disabilities. Provide contact information for a member of your team—preferably a veteran—so that a job candidate who is a veteran can call with questions about how his or her military experience can translate to your company. Train your recruiting and hiring managers on veterans' skill sets, as well as the types of disabilities veterans may have and how they do and do not impact the workplace. They should understand common disabilities among veterans, such as PTSD and TBI, and how to have an appropriate conversation about disabilities and accommodations should a job candidate raise the issue.

—Disabled American Veterans[6]

BREAKOUT BOX

Three Examples of Ways to Celebrate Your Veterans

1. Regularly commemorate military events, such as service branch birthdays, the 9/11 anniversary, Memorial Day, Veterans Day, and Military Spouse Appreciation Day.

2. Display military heritage service and history, such as memorabilia, artwork, and awards and decorations throughout workplaces.

3. Upload videos to your company's YouTube channel depicting your veterans sharing their personal experiences in and about the military. The videos can be organized by thematic questions, such as: Why did you choose to serve? What was your biggest challenge? What do you want civilians to know? How was your transition out of the military? Consider including video tributes from civilian employees sharing their thanks with those who are serving and those who have served.

Ultimately, you are only limited by your imagination when it comes to successfully branding yourself as military friendly and military ready. A consistent messaging strategy should underlie all communications, and should be incorporated in your mission statement, marketing collateral, website, and social media platforms. Remember, those transitioning out of the military will often make up their minds about your company before you even have a chance to talk with them—make sure you are taking all the right steps to create a military-friendly first impression.

As demonstrated, branding yourself as military friendly does not necessarily start and stop with hiring veterans and military spouses. It is also reflected in how you treat veterans who are already part of your organization. With the following case study from PenFed Credit Union, we see that PenFed recognizes that many of their veteran members can benefit from career transition support, and therefore they now provide that to all of their members at no cost.

• • • • • • • • • • •
CASE STUDY

Career Development as a Member
Benefit—A Unique Approach

At PenFed Credit Union, our mission isn't simply to help our members "get by"—our mission is to help our members do better. We exist to help members utilize every ounce of their potential. As part of our emphasis on supporting veterans, as well as our wider credit union membership base (over 1.6 million members and growing steadily), we launched PenFed Career Connect in 2016.

PenFed Career Connect is an innovative initiative that enables our returning military heroes and our entire membership base to take advantage of online job searches and career transition tools. Access to these tools is at no cost to them through a software platform launched in partnership with CareerArc, an HR technology firm.

The Benefits
- Social network integration to increase interviews and offers—connecting returning veterans and credit union members to job opportunities and connections via LinkedIn and Facebook.
- Targeted job matches delivered to email, mobile, and social media.
- Career resources such as résumé development tools.
- Self-assessments to hone skills, values, and career preferences.
- Company research databases, workshops, and guides.
- Specific workshops and guides on transitioning from the military to the private sector.

In just one year, the results of our member benefits and veteran career investments through the launch of PenFed Career Connect has been tremendous, as thousands of members have utilized the platform for their career development and transition needs.

Providing returning veterans and our entire membership with access to world-class career resources not only separates us from our competition as a leading financial institution, but more importantly, enables us to maintain our leadership position in the veteran community. In addition, it showcases the importance of innovation in the careers sector.

—Paul Velky, Senior Vice President of Human Resources at PenFed Credit Union

 LEARNING POINT

Collaborating with local veteran organizations can be part of your military branding strategy. This aligns you with trusted community resources and highlights your commitment to supporting veterans.

BREAKOUT BOX

Five Elements of a Veteran-Friendly Culture

Recruitment campaigns and initiatives may get your organization on the radar for veterans, but once they are through the front door, how does their day-to-day experience match the image you are presenting? More than any individual program or event, here are five fundamental elements toward creating a culture that attracts and welcomes veterans, and provides the opportunity to succeed within your organization.

1. Purpose

    Why does your organization exist? What is your objective? Beyond the bottom line and quarterly performance, the higher purpose of your organization can make all the difference in attracting candidates to your organization and provide the motivation to retain and keep them engaged over time. A clearly defined and widely shared purpose provides the common mission for employees across an organization, aligning plans and objectives. It also helps associates view their role in the context of the larger organization and understand how they can best contribute to delivering on a shared mission.

2. Inclusiveness

    "Do I belong here?" is a question every potential employee will ask themselves in one way or another when joining a new organization. For veterans, this question of fitting in takes on even greater importance if this is their first nonmilitary job. How does your culture welcome new team members and enable each employee to feel comfortable, valued, and empowered to bring their whole selves to the job?

3. Accountability

The military is team-oriented: individuals are counted on to perform as part of a unit. When shifting to a corporate environment, this understanding of teamwork is a strength that can be put at risk if the culture is a bit loose when it comes to accountability. This starts at the top, with leadership that not only talks the talk, but also walks the walk in setting objectives and making sure each member of the team is doing their part to deliver the results.

4. Community

There is incredible power in how a company chooses to engage in their community, and more companies are viewing corporate responsibility and civic engagement not as a program but as part of how they do business. They see the benefit to the bottom line that comes from enabling and empowering employees to reach out, support, and give back to the world around them. For veteran-hires, these efforts provide opportunities to connect with both their community and fellow employees in different ways, and fulfill a desire to contribute and help others in need.

5. Opportunity

Every employee, veteran or not, wants to be given the chance to grow and be successful in what they do. There are many ways employees may define success for themselves, and great company cultures provide those opportunities for employees to learn, develop, and apply their talents, skills, and expertise in meaningful ways that are recognized.

—Patricia A. Lee, Senior Vice President of Human Resources
and Chief Diversity Officer for Wyndham Worldwide

COMMUNITY COLLABORATION

When it comes to creating and maintaining a robust and impactful veteran–hiring program, it really does take a village, so the more like-minded people and groups you can have in your corner, the better. That being said, after 9/11, over forty thousand nonprofit organizations sprung up across our country to provide different services for our veterans and their families. Therefore, it may be difficult for you to identify which groups you should support. Often, consulting with the veteran-employees in your offices is a good start, and you can find other resources online.

LEARNING POINT

If you are determining which veteran organizations to support and you have a VERG in place, start with them. They can discuss the issue together and provide your leadership with their top three choices. Not consulting with them could actually be disrespectful.

BREAKOUT BOX

Use Your Core Strengths to Collaborate with Your Local Community

U.S. Bank partners with many military service organizations through the Community Possible philanthropy and volunteerism platform. Funding support has been provided to organizations including Freedom Alliance and the Mission Continues. The Community Possible giving platform supports initiatives focused on workforce education, job placement, military financial education, and affordable housing for military service members and veterans.

Through U.S. Bank's Housing Opportunities after Military Engagement program, bank-owned homes are donated to military service organizations, which in turn renovate them and donate them mortgage-free to wounded veterans and their families. More than fifteen homes have been donated through the program since it began in 2013. In addition, U.S. Bank provides a free military financial education program to help military families reach their financial goals.

CASE STUDY

America's Warrior Partnership

Communities across the country are all equipped differently to serve military veterans as they transition to civilian life. The resources needed to assist veterans with finding a job or fulfilling other needs are often available, but they can be scattered between disconnected veteran service organizations. Our mission at America's Warrior Partnership is to fill the gaps between unaffiliated groups and nonprofit organizations so a community can offer a holistic range of services to any veteran who needs them.

Our approach centers on empowering communities to empower veterans, which is all about improving the efficiency of the great work that veteran service organizations and nonprofits are already doing. The goal is to establish relationships and leverage technology that organizations can utilize to not only assist veterans with an urgent need, such as employment, but also ensure they feel accepted and supported by their community.

The Community Integration Model

Our signature program is the Community Integration model, which provides communities with the tools and resources they need to offer a customized, integrated range of services that proactively address the needs of local veterans. Nonprofits are the most common type of organization to implement Community Integration, but businesses, government agencies, and other groups have also found the model to be helpful. The model empowers communities through training, mentorship, and structure to conduct proactive outreach by connecting existing resources and providing tools to create collaboration.

Specifically for employment assistance, the Community Integration model connects veteran service organizations with veteran business resource groups, government agencies (such as the VA or the Department of Labor), and local networking groups for entrepreneurs. The structure and connections provided by the service model aim to do more than give one veteran a job—it creates a viable space for businesses and service organizations to build relationships and support veteran-hiring initiatives for years to come.

WarriorServe

Assisting a veteran with employment often also requires helping that veteran with other needs, such as education or housing, so they can ultimately succeed overall. To more effectively provide holistic services to veterans, many of the communities we work with complement our Community Integration model with WarriorServe, a technology platform we developed to streamline the collection and analysis of critical information related to a veteran's case.

One of the most important characteristics of this technology is that it does not replace human interaction. It enhances productivity by allowing organizations to spend more time providing services and less time inputting data into their record system. WarriorServe also provides secure data sharing through an online portal that enhances collaboration between organizations and key community partners. By ensuring everyone involved in a veteran's case has access to the same information, the services provided to that veteran can be proactively and efficiently coordinated.

Empowering Veterans

Our holistic approach to veteran support services has proven to be effective, as seen in the results of our annual survey measuring the success of our programs. The results of our 2017 survey showed that in areas where the Community Integration model is active, 93 percent of veterans feel greater satisfaction and believe their community cares for their well-being. This is a 9 percent increase over our 2016 survey.

This success can be emulated by organizations and communities nationwide. Building relationships between service providers, government agencies, and businesses that champion veteran-hiring initiatives empowers a community to assist veterans with finding the right job that that can help them build a better quality of life. See www. americaswarriorpartnership.org for more information.

—Jim Lorraine, President of America's Warrior Partnership

Many veteran organizations exist to help America's employers connect with transitioning service members, veterans, and military spouses who want civilian jobs. Partnering with these groups can expand your recruiting efforts and provide your company with a pipeline of qualified candidates who meet your hiring needs. But perhaps more importantly, collaborating with veteran groups sends a clear message to your veteran–employees that you care about their community and want to do more. However you want to support veterans, from organizing a coat drive for homeless veterans to starting an internship program for veterans, chances are that a group already exists in your community and can be a resource for you.

BREAKOUT BOX

List of Local Community Collaboration Organizations You Can Join

1. **Veterans Bridge Home.** Focuses on connecting veterans in Charlotte, North Carolina, with North Carolina employers and community resources (www.veteransbridge home.org/).

2. **Vetlanta.** Networks throughout the greater Atlanta community to find organizations with like-minded values that may have opportunities for veterans, including businesses, academia, nonprofit groups, and government organizations (www.vetlanta.org).

3. **Los Angeles Veterans Collaborative.** Administered by the University of Southern California's (USC) Center for Innovation and Research on Veterans and Military Families and comprising hundreds of community stakeholders, agencies, and representatives serving veterans and military families in Greater Los Angeles (cir.usc.edu/lavc).

4. **The Arizona Coalition for Military Families.** A nationally recognized public-private partnership focused on building Arizona's statewide capacity to care for and support all service members, veterans, and their families (arizonacoalition.org).

5. **Home Base Iowa.** Public-private partnership that provides a high level of commitment to Iowa's veterans, transitioning service members, and their families related to transition, employment, and education (www.homebaseiowa.gov).

· · · · · · · · · · ·
CASE STUDY

Home Base Iowa Program Overview

Home Base Iowa (HBI) is one of the most comprehensive state-led public-private partnerships assisting veterans in the nation. This initiative began in November 2013, and in May 2014 legislation was signed that put Iowa among the top tier for veteran state benefits. Since its inception, the program has achieved the following results:

- Over 1,700 business partners have pledged more than eight thousand jobs. All HBI business partners are searchable on the website by name, location, and industry and include a veteran point of contact.
- Over seventy HBI communities, including veteran incentives that complement the statewide incentives. In each community, at least 10 percent of all eligible, hiring businesses are HBI businesses.
- Over twenty colleges and universities that meet specific Certified Higher Academic Military Partners (CHAMPS) criteria for the program, which include on-campus veteran resources and military transitional and financial considerations.
- The program has $1.3 million in pledged donations and features two private sector cochairs who assist with fundraising and business support.
- HBI attended over thirty-five out-of-state career fairs in 2017 and will attend more than forty-five in 2018.
  - ° The program spends $250,000 on marketing and promotional efforts annually.

- The Iowa Business Council has reported that over 2,750 veterans have been hired from program launch to July 2016.
- In April 2017, HBI launched the "Find a Veteran" feature. Veterans create a profile, which includes location and industry criteria. Once an Iowa*WORKS* representative contacts the veteran, screens the résumé, and provides information about the program, the résumé is published and automatically sent to all HBI businesses and communities with matching criteria.
- From January to September 2017, the website accumulated
  ° 78,814 sessions (up from 47,252 in 2016[7])
  ° 61,081 users (up from 37,314 in 2016)
  ° 215,139 page views (up from 125,526 in 2016)
- Since January 2016, HBI has received almost 450 résumés. The program sends out monthly newsletters to over 1,300 veteran subscribers and more than 2,500 partner subscribers. HBI also maintains an active presence on LinkedIn, Facebook, and Twitter.
- Board members meet semi-annually with the governor.

For more information, see www.homebaseiowa.gov.

—Jason Kemp, Program Manager of Home Base Iowa

• • • • • • • • • • •

BREAKOUT BOX

Seven Federal Government Resources Related to Supporting Veterans in the Workplace

1. Department of Defense's Employer Support for the Guard and Reserve (www.esgr.mil)

2. Military Spouse Employment Partnership (www.msepjobs.militaryonesource.mil/msep)

3. Soldier for Life (www.soldierforlife.army.mil)

4. Department of Labor's Veterans' Employment and Training Services (VETS; www.dol.gov/vets/)

5. National Center for PTSD (www.ptsd.va.gov)

6. Department of Veterans Affairs Employment Toolkit (www.va.gov/vetsinworkplace/)

7. Career One Stop Veteran and Military Transition Center (www.careeronestop.org/Veterans/hire-a-vet.aspx)

As you see, many of these collaborative organizations, as well as government agencies, are great resources not only for employers and other community stakeholders, but also for transitioning service members, veterans, and military spouses. Both the employers and job seekers benefit from learning more about what particular communities may have already developed—there is often no need to reinvent the wheel, and you can save time, money, and resources by plugging into an existing infrastructure. This is particularly beneficial if you are an organization just getting your veteran-hiring program off the ground, or if you are a job seeker who does not already have a strong network in a particular community. In this next case study, you will learn about an organization that helps bring together veteran-centric nonprofits in particular communities so that together they can more effectively empower veterans and their families.

 **LEARNING POINT**

Looking for a fun and easy way to support veterans as part of your corporate social responsibility? Support GI Go Fund's Jeans for Troops Day and your employees will help veterans with education, homelessness, and benefits assistance (www.gigo.org/jeansfortroops).

Typically, and as we have described here, community collaboration refers to corporations supporting nonprofit partners in the communities where they do business. And sometimes, as we just saw in the case study of America's Warrior Partnership, community collaboration efforts are led by the nonprofit organizations themselves in an effort to bring all the groups in a particular area that are working on veteran issues under one tent. Needless to say, it can often be very difficult to identify those groups, successfully encourage them to work with others, and keep many different organizations well-informed and motivated.

Recently, partially because of the infrastructure required to do this well, state governments have taken the lead. In the next case study we highlight the actions Arizona has taken to pull together a wide variety of people and resources to better serve their veterans and military families statewide. As you will see, there are many opportunities for businesses to plug into massive efforts like these.

The Arizona Roadmap to Veteran Employment addresses all elements of the employment ecosystem to provide opportunities for service members, veterans, and their families. We are also using technology to promote employment and career opportunities and pathways, including military skills transition and a focus on nontraditional career pathways. To learn more, visit www.ArizonaCoalition.org/employment.

. . . .
CASE STUDY

What Arizona Is Doing

To address the issue of veteran employment in the state of Arizona, the Arizona Department of Veterans' Services (ADVS) and the Arizona Coalition for Military Families (ACMF) partnered to develop the Arizona Roadmap to Veteran Employment. The coalition took the lead in convening stakeholders, collecting data, and fully developing a plan. As the plan developed, the Roadmap began to focus on the interests and needs of different stakeholder groups, relationships between the stakeholders, and the flow of hiring. These stakeholders include job seekers, employment service providers, and employers, as each group plays a key role in advancing veteran employment opportunities.

- **Job seekers**—The Roadmap focuses on the needs of those who are unemployed as well as those who are underemployed. The range goes from people transitioning out of active duty to those serving as drilling National Guard or Reserve members and to those who are already out of the military.

  A key aspect of the Roadmap is connecting these individuals to the array of available support services, whether from the military, government agencies, or community partners. It is very common for people to feel alone in their job search or career development and to not fully access what is available. Too many people end up saying they wish they knew about a resource earlier. One of the key ways to connect people to resources is Arizona's Military and Veteran Resource Network and our Resource Navigators. The network provides the technology platform to match people to resources based on more than two hundred criteria, while over three thousand trained navigators provides the human element for helping people connect to the resource system.

- **Employment service providers (ESPs)**—The Roadmap also focuses on public and private sector ESPs. While the available services may vary from county to county, there are resources available in every county and community statewide. Through the Roadmap, there is a set training protocol to equip ESPs to more effectively serve the military and veteran population. And there is a focus on connecting more job seekers to the resources they provide through matchable resource profiles on the Resource Network.

- **Employers**—The Roadmap engages and supports public and private sector employers in myriad ways to promote both hiring and retention. This includes providing the training and process to become an Arizona Veteran Supportive Employer, a specialized designation.

Several of Arizona's key corporations also partnered with ADVS and ACMF to create the Arizona Corporate Council on Veteran Careers, which is a vehicle to engage the corporate community and promote career opportunities for military members, veterans, and their families.

—Thomas Winkel, Director of Arizona Coalition for Military Families

UNDERSTANDING DEPLOYMENT CHALLENGES

There are a lot of great reasons to hire men and women who continue to support our country in the National Guard or a Reserve unit—they constantly receive training your company doesn't have to pay for, they maintain healthy lifestyles and exercise regularly, and they are constantly receiving leadership training and opportunities at their military units.

One fact of military life is that our Reservists and members of the National Guard have supported the war efforts after 9/11 in an unprecedented manner. It is safe to say that our military simply could not have accomplished all that it did in Iraq and Afghanistan without them.

Of course, some of your veteran-employees who are still serving may be called up to support our nation's efforts overseas. Although this may pose some initial challenges for you, it is actually an opportunity to really show your support for the military and your veterans. When veteran-employees at your company know that you value Reservists and National Guardsmen, that will send a clear message to them that you are military friendly. It will also make them proud to be part of your organization.

LEARNING POINT

U.S. Bank offers eligible employees up to two weeks of paid leave in connection with a family member's military deployment.

Veterans with civilian jobs and ongoing military responsibilities may have civilian salaries that exceed their military wages. If they are mobilized to deploy, and therefore now solely earning their military paycheck, they may end up being paid less than what they have become accustomed to as an employee at your company. This can lead to economic instability if their military wages are not sufficient to cover expenses during deployment.

While not mandatory, some employers pay the difference between these civilian and military salaries during deployments or training exercises. Not only does it show that you truly support the military obligations of your employees, but you are also taking care of their families and reducing stress while they are deployed.

"QUOTABLE"

"It is an honor and privilege to be able to employ more than 1,300 military Reservists, veterans, and military spouses throughout our organization. Because of our many locations, we are able to support our men and women in uniform as they transition into their civilian life or to help with a job transfer when duty calls."

—Yvonne Freeman, Vice President of HR for The Michaels Companies

LEARNING POINT

At Starbucks, members of the Guard and Reserve are provided eighty hours of annual military leave with full pay to support annual training obligations. And when partners are called to active duty, they pay the difference between their Starbucks wages and military wages for up to seventy-eight weeks.

—Herrick Ross, Senior Talent Advisor of Military Talent Acquisition at Starbucks

Remember, their spouses or significant others may now be doing the work for two and juggling an increased number of responsibilities. Childcare, household chores, home upkeep, and any number of everyday activities that were previously divided between two people now all fall on one. There is nothing easy about a military deployment, but there are a number of ways for you to support your employees while they are away to ensure they know how much you value them and their military service.

BREAKOUT BOX

Five Ways to Support Your Deployed Employee

1. Throw a deployment party and include the service member's family. Invite the family to other corporate social events during the deployment.

2. Regularly send care packages put together by coworkers and company leadership, including notes and inspirational quotes from colleagues and team members (don't forget to ask for guidance from the family on what to include in the package).

3. Leave a blue-star flag, which is the symbol of a deployed family member, on that employee's desk while they are deployed.

4. Have the CEO send a letter to them on a monthly basis.

5. Upon their return to the office, give deployed employees a personal letter from the company's CEO and a small gift at a recognition ceremony by their unit leadership and peers.

These are all easy options that cost little or no money and demonstrate your commitment to your Reservists and Guardsmen. Also, in addition to supporting families and deployed service members, these actions may promote a more engaged workforce and result in employee retention.

Deployments can be very challenging for military families, and typically, efforts you make to support them will be very well received. Deployments to war zones can often result in increased family responsibilities, financial issues, fear for a spouse's or parent's safety, anxiety, loneliness, sadness, and feeling overwhelmed.

 **LEARNING POINT**

Since 2008, Walmart has offered differential pay to associates taking a leave of absence for specific military assignments lasting more than three days and through the duration of leave.

This means that if an associate's military salary is less than what they are making at their job at Walmart, the company will pay them the difference while they're on a military leave of absence (MLOA). In May 2017, Walmart announced enhancements to this policy to include any eligible military assignment, including basic training, allowing associates who are considering enlisting in the Armed Forces to do so without fear of losing wages.

—Gary Profit, Senior Director of Military Programs at Walmart

Taking the time to sit down with employees who have been mobilized several weeks before their last day and communicating to them how important they are to you and how you want to support them however you can will make the world of difference to them.

 **LEARNING POINT**

Workforce Transition Advisors

USAA provides a dedicated team of human resource advisors to National Guard and Reserve employees and their families during their entire deployment cycle. These advisors assist employees and their family members with pre-deployment benefits questions and actions, and facilitate the re-employment process. Further, upon their return to USAA, deployed employees receive a personal letter from the USAA CEO or their unit executive leader and a small gift at a recognition ceremony by their unit leadership and peers.

BREAKOUT BOX

Employer Support of the Guard and Reserve (ESGR)

1. ESGR, a Department of Defense program, was established in 1972 to promote cooperation and understanding between Reserve Component Service members and their civilian employers. The program also assists in the resolution of conflicts arising from an employee's military commitment.

2. ESGR is supported by a network of more than 3,750 volunteers in fifty-four committees located across all fifty states, the District of Columbia, Guam, Puerto Rico, and the US Virgin Islands. Volunteers, hailing from small business and industry, government, education, and prior military service, bring a vast wealth of experience to assist employers and service members and their families. Together with Headquarters, ESGR staff, and a small cadre of support staff for each state committee, volunteers work to promote and enhance employer support for military service in the Guard and Reserve.

3. ESGR has served our country for more than forty-five years, fostering a culture in which all employers support and value the employment and military service of members of the National Guard and Reserve. These citizen warriors could not defend and protect us at

home and abroad without the continued promise of meaningful civilian employment for themselves and their families. ESGR continues to adapt to meet the needs of Reserve Component members, their families, and America's employers by joining forces with a network of other national, state, and local government and professional trade organizations.

4. Through military outreach, ESGR volunteers engage with National Guard and Reserve units at the local level all across the country. This effort also includes a robust employer awards program that recognizes those employers who go above and beyond to support their military employees. The awards program culminates in the annual Secretary of Defense Employer Support Freedom Award—the highest federal award a civilian employer can receive for their support of the National Guard and Reserve.

Please meet with your local ESGR representative for a full briefing on Guard and Reserve employee rights and employer responsibilities.

—Travis Bartholomew, Deputy Executive Director
and Chief of National Engagement for ESGR

TWO FINAL KEYS TO ENGAGING AND RETAINING YOUR VETERANS

You have just read a lot of tactical information about how to create a military-friendly and military-ready work environment. Processing and understanding this information, and of course implementing as much as possible, will impact how excited veterans are to apply for work at your organization and then choose to stay there. To that end, there are two very important programs that are best practices for you to implement—these will certainly help your veteran-employees onboard in a successful manner, and also will positively affect their retention rates. In fact, the 2014 Rand report *Veteran Employment: Lessons from the 100,000 Jobs Mission* highlights that many of the participating firms identified the following two initiatives as effective in improving veteran results.[8]

Veteran Mentoring Programs

It is not unusual for companies to utilize a mentorship program for their new employees. Keeping in mind that veterans often do not have corporate experience, a mentoring program specifically for them can be extremely beneficial. Typically, this is a tool you can use to help the veteran-employee adjust to your particular corporate culture and reach their full potential within your organization.

"QUOTABLE"

"Finding employment takes more than just searching for jobs online. It also requires support from individuals experienced in the corporate world and employment space that can help guide a candidate to their next career. Using JobPath's mentorship portal, veterans can connect with HR Representatives, as well as TAP and other government providers, through our built-in text messaging and video chat features to help them build their résumé and assist with their employment search. It is a great way for veterans to connect to leaders in the business community and learn from their expertise, as well as for corporations and their employee resource to give back to our nation's heroes."

—Jack Fanous, Founder and CEO of JobPath

 LEARNING POINT

Mentorship is quite different than supervision or delegation. It is more akin to a partnership that focuses on developing the new employee through support and care.

In addition to providing a smoother transition to the civilian workplace, there are other significant benefits to implementing a veteran-mentoring program. Studies have found that it can lead to increased productivity, career development, and employee retention. This is because the new employees are guided around pitfalls by someone who has already walked in their shoes, and the knowledge they receive significantly speeds up their learning. Ultimately, this support not only affects the morale of your veterans, but can also impact your company's bottom line in a very positive way.

BREAKOUT BOX

Three Benefits for Mentors

1. This opportunity can enhance their leadership and coaching skills.
2. They often feel more valued because their efforts play a direct role in the future success of the organization.
3. They know they are making a difference in a veteran's career.

Developing and implementing an impactful veteran mentoring program requires strategy and commitment. The first step is to create a marketing and recruiting strategy to let your new veteran-employees know about the program and to selectively match mentors with mentees. Then, at the outset of the program, you should provide an orientation for mentors and mentees so both people are on the same page and share mutual expectations. While not mandatory, it is certainly a good idea for your HR professionals to develop instructional guides that detail the orientation material for later reference. Finally, you should support the mentoring relationships by providing developmental activities (this can include guest speakers, networking events, or other activities that the mentors and mentees can attend together) and then evaluating when goals have been met.

BREAKOUT BOX

Ernst & Young's Peer Mentoring Program

EY's Veterans Network helps veterans connect and support one another within our organization, and one of the flagship programs the network runs is a veteran-to-veteran peer mentoring program. This program is especially significant for those who have just left the service. Through this network, veteran new hires are paired with veteran peer advisors to serve as a resource for their integration into the EY community. This program helps ease the transition by providing a designated peer who can assist with career guidance, professional development opportunities, and networking.

—Joseph M. McHugh, Northeast Leader of Complex Program Management
at Ernst & Young LLP

 LEARNING POINT

The mentor does not have to be a veteran, but often they are; a previously integrated and successful veteran-employee with your organization uniquely understands the socialization challenges facing new veteran-hires. If you have a VERG in place, those members often make great mentors.

Just like your overall veteran-hiring program, you should consider having a corporate champion specifically for the mentorship program portion. A robust and impactful mentorship program will make a positive difference in the satisfaction level and retention of your veteran-employees, and it is a best practice to ensure an executive is overseeing the program. Further, you should develop a business case for why your organization should dedicate time and resources to your mentoring program. Five criteria to include in that business case are given below:

1. Employees often grow quicker and feel more engaged when they have a mentor.
2. The organization will experience increased employee retention and decreased turnover.
3. The mentoring system provides an enhanced transfer of knowledge and skills.
4. This training is free and can reduce overall training costs.
5. Providing this resource will make your organization more military friendly—veterans are often your best source for other quality veteran-employees, and their success and comfort at your organization will likely result in them recommending you to their friends.

⚲ LEARNING POINT

American Corporate Partners (ACP) offers a free mentoring program that connects post-9/11 veterans (protégés) with corporate professionals (mentors) for yearlong, one-on-one, customized mentorships. ACP assists veterans on their path towards fulfilling, long-term careers, whether the veteran is job searching or newly employed. ACP partners with seventy-one *Fortune* 500 companies and has helped over 11,000 veterans. For more information, please visit www.acp-usa.org.

A successful veteran mentoring program requires planning, commitment, and follow-through. Fortunately, it truly can affect the growth and engagement of your new veteran-employees, their increased retention and decreased turnover, and the leadership development of your mentors. To learn more about creating a veteran mentor program at your organization, watch this short video course at PsychArmor: https://psycharmor.org/courses/creating-veteran-mentor-program.

BREAKOUT BOX

Meet Veterati, an Organization That Believes Mentoring Is Critical to Hiring and Retaining Veterans

Before the Internet, we had tribes. Tribes were how we survived: strong social bonds, knowledge-sharing, taking care of each other. The Internet has made us more "connected" than ever, but actually, our connections with each other have weakened. We've gone from a village coming together to help a tribe member down on their luck find a job through collective networks and advice, to one person, sitting at a computer, alone, sending out hundreds of job applications hoping one human being might respond. Our tribal bonds are weaker than ever.

Veterati is activating one of history's most powerful tribes, the military and the 94 percent of Americans who support our military, to solve the greatest crisis of opportunity for 1.5 million veterans and 5.5 million military spouses today: finding a job. When we approached this crisis, we didn't think about it traditionally. Our big insight was that 80 percent of jobs don't come through job boards: they come through the people who believe in you, your tribe. So we asked a completely different question: "How do we connect veterans to the people who believe in them? To the tribe that will mentor, sponsor, and champion them to success after they come home from the battlefield?"

Enter Veterati, a digital mentoring platform that empowers veterans and military spouses to book direct phone calls with members of the military-passionate tribe (veterans, military-passionate civilians, and employers who want to hire veterans). Through these conversations, mentors level up veteran talent to become focused, confident, and interview-ready candidates, and land the jobs of their dreams. See www.veterati.com for more information.

—Diana Rau, CEO of Veterati

Veteran-Employee Resource Groups

ERGs are voluntary, employee-led groups made up of individuals who join together based on common interests, backgrounds, or demographic factors such as gender, race, or ethnicity.[9] Veterans are one such group, and establishing a VERG plays a significant role in the recruitment, onboarding, and retention of your veteran-hires. Like other affinity groups, VERGs are professional resource networks created by and for veterans to help them connect and support one another within a particular organization. Not only are veterans tremendous assets to any business, but they can also be great resources to other veterans at your firm, and assist in their retention. The first two to three months at a new job can be challenging for any employee, and particularly so in the case of veterans who are new to the private sector—being able to snap in with a group of people sharing a similar background can be a truly impactful part of a successful onboarding process.

"QUOTABLE"

"The Military and Veterans Business and Employee Resource Group at Harley-Davidson is an employee-led group that promotes the recruiting, professional development, and

alliance of military service members and veterans. It also aims to raise aware-ness, advocacy, and support at work and in the military community."

—Tori Termaat, Director of HR Business Service for the Harley-Davidson Motor Company

---

BREAKOUT BOX

Seven Keys to a Successful VERG

1. Identify a champion in the company to spearhead the project. This person does not necessarily have to be a veteran, but does need to have a passion about supporting veterans. Having a champion also helps also gain buy-in from the CEO and head of HR.

2. Identify funding and personnel resources. Often the champion is a business unit leader and has discretionary funding to support the program.

3. Determine if the program is sustainable and if can it be scaled. You want to avoid a "one and done" scenario.

4. Identify key metrics and outcomes and set up processes to track these measures.

5. Avoid reinventing the wheel and duplication of efforts. If there is a similar existing program, consider collaborating, as strong partnerships produce greater results.

6. Use various social media tools to get the word out. Once a program gets its sea legs, we often find word of mouth is very effective in promoting a program. Definitely use testimonials.

7. Continue to assess the program's efficacy with lessons learned, feedback, surveys, and other measures.

—Michael Veysey, Director of Veterans Programs for Cisco Systems

---

One of the best things about hiring a veteran is that they often come to you with a wide network of other veterans and service members who are still serving. These veteran–employees can be a great resource for iden-tifying candidates for open positions—just imagine how many recommen-dations you can gather by tapping into your VERG. Furthermore, if your organization is trying to identify a nonprofit organization to support, either on a national level or in your local community, your VERG should be the first place you turn to for input. As identified by DAV (Disabled American Veterans), veterans can play an integral role in any veteran–hiring initiative in three distinct ways:[10]

1. VERGs assist HR professionals by reviewing candidate résumés and translating relevant skills and job experience.
2. VERGs provide mentors to new veteran–employees.
3. VERG members act as coaches for job candidates who are transitioning to the civilian workforce by helping them prepare for interviews and understand how their experience and expertise can fit into your company.

CASE STUDY

Ernst & Young Veterans Network

We established the EY Veterans Network in 2010 to support veterans in their career development and their transition from the military to civilian life. Doubling its participation yet again in the past fiscal year, the network has rapidly grown to over nine hundred members. It has also transformed from a local community to a national group, with representation throughout EY service lines and regions in over fifty cities across the United States. Every branch of service (Army, Marine Corps, Navy, Air Force, and Coast Guard), foreign veterans, and nonveteran supporters from all corners of the firm are represented.

Because we are a national firm, we identified regional champions. These regional officers work with the local office to secure financial support or whatever else is needed. Every month we send out a Veteran Dispatch to enable veterans to get active in the firm and community and to keep everyone updated. In March 2016, EY's Veterans Network hosted twenty members of the US Army War College for a one-day information-sharing session on leadership in the private sector and how EY supports veterans as they begin the transition from service to civilian life.

—Joseph M. McHugh, Northeast Leader of Complex Program Management at Ernst & Young LLP

Delta Air Lines

Global Diversity and Inclusion is a corporate-sponsored program that unites individuals and those who support the cultures that are compassionate to them. My company places emphasis on not only recognition, but commitment to each affinity group. Programs within the group continuously communicate information, opportunities, and areas of need. They constantly maintain a focus on evolving and innovation. The inclusion provides connectivity and empowerment between workgroups that extend the foundation of unity.

Each group has officers (employees) who are significant to their affiliation. As the president of the Veterans Business Resource Group, my participation allows me to utilize my knowledge of service and volunteerism in community projects throughout our global work system. The additional roles of other officers include not only their veteran affiliation, but also their expertise in their respective workgroups. This extends opportunities to our members to network on platforms of mentorship, community service, and commitment to camaraderie.

The affinity groups all reflect the same company adage in a mission statement that resonates within the group. This includes core values particular to them but in alignment with the company. New members can register once they have reviewed the information on our portal, accessible through our company intranet. The awesome thing about access is that all affinity groups are located under one main tab for Global Diversity and Inclusion, which now provides other employees the opportunity to join other groups and read about their accomplishments. For example, the Honor Guard is a program that has made world news for the service they provide for the transport of our fallen heroes. This is the ultimate respect that any fallen service member and their families can be given. It is imperative to maintain the dignity and respect that represents each group on a level that is equivalent to their compassion.

—Debra Martin, President of the Veterans Business Resource Group
and Global Diversity at Delta Air Lines

• • • • • • • • • • •

Every organization wants their employees to enjoy working there, to develop their skills and abilities in a healthy way year after year, and to continue expanding their roles and responsibilities over time. As discussed throughout this chapter, there are a number of best practices to implement that can truly affect the retention rate of your employees. And in the veteran space, there is perhaps no company better than USAA to use as an example of this. Granted, USAA is an organization whose entire membership base consists of veterans, but that does not mean they necessarily have to embody so many of the best practices described in this chapter for their veteran–employees— they choose to.

• • • • • • • • • • •
CASE STUDY

Best Practices in Effective Veteran Retention

Can you imagine 50 percent of your workforce leaving your company less than one year after you hired them? That is the rate at which veterans have been leaving their first postmilitary jobs within one year of employment.[11] USAA is one of the nation's top leaders and influencers in the veteran-hiring and retention space; retaining veteran-employees is critical in keeping the organization grounded in its mission and sustaining its culture and values. For this reason, USAA has an enterprise commitment to support transitioning veterans through several initiatives. This support aligns with its mission and benefits the association by reflecting USAA's military membership throughout the organization while seeding future leaders.

Founded by military officers in 1922, USAA has a longstanding commitment to transition veterans and prepare them for meaningful, long-term employment in the organization. USAA recognizes this as a business need and is focused on increasing veteran retention and representation at all levels of the organization through three veteran retention initiatives: veteran onboarding, veteran sponsorship, and their Veteran Transition Leadership Development Program (VetsLeaD).

Veteran Onboarding

USAA's veteran onboarding workshop is specifically intended for veteran-employees who recently left the military and are in their first corporate job. The purpose of the one-day course is to help them adjust to the corporate environment at USAA. Facilitators use a combination of instructor-led discussions and open engagement with a panel of recently transitioned veteran-employees who are succeeding in the organization. The veteran onboarding curriculum was developed by USAA's learning and development team based on a thorough business-needs assessment, and focuses heavily on the change in culture, structure, communications, and career path when transitioning out of the military and into USAA.

Veteran Sponsorship

USAA's Talent Programs team has partnered with their VERG, VETNet, to provide an enterprise veteran sponsorship program (VSP). The VSP, like veteran onboarding, is specifically intended for veteran-employees who recently left the military and are in their first corporate job. The VSP aims to ensure a positive first impression of USAA and an understanding of USAA's culture. The goal of the VSP is to ensure a successful transition by providing accurate and realistic expectations and awareness of helpful resources. A new veteran-employee is paired with an experienced veteran-employee, ideally with a similar military background, who has volunteered to help facilitate the new employee's acclimation into the organization. The VSP ensures transitioning veterans feel like they have a friend at work from the beginning.

VetsLeaD

USAA's VetsLeaD hires and transitions a select cohort of veterans as part of a one-year development program. The veteran onboarding workshop and VSP are both included in the VetsLeaD program, which is also intended for veteran-employees who recently left the military and are in their first corporate job. VetsLeaD employees participate in cross-functional leadership and business acumen learning opportunities within a comprehensive support structure of their cohort, their veteran-employee sponsors, and assigned executive mentors.

Veterans are hired into positions at various skill levels in various lines of business to meet business requirements across the enterprise. VetsLeaD is not a career skills training program; candidates must be qualified for the role and ready to meet the requirements of the job upon hire. Participants convene as a cohort for one to two days of learning and mentoring activities every month for twelve consecutive months. The VetsLeaD curriculum was developed by USAA's learning and development team, in consultation with business leaders, to ensure learning activities bridge the business acumen gap transitioning veterans typically have compared to their civilian counterparts.

VetsLeaD was specifically designed to reduce the 44 percent turnover rate of recently separated veterans in their first postmilitary job, and achieved a 98 percent retention rate.

Conclusion

Deliberate veteran onboarding, thoughtful veteran sponsorship, and the VetsLeaD program all represent a natural extension of USAA's dedication to veterans and their families. Not only does USAA serve the external military community, it also serves its own.

—Sean Passmore, Military Hiring Advisor for Talent Programs at USAA

· · · · · · · · · · ·

RETENTION

Entire reports have been written dedicated solely to veteran retention, and some of those resources are listed in Appendix A. That being said, a number of the practices described earlier in this chapter are considered to be best practices for increasing veteran retention. Ultimately, the more veteran-friendly and veteran-ready your organization is, the more likely it is that your veterans will continue to work there and rise through the ranks. Interviewing and selecting the right candidates, onboarding veterans in a robust way, utilizing VERGs and providing mentoring, supporting your Reservists and Guardsmen, and collaborating with your communities are all aspects of highly effective and impactful veteran-hiring programs that lead to greater retention.

That being said, there are a few specific criteria employers should focus on regarding retention. Of course, pay (including benefits) is one of those factors, as is the case with any other valuable employees. But other criteria tie directly into their military service: opportunities to apply their skills and abilities, and meaningfulness of the work.

As identified by one report, these three issues were consistently ranked as the most important to the surveyed veterans.[12] And it makes perfect sense—when you are part of the military, you rarely have to question the validity of your work, your corporate mission, or whether you are part of a team striving to do great things. One of the virtues of military service is that its members are often handed significant responsibilities at early stages of their careers. While this makes them a great asset, it can be a challenge for employers whose positions do not carry the same levels of responsibility. Therefore, midlevel managers should be aware that their veteran–employees are typically eager to work hard and shoulder more responsibility than their civilian counterparts. A more detailed description of this is provided in the final case study of this chapter below.

Figures 6.1 and 6.2 demonstrate the main reasons why surveyed veterans left their jobs, and what employers could have done to keep them. As you will see, employers have direct control over many of the top reasons listed for job attrition (Figure 6.1). Similarly, employers have a similar amount of control over the factors influencing whether veterans stayed at their first job after the military, as depicted in the Figure 6.2.

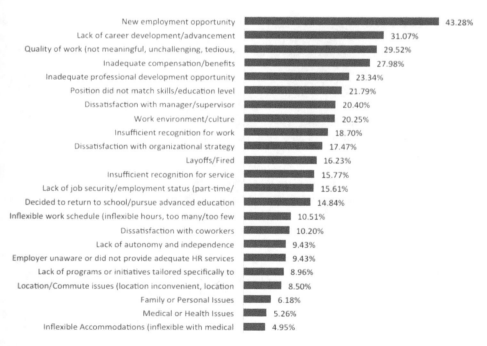

New employment opportunity	43.28%
Lack of career development/advancement	31.07%
Quality of work (not meaningful, unchallenging, tedious,	29.52%
Inadequate compensation/benefits	27.98%
Inadequate professional development opportunity	23.34%
Position did not match skills/education level	21.79%
Dissatisfaction with manager/supervisor	20.40%
Work environment/culture	20.25%
Insufficient recognition for work	18.70%
Dissatisfaction with organizational strategy	17.47%
Layoffs/Fired	16.23%
Insufficient recognition for service	15.77%
Lack of job security/employment status (part-time/	15.61%
Decided to return to school/pursue advanced education	14.84%
Inflexible work schedule (inflexible hours, too many/too few	10.51%
Dissatisfaction with coworkers	10.20%
Lack of autonomy and independence	9.43%
Employer unaware or did not provide adequate HR services	9.43%
Lack of programs or initiatives tailored specifically to	8.96%
Location/Commute issues (location inconvenient, location	8.50%
Family or Personal Issues	6.18%
Medical or Health Issues	5.26%
Inflexible Accommodations (inflexible with medical	4.95%

Figure 6.1. Reasons for leaving first postmilitary job

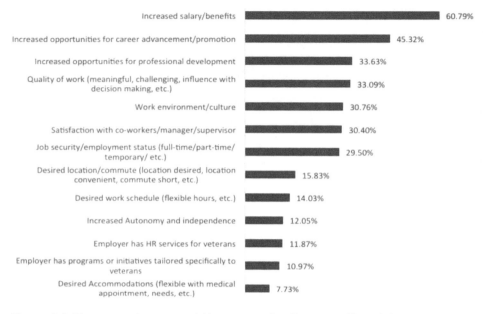

Figure 6.2. Reasons veterans would have stayed at first postmilitary job

---

BREAKOUT BOX

Retention Is an Issue for Employees and Employers

It is critical to note that the issue of retention is not a one-way street, and that it is just as important for job seekers and employees as it is for employers. Ideally, no job seeker will take a job that they do not want, as this will most likely lead to frustration and an early departure, which is typically a waste of time for employee and employer. Therefore, it is imperative for you, as transitioning service members, veterans, and military spouses, to spend time identifying what it is you truly want to do, and then to pursue organizations in that industry. Remember, the government has already spent a lot of time and money training you to a certain level of expertise in your field—if you like that area, take the time to secure an employment opportunity that matches your military training and experience and you will likely be quite satisfied with that employer.

All employees need to be fully engaged to operate at their highest level at work and veterans are no exception. As we wrap up this chapter, here is a case study by Ryan Manion of the Travis Manion Foundation that provides impactful guidance on engaging veterans to increase their retention levels.

How to Effectively Engage Veterans to Ensure Long-Term Success

For a veteran to thrive in the workplace, they must feel like their career leverages personal strengths, serves a higher purpose, and contributes to the development of strong relationships with others. While these three categories are required for the success of any employee, they are particularly crucial for veterans, whose years of service are explicitly and implicitly defined by these markers of engagement, meaning, and positive relationships.

To ensure that the conditions for all three components exist, companies must make an investment in veterans. But this investment will pay off in spades over time, because veterans are programmed to work hard, deliver results, and remain loyal, which in turn leads to better retention rates than their civilian counterparts. Companies need not make this investment alone. There are great nonprofits that will serve as partners to achieve all three components for veteran-employees.

1. **Leverage their strengths.** Many employers understand that years in the military teaches veterans the strengths of discipline, a strong work ethic, and leadership. While it's tempting to paint veterans using broad brush strokes like these, it's important to understand that each veteran possesses individual strengths that must be leveraged in order for them to stay engaged. Every veteran received training in a specialty that can be utilized postmilitary; many, however, are ready to begin a career in a completely new field. It's important to treat each veteran as a unique individual with unique passions and strengths in order to achieve long-term engagement. At the Travis Manion Foundation (TMF), we host workshops where veterans take a personal strengths assessment and discuss how to map those strengths to their next career. Understanding one's strengths is a critical first step to leveraging them. Companies don't have to be experts in strength assessments, they just need to find a partner that can help with this important first step toward employee engagement.

2. **Explain the higher purpose.** In the military, it is clear how each individual contributes to the overall mission. As a service member serving a nation at war since 9/11, the stakes are high and the work feels important. In a corporate setting, employers must maintain this premium placed on purpose by explaining how an individual veteran's role serves others and contributes to the greater good and higher mission. In addition to the company's direct mission, offer opportunities for employees to serve their community. This can include providing paid time off to participate in a service project or running a giving campaign that supports a good cause. Partner with a nonprofit organization that provides support so that employees' time is spent efficiently and the burden of participation in philanthropic or voluntary initiatives is not cumbersome. For example, at TMF we train and support veterans that want to mentor youth about character and leadership. These are two areas that veterans are uniquely qualified to teach. And through our support, veterans are able to maximize their time executing the program rather than developing curriculum or performing other administrative and logistical tasks. There are many great nonprofits that support organizations that want to give back. Identify those best-in-class nonprofits and partner up to ensure that veterans feel that sense of purpose, both during the work day and during the activities that bookend it.

3. **Develop strong relationships with others.** Another key component to military life is camaraderie. While it's difficult to match the close relationships formed from sharing hardships and other factors unique to military life, companies must find ways for veterans to get to know their coworkers, both veterans and nonveterans, on a personal basis. Many companies form an affinity group or VERG to encourage social interaction and mentorship among veterans. This is a great start. Go one step further by creating events that bring all employees together to serve a common cause. With TMF's support, our partners organize annual 5ks to memorialize those who have served and sacrificed since 9/11 as well as service projects during Veteran's Day week. Through shared experience, these veterans get to know each other and their nonveteran counterparts in a low-stress, high-impact environment. Nothing bonds people together like serving and honoring others.

—Ryan Manion, President of the Travis Manion Foundation

ENDNOTES

1. Institute for Veterans and Military Families, *Leading Practice: Measuring the Impact of Veterans in the Workplace,* (Syracuse: Insitute for Veterans and Military Families, 2012), http://toolkit.vets.syr.edu/wp-content/uploads/2012/12/LP-Tracking-Veterans.pdf.

2. Rajiv Chandrasekaren, Michel du Cille, and Zoeann Murphy, "A Legacy of Pain and Pride," *Washington Post,* March 29, 2014, http://www.washingtonpost.com/sf/national/2014/03/29/a-legacy-of-pride-and-pain/.

3. Anna Zogas, *Costs of War: US Military Veterans' Difficult Transition Back to Civilian Life and the VA's Response* (Providence, RI: Watson Institute at Brown University), http://watson.brown.edu/costsofwar/files/cow/imce/papers/2017/Zogas_Veterans%27%20Transitions_CoW_2.1.17.pdf.

4. The Bush Institute, *I Am a Post 9/11 Veteran* (Dallas: George W. Bush Presidential Center), https://gwbcenter.imgix.net/Resources/gwbi-msi-i-am-a-post-911-veteran.pdf.

5. Phillip Carter et al., *Lost In Translation: The Civil-Military Divide and Veteran Employment* (Washington, DC: Center for a New American Security, 2017), www.cnas.org/publications/reports/lost-in-translation.

6. Disabled American Veterans, *The Veteran Advantage: DAV Guide to Hiring and Retaining Veterans with Disabilities* (Cold Spring, KY: Disabled American Veterans, 2018), https://www.dav.org/wp-content/uploads/HiringGuide.pdf.

7. All 2016 numbers have been adjusted to account for a major Vietnam spam attack.

8. Kimberly Curry Hall et al., *Veteran Employment: Lessons from the 100,000 Jobs Mission* (Santa Monica: RAND Corporation, 2014), https://www.rand.org/pubs/research_reports/RR836.html.

9. Shelton Goode and Isaac Dixon, "Are Employee Resource Groups Good for Business?," *HR Magazine,* August 25, 2016, https://www.shrm.org/hr-today/news/hr-magazine/0916/pages/are-employee-resource-groups-good-for-business.aspx.

10. Disabled American Veterans, *Veteran Advantage,* 9–15.

11. Rosalinda Maury, Brice Stone, and Jennifer Roseman, *Veteran Job Retention Survey Summary (Washington, DC: Institute for Veterans and Military Families, 2016),* https://ivmf.syracuse.edu/wp-content/uploads/2016/10/VetAdvisor-ReportFINAL-Single-pages.pdf.

12. Maury, Stone, and Roseman, *Veteran Job Retention.*

CHAPTER 7

Understanding the Visible and Invisible Wounds of War

Many wounded warriors have injuries that are visible, but many have injuries that are not immediately noticeable. It is important to remember that each warrior is unique—some warriors will have similar injuries, but different reactions. Some warriors recover to the extent that if you can't see a prosthesis, you may never know that they are injured. But just because an injury is not visible does not mean that the injury is any less difficult to endure.

—Wounded Warrior Project[1]

BREAKOUT BOX

Understanding Visible and Invisible Wounds of War

The myth of the broken veteran has been perpetuated by Hollywood with films like *Rambo*, despite a more-than-critical mass of actual case studies disproving its generalizability. In fact, post-traumatic stress disorder (PTSD) impacts about 7–8 percent of the general US population in their lifetime (approximately 2.5 million people), which includes victims of crime and violence, first responders, and survivors of traumatic experiences, none of whom we generally regard as powder kegs waiting to explode in the workplace. Combat veterans do experience the uniquely profound psychological consequences of sustained exposure to imminent harm, but . . . access to resources and military cultural competency[2] help mitigate those effects, particularly in workplaces where veteran-specific support (e.g., policies that allow time off to attend medical appointments, or peer support networks for veterans in the company) is available. Ultimately, a wounded veteran who is fully qualified for a job and simply wants reasonable accommodations and an opportunity to prove their worth to the company will likely possess the same extraordinary tenacity, selflessness, and loyalty in the workplace that got them through the combat experience and rehabilitation.

—Sherman Gillums, Jr., Chief Strategy Officer of American Veterans (AMVETS)

The military operations in Afghanistan and Iraq represent the longest sustained US combat operations since the Vietnam War and have brought new focus to the needs of wounded, ill, and injured (WII) service members and their families. Troops are seeing more-frequent deployments with shorter rest periods in between. Many of the challenges they face in the theater of war include firefights, roadside bombs and improvised explosive devices (IEDs), suicide bombers, and seeing fellow Soldiers killed or injured.

WII service members are not limited to those injured in combat. As the name denotes, those who were injured or fell sick during training activities or other aspects of active duty are all included. Although there are many other terms used to refer to this same population, such as "wounded warriors," "disabled veterans," and "recovering warriors," we will simply use WII to ensure we are being as inclusive as possible.

 **LEARNING POINT**

These terms [wounded, ill, and injured] are used as general classifications of service members or veterans with regard to their medical condition. Injury means any skin, tissue, or organ damage inflicted by an external force. Wounded generally means any injury inflicted by an external force during combat. Combat wounded are a subset of all injured individuals. Ill means any disease process that changes an individual from healthy to not healthy.

—Department of Veteran Affairs[3]

Although it may sound odd at first, I am actually very lucky to have such a visible physical injury (although I also suffer from PTSD and a TBI). Especially early on in my recovery, people could tell that I had been injured in war. This led to a lot of well-wishing, support, and even job offers. As you will learn, the majority of WII service members and veterans suffer from the invisible wounds of war (e.g., vision impairment, back pain, hearing loss, mental heath issues), and will never receive the immediate recognition that I received. According to the Wounded Warrior Project, "These unseen injuries/disabilities are no less significant than those that are visible. In fact, the non-visible injuries can often cause more confusion and distress to service members, because they are not as easily understood. If others can't 'see' your injury or disability, they are less likely to know what you might need to be successful."[4]

"QUOTABLE"

"Despite the fact I was wounded, dozens of times I have had people say to me, when I tell them I was wounded in combat, 'Well, you look OK to me.' It's kind of a compliment, but it's also grounded in some serious and erroneous assumptions about what it means to be wounded. I had several pieces of shrapnel go through my torso and broke several bones—but those would not be visible to someone unless I took my shirt off!"

—Michael Zacchea, Director of the UConn Entrepreneur Bootcamp
for Veterans with Disabilities

● ● ● ● ● ● ● ● ● ●
CASE STUDY

Health and Wellness Programs for Veteran Employees

Physical health and activity are fundamental elements of military life. Given the importance of physical health and activity to those who have served in the military, it is advisable to make a special effort to ensure veterans are aware of a company's health and wellness–focused programs and benefits. Outreach can be conducted through general information sharing, networking, or special events, like health and wellness information fairs, or more specifically through a company's VERG or veteran-specific communications.

Involvement in a company's health and wellness programs will have special benefits to the veteran. Programs will involve them in group activity, something veterans are very familiar with given their experience working closely with one another in military units. Also, participation will provide a convenient outlet to establish consistent health and wellness habits, as they did in the military through activities such as morning PT workouts. Physical activity has numerous physical and psychological benefits and, specifically for combat veterans, has been shown to reduce the effects of post-traumatic stress.

Veterans with Disabilities

Tremendous advances in adaptive sports equipment and specially trained instructors make it easier than it has ever been to offer health and wellness programs to veterans with disabilities. Even veterans with severe injuries, such as single or multiple amputations, spinal cord injury and paralysis, TBI, or blindness, can easily engage in health and wellness programs. Often, the benefits of participation are much greater than in the general population. In fact, Disabled Sports USA, a national nonprofit that has offered adaptive sports to military veterans for over five decades, offers opportunities in over fifty sports for veterans with severe injuries. These activities include skiing, snowboarding, golfing, hiking, cycling, wheeling, hand cycling, running, swimming, climbing, water skiing, scuba diving, sailing, kayaking, fishing, and more.

While some adaptive sports require sophisticated equipment, like sit-down mono-skis for skiers with no legs or lower limb paralysis, often the adaptations can be quite simple. For example, if your company has a workout facility, putting a toe strap on a stationary cycle pedal can enable someone who has had a single- or double-leg amputation to effectively use the device to exercise. A hand crank or hand ergometer device on a table can enable a paraplegic in a wheelchair to use their arms to achieve aerobic exercise. Tracked exercise equipment that strengthens muscles is available that allows independent use of individual limbs in the event that the user is missing an arm or leg. Often, simply engaging the participating veterans directly can lead to simple workout-facility accessibility modifications that not only make participation possible, but communicate to veterans with disabilities that they are valued, equal members of the team.

Numerous resources are available online and at programs around the country to provide sports and recreation to veterans and others with disabilities:

- Disabled Sports USA (www.disabledsportsusa.org)
- US Paralympics and Paralympic Sports Clubs (www.usparalympics.org)
- Semper Fi Fund and Team Semper Fi (www.semperfifund.org)
- Paralyzed Veterans of America (www.pva.org)
- Disabled American Veterans (www.dav.org)

Additional information on health and fitness activities for people with disabilities can be found at the National Center for Physical Activity and Disability (https://www.nchpad.org/).

—Kirk Bauer, Executive Director of Disabled Sports USA

• • • • • • • • • • •

For a lot of us, especially those with serious physical injuries, critical advances in battlefield medicine means that we are surviving injuries that would have killed Soldiers not so long ago. On the flip side, this means that our recoveries often take an extremely long time. In my case, it has been eleven years since I was shot—I had my most recent surgery last year and hope to have more next year.

After World War II, veterans came back to a booming economy, and so many Americans had served that they were fully integrated back into society. After the Vietnam War, many of veterans were treated horribly upon their return, which remains a stain on our nation's honor. But now, coming back from Iraq and Afghanistan, veterans are called heroes and heralded at every turn, but we are often left out in the cold in perhaps the most important arena—finding enriching jobs where we once again serve as productive members of society. While the veteran unemployment rate is at the time of publication around 4 percent and approximately the same as the nonveteran unemployment rate, many veterans feel underemployed and leave their first

jobs out of the military within one year.[5] And for those who are more seriously injured, WII veterans consistently struggle with higher rates of unemployment compared to the rest of the veteran population.[6]

There are a variety of reasons for this, including health and medical
problems, enrollment in a school or training program or retirement. Further
reasons include misperceptions by employers related to PTSD and TBI, confusion among the WII population about what opportunities exist for us, and
the realistic effects of injury or illness as they relate to continued employment. In this chapter we hope to clear up a lot of this confusion, and to
provide a number of valuable resources to employers and job seekers.

 LEARNING POINT

The Injured Marine Semper Fi Fund has developed a new video series, including the docu-
mentary *In Your Corner*, to address issues that service members face. These videos share
unique insights and powerful advice and support for the mission to bring veterans back to the
workforce by providing resources and, most importantly, hope to service members and their
families. These videos can be found online at www.SemperFiFund.org.

BREAKOUT BOX

While most "wounds of war" are not conspicuous, those that are (paralyzed or missing limbs,
disfigurement) can create unease or tension among supervisors or coworkers who find these
grim reminders of courageous military service too much to face in the workplace. The only way
to combat this is through education, sensitivity training, and leadership by example that seeks
to acclimate employees to unfamiliar characteristics, whether those characteristics are related
to race, gender, religion, or disability incurred during combat.

—Sherman Gillums, Jr., Chief Strategy Officer of American Veterans (AMVETS)

GOVERNMENT RESOURCES

There are a number of free government resources related to WII that
employers and job seekers should be aware of. While it is impossible to discuss each of them here, you can learn a lot through some basic research, and
these sources will often lead to more options for you.

America's Heroes at Work is a Department of Labor initiative that focuses
on hiring, retaining, and promoting veterans, which includes a focus on WII

veterans.[7] The Department of Labor has compiled a list of free, vetted tools and resources to keep at your fingertips. While certainly not all-inclusive, their list is designed to be a quick go-to reference guide for helpful sources of information, including answers about accommodation, disability employment, and PTSD and TBI.

The Department of Labor's Veterans' Employment and Training Service (VETS), through cooperative efforts with and grants to each state, offers employment and training services to eligible veterans with service-connected disabilities through its Disabled Veterans' Outreach Program (DVOP).[8] DVOP specialists provide outreach and offer assistance to disabled and other veterans by promoting community and employer support for employment and training opportunities, including apprenticeships and on-the-job training. The Department of Labor provides grant funds to each state's employment service to maintain DVOP specialist positions in the state. The staffing formula and current appropriations level support about 1,500 DVOP specialists nationally.

BREAKOUT BOX

Military Wounded Warrior Units

Each military service branch has a command unit charged with providing leadership to and facilitating the integration of nonmedical and medical care to WII service members in order to maximize their recovery as they return to duty or transition to civilian life. Here are the websites for each of those:

- Army Warrior Care and Transition Program (www.facebook.com/pg/ArmyWCT)

- Air Force Wounded Warrior (AFW2) Program (www.woundedwarrior.af.mil)

- Navy and Coast Guard Wounded Warrior Safe Harbor (www.navywoundedwarrior.com)

- Marine Corps Wounded Warrior Regiment (www.woundedwarrior.Marines.mil)

- US Special Operations Command's Care Coalition (www.socom.mil/care-coalition/)

The Department of Labor's Job Accommodation Network (JAN) is the leading source of free confidential guidance on disability issues. Call them at (800) 526-7234 or visit AskJAN.org.

The federal government's Computer/Electronic Accommodations Program (CAP) is a centrally funded effort that provides technology and reasonable accommodations to some wounded warriors. Call (833) 227-3272 or (703) 614-8416, email cap@mail.mil, or go to CAP.mil. CAP's mission is to provide assistive technology and accommodations to support individuals with disabilities and WII service members throughout the federal government in accessing information and communication technology.

The VA's Special Employer Incentives (SEI) program provides assistance to employers who hire veterans. The SEI program connects qualified veterans with a specific role at your organization. Veterans who successfully complete the hiring program are expected to stay on at your organization. With this program, you can hire a qualified trainee at an apprenticeship wage. Employers are reimbursed for up to half the veteran's salary to cover certain supplies and equipment, additional instruction expenses, and any loss of production. The veterans receive immediate income and benefits as employees, valuable skills learned in a practical setting that meets the employer's specifications, and one-on-one support from a VA counselor to assist with training or work-related needs. To access the flyer about the SEI program, go to benefits.va.gov/VOW/docs/seiflyerfinal.pdf. To learn more about SEI program, go to benefits.va.gov/vow/for-employers.asp.

VETERAN SERVICE ORGANIZATION (VSO) RESOURCES

Just like with other veteran issues, there are a number of VSOs that provide a variety of resources for job seekers from the WII community and employers. Of course, it is impossible to detail all of them here, so in this chapter we focus on several national and well-known programs that have a significant history of dedicating time, resources, and efforts to supporting WII veterans and their families. In addition to reading about them here, we encourage you to contact them directly and connect with a representative in your area.

Wounded Warrior Project

The Wounded Warrior Project (WWP) serves veterans and service members and their families who incur a physical or mental injury, illness, or wound coincident to their military service on or after September 11, 2001, by providing free programs and services to address the needs of wounded warriors and fill gaps in government care. WWP's services generally stretch across the four pillars of engagement and mind, body, and economic empowerment. One of WWP's most notable programs is the Warrior Care Network, which is a unique partnership between WWP and four national academic medical centers of excellence: Emory Healthcare, Massachusetts General Hospital, Rush University Medical Center, and UCLA Health. At no cost to the veterans, and in cooperation with the VA, this program connects thousands of warriors with world-class care.

WWP's Warriors to Work program is a robust resource for both sides of the employment equation. For the job seekers, it provides career guidance and support services to wounded warriors, their families, and caregivers interested in transitioning to the civilian workforce. Specifically, they help their constituents set attainable goals, build effective résumés, prepare for interviews, and network with local employers. They also support employers by helping them connect with qualified candidates, providing information and education about combat-related injuries and reasonable accommodations, facilitating a productive onboarding process, and developing a long-lasting relationship throughout the life cycle of employment. To learn more and to gain access to a variety of employer resources, visit woundedwarriorproject.org/programs/warriors-to-work.

Disabled American Veterans

Disabled American Veterans (DAV) provides a lifetime of support for veterans of all generations and their families, helping more than 1 million veterans in positive, life-changing ways each year. The organization provides more than 670,000 rides for veterans attending medical appointments and assists veterans with more than 292,000 benefit claims annually. With almost 1,300 chapters and nearly 1.3 million members across the country, DAV is also a leader in connecting veterans with meaningful employment, hosting job fairs, and providing important employment resources employers and job seekers alike. Learn more at dav.org/veterans/employment-resources/employers.

Paralyzed Veterans of America

Paralyzed Veterans of America (PVA) was founded over seventy years ago and provides unique expertise on a wide variety of issues involving the special needs of veterans who have experienced spinal cord injury or dysfunction. Despite that specialization, in 2007 PVA launched its vocational rehabilitation and employment program to assist *any* veteran or service member, spouse, or caregiver across the country. Through the generous support of both private and public partnerships, their Paving Access for Veterans Employment (PAVE) program now has offices in VA medical centers in Tampa, Richmond, San Antonio, Chicago, Minneapolis, Long Beach, and New York City. This is a no-cost program that offers assistance with a variety of customized job search strategies to position their clients for success. The PAVE program strives to place at least one client every day, and helps with effective job search strategies, job leads, networking opportunities, résumé development, and more. To learn more, go to pva.org/veterans-employment.

American Red Cross

The American Red Cross is a robust supplier of free, professional volunteer services to our recovering wounded warriors and their families in military treatment facilities and VA hospitals. It provides both clinical and nonclinical care and aid in more than 78 military treatment facilities and 160 VA hospitals and clinics worldwide. The Red Cross also assists veterans and their families in preparing, developing, and obtaining sufficient evidence to support claims for veterans' benefits. They further assist claimants seeking to appeal to the Board of Veterans' Appeals (BVA) through Red Cross staff at the BVA, as well as a network of state work-share representatives who are accredited by the VA to work on behalf of the Red Cross. Learn more at redcross.org/get-help/military-families/services-for-veterans.

BREAKOUT BOX

What Steps Can Employers Take to Recruit and Retain WII Veterans?

There are many steps employers can take to recruit and retain WII veterans. As with any targeted population, a clear company vision is critical. It must be communicated from the top down and understood from the bottom up. Communicating a clear vision will help those responsible to create goals and report challenges and successes. This can be accomplished by taking the following steps:[9]

- Create a committee on veteran or WII-veteran-hiring. Include people from different parts of the organization and be sure veterans and/or military spouses are included. During this process, identify members within the organization who can provide mentorship to new hires.

- Educate human resource managers, supervisors, and talent acquisition staff on the challenges facing today's wounded veterans, including common injury types, such as post-traumatic stress disorder (PTSD) and traumatic brain injury (TBI)—and on the fact that these injury classifications are not limited solely to military personnel.

- Learn how to write effective position descriptions to make the transition from the military to the civilian workforce easier to understand and less complicated for both the future employee and your current staff.

- Institute effective accommodation policies and practices, including the promotion of flexible workplace strategies. Be sure all employees are made aware of the organization's resources for discussing and accessing accommodations.

- Recruit from reliable sources, such as the WWP Warriors to Work program, and use these sources to support your mission of hiring and retaining the best talent.

—Wounded Warrior Project[9]

PTSD AND TBI IN THE WORKPLACE

"QUOTABLE"

"One out of five Americans—not just veterans, but Americans in general—has a diagnosable mental health condition. While those who serve in harm's way may be more likely to experience mental health challenges, research indicates that they are more likely to recognize the signs of emotional suffering in themselves and their loved ones. Encouraging an open conversation about the mental health challenges we all face and the resources available in companies and communities creates a healthier workforce overall. Our veterans can lead the way."

—Barbara Van Dahlen, Founder and President of Give an Hour

Studies show that a significant number of hiring mangers worry that veterans with PTSD may face challenges assimilating into civilian jobs. In a June 2010 poll, the Society for Human Resource Management (SHRM) found that 46 percent of the HR professionals responding said PTSD and other mental health issues pose hiring challenges. Just 22 percent said the same about combat-related physical disabilities.[10] Common concerns are that employees with PTSD will pose a safety threat to other workers, will require costly accommodations, and will take too much of their managers' time.

Understanding PTSD is an important step for anyone who interacts with veterans at your organization. It will help you not only better understand and support the veterans within your organization, but also break the stigma often associated with recruiting and hiring military veterans, particularly those who have served in combat. Veterans are resilient individuals, add value to any team, and should not be defined by invisible wounds of war.

BREAKOUT BOX

Creating Emotionally Healthy Work Environments

1. Provide basic information and training regarding the myths and realities about mental health in general—and veteran mental health specifically—for all employees across your company.

2. Identify veterans in your company or in the surrounding community who are comfortable talking about their own experiences with trauma and recovery. All of your employees will benefit since many civilians have experienced trauma and are reluctant to share or seek proper help for their challenges.

3. Identify leaders within the company or the community who are willing to talk about their own nonmilitary traumas or mental health challenges and let them present at town hall events or brown-bag lunches.

4. Ensure that mental health resources are available and accessible for all employees and that programs offered to employees. Employee assistance program (EAPs) or other services are knowledgeable about the issues that may affect veterans and their families.

5. Affinity groups are becoming very popular, not just for veterans, but for any employees dealing with mental health challenges. Affinity groups allow employees to share struggles or experiences and provide support to each other.

6. Ensure that managers are trained to recognize signs of emotional suffering that may affect any employee. Provide basic training on how to support employees who are seeking mental health services, either through company resources or in the community.

—Barbara Van Dahlen, Founder and President of Give An Hour

What Is PTSD?

We are not sure why some people develop PTSD and why others do not—this has baffled researchers for a long time. PTSD is a psychiatric disorder that can occur following the experience or witnessing of life-threatening events, such as natural disasters or fire, terrorist incidents, car accidents, violent crime, military combat, or physical or sexual assault in childhood or as an adult. It is also possible for the person to be exposed to the event vicariously, such as with a chaplain or mental health professional, although this scenario is far less frequent. Over 60 percent of men have experienced a traumatic event in their lives, and over 50 percent of women have also, which means that most of the people you meet every day have probably experienced trauma.[11]

BREAKOUT BOX

What Causes PTSD?

According to the DSM-5, a diagnosis for PTSD requires one of the following four specific types of trauma exposure:

1. Directly experiencing a traumatic event;

2. Witnessing, in person, an event that happened to someone else;

3. Learning about the violent or unexpected death of a friend or family member; or

4. Experiencing repeated or extreme exposure to aversive details of traumatic events.

Further, a trauma survivor must have experienced intense fear, helplessness, or horror from the event.[12]

For most people, the reactions to these traumatic events will lessen within the first few days or weeks after the traumatic event. But for people with PTSD, these reactions don't go away. PTSD is characterized by specific categories of symptoms that exist for more than one month and cause significant distress or impairment.

BREAKOUT BOX

Traumatic Events Associated with PTSD

The traumatic events most often associated with PTSD for men are rape, combat exposure, childhood neglect, and childhood physical abuse. The most common traumatic events for women are rape, sexual molestation, physical attack, being threatened with a weapon, and childhood physical abuse.[13]

Symptoms of PTSD

There are a variety of symptoms of PTSD, and all of them have the potential to interfere with everyday activities, both inside and outside the workplace. However, not all PTSD cases are the same or severe, and many people with PTSD don't face workplace challenges at all.

That being said, the symptoms of PTSD fall into four distinct categories. The first category is reliving or re-experiencing the event. These are unwanted memories where the individuals feel that they are right back in the moment of the traumatic event. Typical triggers include a combat veteran hearing a car backfire, a victum of a motor vehicle accident driving by a car accident, or a rape victim seeing a new report of a recent sexual assault.[14] During a flashback, the memories feel incredibly real. Victims can also experience dreams or nightmares directly related to the traumatic event.

The second category is avoidance, which is evidenced by individuals taking actions to avoid situations that trigger memories from the traumatic event. They often avoid activities, places, people, or conversations that are reminders of the event. They do everything they can to avoid reliving that pain and anything that might trigger those thoughts.

 LEARNING POINT

You might see combat veterans with PTSD avoiding crowded situations, including restaurants, movie theaters, grocery stores, and other places with loud noises where they feel like they are not in control.

The third category involves negative changes in moods, feelings, or beliefs. Many with PTSD feel very unsafe, anxious, and depressed. They may start to experience a lot of guilt and shame and begin to withdraw. They may also feel significant anger and irritation at others and lash out. All of these reactions negatively affect their interactions with others and ability to maintain relationships. These symptoms are sometimes referred to as "numbing symptoms" because they are also characterized by diminished interest or participation in significant activities. The individuals experience feelings of detachment or estrangement from others, an inability to experience positive emotions, and an inability to recall important aspects of the trauma.

The fourth category is hypervigilance or feelings of increased emotional arousal, because people with PTSD may feel constantly alert after the traumatic event. They can be startled extremely easily (e.g., a car backfiring, a balloon popping, or fireworks going off can cause them to dive to the ground or react dramatically). They often do not feel safe, and therefore feel anxious and jittery much of the time. In an office environment they may need to sit with their back to the wall or in a position where they can see people entering and exiting the room.

BREAKOUT BOX

Persistent Symptoms of Hypervigilance

1. Sleep disturbance and not being able to sleep well,

2. Irritable behavior and outbursts of anger,

3. Problems with concentration,

4. Reckless or self-destructive behavior, and

5. Exaggerated startle response.

 LEARNING POINT

There is a very good chance that your employees with PTSD may feel a lot of guilt regarding the symptoms and how they affect others around them. Guilt about the traumatic incident is compounded by guilt over isolating themselves, guilt over avoiding those things they used to love, and feeling so anxious and irritated about everyday life.

BREAKOUT BOX

How Common Is PTSD?

PTSD affects millions of individuals across the country, and the vast majority of these people never served in the military. Whether you know it or not, chances are that you are already used to working with and around people with PTSD. Almost 8 percent of Americans will experience PTSD at some point in their lives, and in a country as large as ours, that comes out to over 25 million people.[15] About 8 million adults have PTSD during a given year, and this is only a small portion of those who have gone through a trauma.[16] There is no exact number detailing how many of our veterans have PTSD. However, the higher estimates find that 20 percent of those who served in Iraq or Afghanistan have PTSD. Out of the 2.7 million service members who deployed, that comes out to 540,000 veterans with PTSD. So, what we see in the military community is just a slice of the overall American population.

How PTSD May Present at Work

Naturally, your employees with PTSD may be affected by it while at work. Similar to other disorders or illnesses, each case is specific to that person. The individuals with PTSD coming in to work may have everything under control, or may need help from you and their coworkers. In fact, your efforts to support them could make a significant difference in their overall recoveries. As you read through this list, many of these issues will probably sound familiar to you—multitasking, personal devices, and overscheduling have led to an increased frenzy in both our personal and professional lives. Many of us may face these issues in everyday life.

BREAKOUT BOX

Problems Associated with the Workplace for Those Who Have PTSD[17]

- Memory problems
- Lack of concentration
- Difficulty retaining information
- Feelings of fear or anxiety
- Poor interactions with coworkers
- Unreasonable reactions to situations that trigger memories
- Absenteeism
- Trouble staying awake
- Panic attacks

Because PTSD is caused by a wide variety of situations and can manifest itself in any number of ways, there is no silver bullet for providing the proper support to those who may be struggling with it. A rape victim may feel extremely nervous around particular coworkers, a combat veteran may struggle with people walking behind her where she cannot she them, and someone who was in a debilitating car accident may not be sleeping well at night due to graphic nightmares causing him to relive that horrible incident. But your understanding and compassion could significantly help them be productive members of your team. Being aware of the common problems associated with PTSD in the workplace and implementing proven solutions will be quite helpful.

LEARNING POINT

U.S. Bank offers paid days off to newly hired veterans to attend to service-related medical conditions or participate in reintegration activities.

LEARNING POINT

Although our society has made a lot of progress related to understanding PTSD over the last decade, there is still a significant stigma attached to it. This is especially true in the military community. Veterans may not want to talk about PTSD in the workplace because

- They may not want to relive that trauma;

- They might not want anyone to think they are weak; or

- They may be concerned that they may be risking their position if they disclose to you.

BREAKOUT BOX

Questions for Employers to Consider

Employees with PTSD can ask for an accommodation any time they need it to perform the essential functions of the job. The employee can make a request verbally or in writing and is responsible for providing documentation of a disability. If the employee does so, here are some questions to consider:[18]

- What limitations is the employee with PTSD experiencing?

- How do these limitations affect the employee and the employee's job performance?

- What specific job tasks are problematic as a result of these limitations?

- What accommodations are available to reduce or eliminate these problems? Are all possible resources being used to determine possible accommodations?

- Has the employee with PTSD been consulted regarding possible accommodations?

- Once accommodations are in place, would it be useful to meet with the employee with PTSD to evaluate the effectiveness of the accommodations and to determine whether additional accommodations are needed?

- Do supervisory personnel and employees need training regarding PTSD?

PTS versus PTSD

There is a technical difference between post-traumatic stress (PTS) and PTSD. PTS is a common and normal response to a traumatic or stressful event. With PTS, one may experience symptoms such as a racing heart, shaking hands, sweating, or feeling afraid and nervous. Significantly, symptoms of PTS usually subside a few days after the event and don't cause any prolonged meaningful interference with one's life. PTSD, also a normal response to a traumatic event, is more long-term and the symptoms exist for at least one month.

However, there is a growing movement in the veteran community to drop the D from PTSD and simply refer to the condition as PTS. The general reasoning is that because there is still a significant stigma attached to PTSD, keeping the D, which stands for "disorder," in its name will further disincentive veterans from seeking the care that they need and deserve. So, while the term PTSD is still technically correct and will be used by health experts and insurance companies, you will notice a growing number of people simply saying "PTS."

 **LEARNING POINT**

If veterans in your office refer to their condition as PTS, you should also. They are signaling to you their term of choice and you have nothing to gain by continuing to refer to it as PTSD.

Helping Veterans with PTSD Succeed

Veterans, and anyone else experiencing PTSD, may face difficulties in their work environments. However, you can play a significant role in their recoveries by making small adjustments and reasonable accommodations. Your support here will not only help these employees, but make your office a better place overall. Here are three of the most common symptoms of PTSD in the workplace and how you can make a difference.

Difficulty Concentrating

Difficulty concentrating is a classic symptom of PTSD, and obviously one that can be a real detriment in the workplace. When your employee has identified this issue to you, there are a number of easy and inexpensive (or free) steps you can take to help. To reduce distractions in the work area if a private office is not an option, you can allow the use of white noise machines, allow your employee to listen to soothing music, provide a noise-canceling headset, or help plan for uninterrupted work time.

Memory Loss

Recent studies have shown that combat veterans can actually experience physical changes to the hippocampus, a part of the brain involved in learning and memory, as well as in handling stress.[19] PTSD patients report difficulty remembering facts or lists and gaps in memory lasting from minutes to days that are not caused by ordinary forgetting.[20] There are however, a number of accommodations you can easily implement that can help tremendously.

BREAKOUT BOX

Accommodations or Strategies to Combat Memory Issues in the Workplace[21]

- Provide written as well as verbal instructions.
- Provide written checklists.
- Use a wall calendar.
- Use a daily or weekly task list.
- Provide verbal prompts and reminders.
- Use electronic organizers, handheld devices, and apps.
- Allow the employee to record meetings and trainings.
- Provide printed minutes of meetings and trainings.
- Allow additional training time for new duties.
- Provide a mentor for daily guidance.
- Provide reminders of important deadlines via emails, memos, and weekly supervision.
- Use notebooks, planners, or sticky notes to record information for easy retrieval.
- Provide cues (labels, color-coding, or bulletin boards) to assist with locating items.
- Post written instructions for using equipment.

Sleep Disturbances and Fatigue

Many people have trouble sleeping and this is especially true if they have PTSD. This is an unfortunate reality for a number of reasons. Because some veterans are hypervigilant, they constantly feel on guard and the need to protect themselves; it is difficult to fall asleep while feeling this way. Similarly, people with PTSD often have negative thoughts and it is difficult for them to fall asleep while competing with that. Also, nightmares are common for people with PTSD—these nightmares wake people up in the middle of the night, and a fear of those nightmares can also cause people to feel very nervous about falling asleep. Needless to say, your veteran employees who are not sleeping well at night will face challenges in the workplace.

BREAKOUT BOX

It's Possible to Unintentionally Discriminate against a Disabled Worker

Discrimination can include not providing a reasonable accommodation for known limitations caused by a disability. "Reasonable accommodations" can include job restructuring; a part-time or modified work schedule; reassignment to a vacant position; adjustment to training materials or policies; acquisition or modification of equipment or devices; providing qualified readers or interpreters; or modifications that will make the workplace accessible.

Make sure your hiring managers and supervisory officials are trained in compliance with the Americans with Disabilities Act and the Americans with Disabilities Amendments Act; the Family and Medical Leave Act; and the Uniformed Services Employment and Reemployment Rights Act (USERRA). [22]

Flexible Work Schedules

If your veteran employees are receiving care from the VA, they likely will have little flexibility when it comes to their appointments, even for therapy. Allowing them to change their work schedules in order to attend their appointments will be helpful for the morale of your employees, but also will be mentally and physically beneficial to them (and ultimately to your team).

Allowing for a flexible start time or work-from-home options are probably the most beneficial accommodations for sleep disturbances. If your employee wakes up from a terrifying nightmare and cannot fall back asleep for a couple of hours, the opportunity to sleep in an extra hour or two can make a huge difference in their productivity. If your employees are facing an upcoming anniversary of that traumatic incident, they may face significant sleep issues at that time. Working with their schedule at that time could be very helpful. Also, recent studies have drawn a strong relationship between workplace daylight exposure and an office worker's sleep, activity, and quality of life—if it is possible to increase the natural lighting in your office, you should consider that option.[23]

BREAKOUT BOX

Dispelling Myths around PTSD in the Workplace

Myth 1: Support and accommodations in the workplace are too costly.

FACT: According to an accommodations study, 56 percent of accommodations cost absolutely nothing![24] Of those accommodations that do have a cost, the typical one-time expenditure by employers was only $600.

Myth 2: It's a legal liability to hire someone with a disability because it is impossible to fire them.

FACT: The decision to terminate any employee carries with it the risk of possible legal challenges. It is best to have clear procedures and policies in place to ensure that all employees are getting the feedback they need in order to perform their jobs to the best of their abilities. The ADA does not protect an employee with a disability from being fired because of poor job performance; it protects them from being fired simply because of their disability. An employer can discipline an employee with PTSD who violates conduct standards or fails to meet performance standards, even if the behavior exhibited is caused by the employee's disability. However, an employer is obligated to consider reasonable accommodations to help the employee.

Myth 3: People with PTSD are violent and unpredictable.
FACT: PTSD symptoms range all the way from very mild and almost unobservable to very severe. The belief that violence and unpredictability are associated with serious mental problems is common, but untrue. In reality, the presence of PTSD or a psychological condition does not necessarily make someone prone to violence. Therefore, someone with PTSD or any other psychological condition should not be viewed as a threat in the workplace.

Myth 4: Once people develop PTSD, they will never recover.
FACT: Studies suggest that most people with PTSD and other mental illnesses get better, and many recover completely.[25] Recovery refers to the process in which people are able to live, work, learn, and participate fully in their communities. For some individuals, recovery is the ability to live a fulfilling and productive life. For others, recovery implies the reduction or complete remission of symptoms.

Myth 5: PTSD is a sign of weakness of character.

FACT: PTSD is a common human reaction to very traumatic situations. PTSD seems to be caused by complex chemical changes in the brain when an individual witnesses or experiences a traumatic event. The symptoms of PTSD appear to be frequently experienced in situations where someone perceives they have been exposed to a life-threatening event, although symptoms and reactions vary from person to person.[26]

I have both PTS and a TBI, and I challenge any employer to find a reason why I wouldn't make a good addition to their workforce. Like tens of thousands of others like me, I realized that PTS counseling was a good thing and something I embraced, I work out regularly because physical fitness is critical to a healthy brain and healthy lifestyle, and I engage in peer mentoring, both to help others and to help myself. For those who instinctively feel reservations about hiring a veteran because of a fear of PTS, I hope you take the time to learn what PTS is and what it isn't.

VETERAN RESOURCE CENTER FOR PTSD

There are a variety of governmental, private, and nonprofit resources available to veterans for different issues related to PTSD:

- The VA National Center for PTSD (www.ptsd.va.gov).
- The Warrior Care Network, WWP's collaboration with Emory Healthcare, Massachusetts General Hospital, Rush University Medical Center, and UCLA Health's Operation Mend (www.woundedwarriorproject. org/programs/warrior-care-network).
- Give An Hour, a national nonprofit organization providing free counseling through their network of licensed mental health professionals, including seven thousand psychologists, social workers, psychiatrists, marriage and family therapists, drug and alcohol counselors, pastoral counselors, and other professional counselors (www.giveanhour.org).
- Vets4Warriors, a national nonprofit organization providing 24/7 confidential conversations in a stigma-free environment to active duty, National Guard and Reserve service members, veterans, retirees, and their families and caregivers who need to talk to someone who has been through similar situations and can help them get answers to their questions (vets4warriors.com).
- Sleep and PTSD, a specific section within the VA website dedicated to suggestions for veterans with PTSD and sleep issues (www.ptsd.va.gov/public/problems/sleep-and-ptsd.asp).

- The Soldiers Project, comprehensive list of resources for veterans for numerous issues related to PTSD and treatment options (www. thesoldiersproject.org/resources-for-veterans-and-their-loved-ones/).
- VA Vet Centers across the country provide a broad range of counseling, outreach, and referral services to combat veterans and their families (www.vetcenter.va.gov).
- Veterans' Voices on PTSD, a group that shares honest and candid descriptions from veterans of what life was like for them with PTSD (veterans-voices.net/tag/ptsd).
- Make the Connection (www.maketheconnection.net/conditions/ptsd).
- Marcus Institute for Brain Health, an institution that welcomes veterans of any discharge status and provides specialty care for military veterans and retired athletes struggling with mild to moderate TBIs (including concussions) and changes in psychological health (www.ucdenver.edu/anschutz/patientcare/marcusinstitute).
- WWP's Combat Stress Recovery Program, a program that addresses the mental health needs of warriors returning home from war. Teammates provide ongoing assistance to help set and achieve goals and gain access to resources (www.woundedwarriorproject.org/programs/combat-stress-recovery-program).

BREAKOUT BOX

Disability or Injury ≠ Inability

It is estimated that approximately fifty-four million Americans have some form of disability. Disabilities come in many forms: visual, auditory, verbal, cognitive, psychological, and physical. If you are a veteran with a disability, you may not think of yourself as a person with a disability. Instead, maybe you are quick and proud to refer to yourself as a disabled veteran or a wounded service member. Language matters when it comes to understanding all the legal protections and entitlements and accessing eligibility-based services and resources within the community. This is especially true when considering education or entering the workforce. Whether you are newly injured or you acquired a disability many years ago, the way in which you deal with it may have a great impact on your future education and employment opportunities. Many veterans with significant disabilities have difficulty accepting the fact that they are not the same as they once were. It is important for you to take the time to fully understand how your particular disability impacts you—especially if you are considering returning to school or work. After all, you were not born with this disability. Part of your recovery, rehabilitation, and reintegration into the workforce or an academic setting will be to understand your disability, how it impacts you, and what functional limitations you might experience.[27]

Traumatic Brain Injury

Every year, TBIs contribute to a substantial number of deaths and cases of permanent disability. An estimated 1.7 million people annually sustain a TBI in America. A traumatic brain injury is caused by a blow to the head, a penetrating skull injury, or some sort of acceleration or deceleration of force from a sudden stop or impact that moves the brain around in the skull. TBIs can be mild, moderate, or severe (Table 7.1). Most TBIs are mild and are often referred to as concussions. Over 85 percent of people with concussions recover completely and very quickly.

Although not all blows to the head lead to a TBI, they are common both in the civilian world and in the military. They are commonly caused in everyday life by car accidents, sports, falls, and assaults. In combat, they are typically from exposure to a blast (roadside bombs), indirect fire (incoming rockets or mortars), and direct fire (penetrating injuries such as shrapnel going into your brain or being shot in the head). Service members also frequently fall from vehicles and aircraft. Since 2000, almost 360,000 service members have incurred a traumatic brain injury.

Not all people with a TBI will need accommodations to perform their jobs and the most commonly requested accommodations are inexpensive. However, these accommodations can be an integral part of the employee's peak performance. Simple accommodations exist that can help with physical limitations, visual problems, and attendance issues, as well as assist with maintaining stamina and concentration during the workday, staying organized, and handling stress and emotions. Learn more at Brainline or JAN.[28]

BREAKOUT BOX

Questions for Employers When Determining Accommodations for TBI

The following is only a sample of the questions employers should consider when determining appropriate accommodations:[29]

- What limitations is the employee with TBI experiencing, and how do these limitations affect the employee's job performance?
- What specific job tasks are problematic as a result of these limitations?
- What accommodations are available to reduce or eliminate these problems?

- Has the employee with TBI been consulted regarding possible accommodations?

- Do supervisory personnel and employees need training regarding TBI?

 LEARNING POINT

Your employee may not be aware that they have a TBI and may not have been diagnosed with one. Also, employees suffering from TBIs may be hesitant to seek support. Some warning signs of TBIs include headaches, blurry eyesight or sensitivity to light, mood swings, low threshold for managing stress, hostility, outbursts, avoidant behavior, absenteeism, forgetfulness, difficulty with concentration, and an inability to maintain organization.

BREAKOUT BOX

Supporting Your Employee with a TBI

If your veteran employee has identified that they have suffered a TBI, there are some easy steps you can take to support them:

1. To help concentration issues and headaches, you can dim the lighting or take advantage of natural lighting, allow for white-noise makers, and be aware of environmental noises.

2. For memory issues, you can provide them regular reminders, provide directions verbally and in writing, and allow them to record meetings.

3. For mood issues, you can allow the use of support animals, provide breaks, and allow flexible work schedules and work-from-home options.

4. Be a careful and empathetic listener—disclosing their TBI to you is a sign of courage.

 LEARNING POINT

If necessary, you can discipline veterans with a TBI or PTSD just like any other employee. In fact, you cannot treat them differently than others when performance issues arise. You also cannot require a veteran applicant or employee to undergo a medical exam unless you require the same medical exam for others under the same circumstances and the medical exam is related to their position.

Table 7.1. Levels of severity of TBIs

Level of Severity	Loss of Consciousness	Length of Symptoms	Length of Amnesia
Mild	None or less than 30 minutes	Less than 24 hours	Less than 24 hours
Moderate	More than 30 minutes and less than 24 hours	More than 24 hours and less than 7 days	More than 24 hours and less than 7 days
Severe	More than 24 hours	More than 7 days	More than 7 days

EMPLOYER RESOURCE CENTER FOR TBI

- Mayo Clinic, *Understanding Brain Injury: A Guide for Employers (Rochester, MN: Mayo Clinic, 2011),* http://www.ndrn.org/images/Documents/webcats/mc1298.pdf.
- "Accommodating Employees with Traumatic Brain Injury," *Brainline,* May 21, 2012, https://www.brainline.org/article/accommodating-employees-traumatic-brain-injury. Detailed fact sheet developed in cooperation with the Department of Labor's Office of Disability Employment Policy, the Job Accommodation Network, VETS, the Defense Centers of Excellence for Psychological Health and Traumatic Brain Injury, and the Defense and Veterans Brain Injury Center.
- Job Accommodation Network, *Employees with Brain Injuries, Office of Disability Employment Policy,* March 4, 2013, https://askjan.org/media/downloads/BrainInjuryA&CSeries.pdf.
- Defense Centers of Excellence (DCoE) for Psychological Health and Traumatic Brain Injury is a division of the Defense Health Agency that provides the Military Health System with current and emerging psychological health and traumatic brain injury clinical and educational information (www.dcoe.mil).

VETERAN RESOURCE CENTER FOR TBI

Just like with PTS and PTSD, there are a variety of governmental, private, and nonprofit resources available to veterans for different issues related to TBI:

- "Understanding Your Employment Rights under the Americans with Disabilities Act: A Guide for Veterans," Equal Opportunity Employment Commission, https://www.eeoc.gov/eeoc/publications/ada_veterans.cfm.
- "TBI Basics," Defense and Veterans Brain Injury Center, http://dvbic.dcoe.mil/article/tbi-basics.
- The VA Polytrauma System of Care provides comprehensive care and tailored rehabilitation for veterans and returning service members with TBI and other injuries to more than one physical region or organ system of the body (www.polytrauma.va.gov/index.asp).

• Take an online symptom management assessment to evaluate how you are handling your TBI symptoms and hear from other veterans and service members dealing with TBI (www.afterdeployment.dcoe.mil/ topics-traumatic-brain-injury).

BREAKOUT BOX

Helping Yourself

You can take the following steps to help manage your TBI symptoms:[30]

• Get enough sleep.

• Write things down or use electronic reminders if you have trouble remembering.

• Establish a regular daily routine.

• Check with someone you trust when making decisions.

• Avoid alcohol. It could slow down the healing process and make symptoms worse.

• Avoid caffeine, cold medications that treat nasal congestion, or other products that contain pseudoephedrine, which may increase the symptoms.

• Recognize triggers. Keep a record to help identify situations that are more likely to worsen your symptoms.

• Take up a hobby or a recreational activity.

• Talk to others to keep you from feeling isolated and to give friends and loved ones a chance to support you.

• Remember that symptoms are a normal part of the recovery—and that they will get better.

· · · · · · · · · · ·
CASE STUDY

Disabled American Veterans (DAV)

DAV is a very prolific charity when it comes to supporting disabled veterans, helping more than one million veterans in life-changing ways every year. This includes organizing nearly 150 job fairs annually, where veterans can meet directly with employers seeking top-notch talent. As a result, tens of thousands of veterans have found employment.

Working closely with hundreds of employers and thousands of job seekers who are veterans with disabilities, DAV discovered a significant knowledge gap when it comes to hiring and retaining disabled veterans. First, many employers don't realize that of the approximately four million veterans with a service-connected disability, the vast majority have disabilities that are not visible. And far too many veterans with disabilities fear discrimination in the workplace, worried that employers and coworkers will conclude they are not capable of performing on the job. Indeed, a survey of veterans with disabilities transitioning to the civilian workforce estimated 57 percent feared hiring discrimination related to their disability, while 71 percent of those with a diagnosed mental health condition had no intention of disclosing this information in an employment situation.

The reality is that most accommodations that will help veterans with disabilities succeed in the workplace cost little or nothing to implement. These can include time off for medical appointments, an adjustable workstation or ergonomic chairs for veterans with back or spinal injuries, or a flexible work schedule or telecommuting for veterans with ongoing treatment. And, despite the fact that too many employers worry about the impact of PTSD in the workplace—30 percent according to a survey conducted by DAV and Military.com[31]—the vast majority of people with PTSD can succeed in the workplace with little, if any, accommodations.

The need for greater understanding by employers, including the thousands of employers committed to ensuring veterans with disabilities integrate and succeed as part of their workforce, led DAV to develop *The Veteran Advantage: DAV Guide to Hiring and Retaining Veterans with Disabilities*. It provides insights, best practices and practical strategies for employers looking to recruit and hire veterans with disabilities— such as adding disabled veterans to recruitment teams, putting in place a mentoring program, training hiring managers on veterans' skill sets and the types of disabilities they may have, and including information about accommodations in onboarding procedures. To access *The Veteran Advantage* and other resources, visit www.jobs.dav.org.

BREAKOUT BOX

Representative List of Organizations Supporting WII Veterans and Caregivers

- Military Order of the Purple Heart (www.purpleheart.org)
- Disabled American Veterans (DAV) (www.dav.org)
- Wounded Warrior Project (WWP) (www.woundedwarriorproject.org)
- Disabled Sports USA (www.disabledsportsusa.org)
- Fisher House Foundation (www.fisherhouse.org)
- American Red Cross Military and Veteran Caregiver Network (milvetcaregivernetwork.org/)
- Hope for the Warriors (www.hopeforthewarriors.org)
- PsychArmor (psycharmor.org/)
- Gary Sinese Foundation (www.garysinisefoundation.org/#SnowballModal)
- Paralyzed Veterans of America (PVA) (www.pva.org)
- Injured Marine Semper Fi Fund (www.semperfifund.org)
- Homes for Our Troops (www.hfotusa.org)
- Military Warriors Support Foundation (www.militarywarriors.org)
- Vets4Warriors (vets4warriors.com)
- Project Healing Waters Fly Fishing (www.projecthealingwaters.org)
- K9s for Warriors (www.k9sforwarriors.org)
- DogTag Bakery (www.dogtaginc.org)
- R4 Alliance (www.r4alliance.org)
- Warriors Ethos (www.warriorsethos.org)
- 22Kill (www.22kill.com)
- Bob Woodruff Foundation (www.bobwoodrufffoundation.org)
- Green Beret Foundation (www.greenberetfoundation.org)
- Give an Hour (www.giveanhour.org)
- Blinded Veterans Association (www.bva.org)
- Entrepreneurship Bootcamp for Disabled Veterans (EBV) (ebv.vets.syr.edu)
- United States Veterans Chamber of Commerce (USVCC) (www.USVCC.org)

ENDNOTES

1. Wounded Warrior Project, *Working with Wounded Warriors Participant Guide*, 37.
2. For example, see "Veterans Employment Toolkit," Challenges and How to Help, Department of Veterans Affairs, last modified August 24, 2015, https://www.va.gov/VETSINWORKPLACE/challenges.asp.
3. Department of Veteran Affairs, VA Handbook 0802: Federal Recovery Coordination Program (Washington, DC: Department of Veteran Affairs, 2011), https://www.va.gov/vapubs/viewPublication.asp?Pub_ID=537&FType=2.
4. Wounded Warrior Project, *Working with Wounded Warriors Participant Guide*, 37.
5. Natalie Gross, "Despite Decreasing Veteran Unemployment Rate, Underemployment Remains a Problem," Rebootcamp, March 7, 2017, https://rebootcamp.militarytimes.com/education-transition/2017/03/07/despite-decreasing-veteran-unemployment-rate-underemployment-remains-a-problem/; and Bureau of Labor Statistics, "Employment Situation of Veterans Summary," Department of Labor news release no. USDL-18-0453, March 22, 2018, https://www.bls.gov/news.release/vet.nr0.htm.
6. Wounded Warrior Project, *2017 Wounded Warrior Project Survey: Report of Findings* (Jacksonville, FL: Wounded Warrior Project, August 25, 2017), https://www.woundedwarriorproject.org/media/172072/2017-wwp-annual-warrior-survey.pdf, x.
7. "Veterans Hiring Toolkit," Veterans' Employment and Training Service, Department of Labor, accessed April 20, 2018, https://www.dol.gov/vets/ahaw/Resources.htm.
8. "Employment Services for Veterans," Veterans' Employment and Training Services OASVET Fact Sheet no. 97-2, Department of Labor, accessed April 20, 2018, https://www.dol.gov/vets/programs/fact/vet97-2.htm.
9. Wounded Warrior Project, https://www.woundedwarriorproject.org/media/1581/warriors-to-work-a-resource-for-employers_rev5615.pdf.
10. Dori Meindert, "Hidden Wounds," *HR Magazine,* July 1, 2011, https://www.shrm.org/hr-today/news/hr-magazine/pages/0711meinert.aspx.
11. Jessica Hamblen, "PTSD 101: PTSD Overview," education course, Department of Veteran Affairs, https://www.ptsd.va.gov/professional/continuing_ed/flash-files/ptsd-overview-course/launcher.html#.
12. "DSM-5 Criteria for PTSD," *Brainline*, February 22, 2018, https://www.Brainline.org/article/dsm-5-criteria-ptsd.
13. Nebraska Department of Veteran's Affairs, "What Is PTSD (Posttraumatic Stress Disorder)?," 2007, http://www.ptsd.ne.gov/what-is-ptsd.html.
14. Nebraska Department of Veteran's Affairs.
15. Nebraska Department of Veteran's Affairs.
16. National Center for PTSD, "How Common Is PTSD?," Department of Veteran Affairs, October 3, 2016, http://www.ptsd.va.gov/public/ptsd-overview/basics/how-common-is-ptsd.asp.
17. Amy Menna, *Post Traumatic Stress Disorder and the Workplace: What Employers and Coworkers Need to Know* (Camden, ME: A Gift from Within, August 24, 2012), http://www.giftfromwithin.org/html/PTSD-Workplace-What-Employers-Coworkers-Need-To-Know.html.

18. Job Accommodation Network, "Employees with Post Traumatic Stress Disorder," Accommodation and Compliance Series, October 8, 2015, p. 6, https://askjan.org/media/downloads/PTSDA&CSeries.pdf.

19. J. Douglas Bremner and Meena Narayan, "The Effects of Stress on Memory and the Hippocampus throughout the Life Cycle: Implications for Childhood Development and Aging," *Development and Psychopathology* 10, no. 4 (December 1998): 871–85.

20. J. Douglas Bremner, "The Invisible Epidemic: Post-traumatic Stress Disorder, Memory and the Brain," Pandora's Project, March 2000, http://www.pandys.org/articles/invisibleepidemic.html.

21. Job Accommodation Network, "Employees with Post Traumatic Stress Disorder," 7.

22. Hiring Our Heroes, "Accommodating Veterans with Disabilities," Employer Roadmap, 2017, https://www.vetemployerroadmap.org/wounded-veterans/2017/3/27/accommodating-veterans-with-disabilities.

23. Christopher Bergland, "Exposure to Natural Light Improves Workplace Performance," *Athlete's Way (blog), Psychology Today,* June 5, 2013, https://www.psychologytoday.com/blog/the-athletes-way/201306/exposure-natural-light-improves-workplace-performance.

24. Job Accommodation Network, *Workplace Accommodations: Low Cost, High Impact, Office of Disability Employment Policy,* September 1, 2009, https://kcdcinfo.ks.gov/docs/default-source/default-document-library/low-cost-high-impact.pdf.

25. "Post-Traumatic Stress Disorder," Mental Health America, online brochure, accessed April 20, 2018, http://www.mentalhealthamerica.net/conditions/post-traumatic-stress-disorder.

26. "Post-Traumatic Stress Disorder," Mental Health Information, National Institute of Mental Health, last modified February 2016, https://www.nimh.nih.gov/health/topics/post-traumatic-stress-disorder-ptsd/index.shtml.

27. Wounded Warrior Project, *Warriors to Work Planning Guide,* 45.

28. America's Heroes at Work, "Accommodating Employees with Traumatic Brain Injury," *Brainline,* May 21, 2012, https://www.brainline.org/article/accommodating-employees-traumatic-brain-injury; and Job Accommodation Network, "Veterans and Service Members," https://askjan.org/topics/veterans.htm.

29. "Accommodating Employees with Traumatic Brain Injury," *Brainline,* May 21, 2012, https://www.brainline.org/article/accommodating-employees-traumatic-brain-injury.

30. "Effects of Traumatic Brain Injury," Make the Connection, last modified April 20, 2018, https://maketheconnection.net/conditions/traumatic-brain-injury.

31. Steven Wilson, "Survey Reveals Experiences for Disabled Veterans, Their Employers," Disabled American Veterans press release, February 23, 2017, https://www.dav.org/learn-more/news/2017/survey-reveals-experiences-disabled-veterans-employers/.

CHAPTER 8

Military Spouse Employment

Military spouses bring strength, resilience, and common-sense wisdom to the workplace. Their ability to step in and blend in from day one is a remarkable asset and their strong sense of community adds that special something extra to the working environment that all organizations need for success.

—Suzie Schwartz, President of Victory Media Military Spouse Programs and spouse of General Norton Schwartz, retired Air Force Chief of Staff

MILITARY SPOUSE EMPLOYMENT

BREAKOUT BOX

Why Hire Military Spouses?

Resilient, adaptable, civically engaged, educated, socially aware, multi-tasking capable, resourceful, diverse, entrepreneurial, and team-oriented—descriptors any manager would want regarding their team members or new hires. These are typical traits and qualities military spouses possess. Hiring managers want to add talent to their organization that raises the overall productivity of the team. And those same managers also want their employees to be loyal, dedicated, hard-working, and resourceful to accomplish any task that comes their way.

That is exactly the kind of talent Prudential has found in military spouses. Due to permanent change of station (PCS) moves, many military spouses have gaps in employment, lack of career progression, what appears to be job-hopping, and other red flags that cause recruiters to weed out their applications. Jim Beamesderfer, vice president of veterans initiatives at Prudential, says, "Military spouses have a lot of the red flags the average screening process weeds out if the recruiter doesn't understand the back story—the reason why. We encourage our hiring managers and recruiters to think differently." This has allowed Prudential to hire several military spouses who have now been with the company a few years—and they are some of the most dedicated and loyal employees.

Reflecting on the reasons to consider hiring military spouses, Chuck Sevola, head of veterans initiatives at Prudential, says, "Military spouses have the skills and experiences to add value to most any organization—they often only need an opportunity. Once given that chance, you will find some of the best and most loyal employees you could ever want in your organization."

—Prudential Financial

Background Information

Like our service members and veterans, military spouses are diverse, coming from all walks of life and different stages of career. Being married to someone in the military has most likely affected their life and career trajectory; however, unlike their active duty counterparts, there is very little emphasis on hiring military spouses, and many HR managers are unaware of their backgrounds or the noteworthy reasons to hire them. We aim to remedy that issue in this chapter!

According to the Department of Defense, there are approximately 642,000 spouses of active duty service members. Of that population, approximately 92 percent are women. Therefore, any figures we use in this chapter will be based on female military spouses—the relatively small number of male spouses makes it difficult to conduct statistically reliable analyses. Further, this chapter will also focus on the female spouses of *active duty* service members—once military personnel transition to veteran status, these spouses typically no longer face the challenges (such as periodically moving because of military orders) that separate them from civilians.

BREAKOUT BOX

Active Duty Military Spouse Demographics[1]

- Active duty military spouses are predominantly female (95 percent).

- They are significantly younger than to their civilian and veteran counterparts: on average, 33 years of age, compared to 47 years of age for civilian spouses and 60 years of age for veteran spouses.

- The active duty military spouse community has a larger proportion of ethnic and racial minorities than the broader civilian population.

- They are more likely to have children (18 and under) at home compared to their civilian counterparts (74 percent versus 59 percent).

- They are more likely to have moved within states, across states, and abroad than their civilian and veteran counterparts. This increased likelihood of moving from one geographic location to another interacts with economic issues for these families, as indicated by an average personal income that is over 38 percent less than that of their civilian counterparts.

Since 9/11, many military families have faced multiple deployments and significant periods of separation as a result of those deployments. Department of Defense studies reveal that 81 percent of military spouses have experienced a deployment during their service member's career,[2] and that the deployments average 7.7 months.[3]

Another aspect of military life is the requirement to move frequently. When service members and their families relocate to another military base, this is called a permanent change of station (PCS) move, and it requires the entire family to uproot and start their life again in another town that could be thousands of miles away. In addition to the obvious career-related challenges military spouses face when this happens—such as identifying new opportunities for jobs, creating new professional networks, and having to explain why they had to leave their last job after only two or three years—many military bases are located more than fifty miles from major urban locations, which limits both the quantity and types of jobs available to military spouses.

BREAKOUT BOX

Five Key Points You Should Know about Military Spouse Employment[4]

1. Unemployment and underemployment continue to be significant challenges for most military spouses. Many are in part-time or seasonal positions when they would prefer full time or permanent work.

2. Military spouses with degrees face the greatest challenges in nearly every measurable employment category. They face the highest rates of unemployment and the most difficulty finding meaningful work.

3. Moves between duty stations play havoc on careers. Not only do most military spouses have to quit jobs because of a move, they face long periods of unemployment after the move.

4. Like most American families, military families want and need two incomes—something that is much harder for military families to achieve.

5. The lack of employment opportunities creates stress and influences a family's decision to stay in or leave the military—factors that ultimately hurt military readiness, retention and recruiting.

It is also important to note that approximately one-third of military spouses work in a field that requires licensure. This includes teachers, nurses, attorneys, aestheticians, doctors, real estate professionals, and others. For these spouses, that means that every time the military moves their family to another state, they have to initiate and complete the process of becoming state certified.

"QUOTABLE"

"Our military spouses face very unique challenges, yet many have continued to serve as the very fiber that keeps military families connected and thriving. We have to find ways that installation and base commanders can build better opportunities with local agencies, municipalities, and companies to create more experiences and opportunities for the spouses seeking employment."

—Victor LaGroon, Director of the Office of Veterans Affairs for the City of Chicago

Although these licensing requirements are designed to ensure that practitioners meet a certain level of professional competency, it is often a very confusing and laborious process. As the Departments of Treasury and Defense have noted, each state determines its own requirements for licensing and certification, which results in variation across state lines and a lack of license portability. These administrative and financial processes can act as a significant and time-consuming obstacle to employment for military spouses especially and repeatedly, as many military spouses undergo multiple moves and relocations.[5]

As the IVMF study reveals, 78 percent of spouses who reported that they had experienced a military move during their active duty spouse's career, only 11 percent acquired a new professional license or credential after their last move.[6]

BREAKOUT BOX

Barriers to Military Spouse Employment[7]

1. **Frequent Relocations**—Active duty families move on average once every two to three years: 2.4 times more often than civilian families. The frequency of relocations increases the number of job changes a military spouse will face, the number of gaps in employment, and chances for repeated periods of unemployment over time.

2. **Underemployment**—Because of the labor market (e.g., moving to remote locations or overseas), licensure requirements, and the need to take over parenting responsibilities while a spouse is deployed or because of unpredictable military schedules, military spouses frequently find themselves working in positions for which they are overqualified by virtue of their educational background or work experience.

3. **Licensure Transferability**—As many as 35 percent of spouses work in a field that requires licensure. According to a 2012 survey of active duty spouses, of the 78 percent of spouses who reported they had experienced a military move during their husband or wife's active duty career, only 11 percent acquired a new professional license or credential after their last move.

4. **Childcare Access and Cost**—More than two-thirds (67 percent) say lack of childcare has impacted their ability to pursue employment or education.

5. **Unpredictable Lifestyle**—Military spouses often wrestle with challenges around single parenting due to spouse deployments, separations, or long, unpredictable work schedules. When spouses do seek employment, their résumés may appear inconsistent due to working in multiple unrelated positions, they may have multiple or lengthy gaps in employment, or they may have worked in jobs that are unrelated to their education or prior work experience.

6. **Parenting Responsibilities**—Active military spouses are more likely to have children 18 and under at home compared to their civilian counterparts (74 percent versus 59 percent). Having young children creates the need for childcare and impacts the ability to work, particularly when a spouse is deployed or unable to assist with childcare responsibilities.

7. **Age Barriers**—Active military spouses are significantly younger than their civilian and veteran counterparts—active duty military spouses are on average 33 years old, compared to civilian spouses, who average 47 years, and veteran spouses, who average 60. Their youth impacts employment because they are more likely to have young children at home, require childcare, have just completed school, or have either no or limited employment experiences prior to becoming a military spouse.

UNEMPLOYMENT AND UNDEREMPLOYMENT

Underemployment is a serious challenge for military spouses, caused by a combination of issues associated with the military lifestyle. As detailed in the *Military Spouse Employment Report*, a large percentage of military spouses are underemployed based on two key definitions—education and experience. Underemployment with respect to education refers to those possessing more formal education than their position requires (this applies to 33 percent of their survey sample). Underemployment with respect to experience relates to possessing more years of experience than the position requires (this applies to 10 percent of their sample). And many military spouses are underemployed with respect to both education and experience at their current or most recent position (approximately 47 percent of their sample). In sum, 90 percent of their employed military spouse respondents reported being underemployed with respect to education, experience, or both.[8]

 **LEARNING POINT**

Underemployment, especially with regard to levels of education, is widespread among military spouses. Spouses with a college or postgraduate degree appear to be most impacted by the transient nature of military life: not only are they more likely to be unemployed, they also face longer periods of unemployment and are more likely to be underemployed.

According to Hiring Our Heroes, overall military spouse unemployment has declined in recent years, from 23 percent in 2015 to 16 percent in 2017.[9] While significant, this decline in the military spouse unemployment rate does not close the gap between military spouse unemployment and that of their civilian counterparts. At 16 percent, the military spouse unemployment rate still quadruples the unemployment rate for all adult women (4 percent in May 2017) and triples the unemployment rate for women between the ages of 20 and 25. Regarding underemployment, Hiring Our Heroes has further identified some significant statistics through their recent survey:[10]

- More than 18 percent of employed spouses surveyed have seasonal or temporary jobs; 82 percent of those spouses would prefer a permanent position.
- Of military spouses who are employed, 25 percent are working more than one job for pay.
- Approximately 70 percent of employed spouses do not believe that their education or past work experience is being fully utilized in their current job.
- Nearly two-thirds (63 percent) of employed military spouses indicated that they had held previous positions that required greater skills or responsibilities.

BREAKOUT BOX

The Military Spouse Perspective[11]

Through its 2017 survey of military spouses, Hiring Our Heroes identified a host of unique factors that impact a military spouse's new job prospects:[12]

1. Forty-one percent of military spouses say their greatest employment challenge is employers not wanting to hire them because they may move in the future.

2. Thirty-four percent cite the lack of a flexible work schedule, often a crucial factor during a service member's deployment.

3. Thirty-two percent cite finding affordable childcare, which can include navigating childcare wait lists following a move without extended family nearby.

4. Twenty-nine percent report insufficient pay.

5. Twenty-eight percent report difficulty explaining gaps in their résumé.

6. Twenty-six percent cite the lack of jobs on or near the military base.

HIRING MILITARY SPOUSES

It is evident that military spouses face some significant challenges when it comes to full-time employment. Knowingly or not, they have made significant sacrifices by marrying into the military. While there is a certain percentage that are not seeking full-time careers, the vast majority are. Typically, military spouses are well qualified to provide great services to employers, and derive great satisfaction from that work.

BREAKOUT BOX

Top Ten Reasons Military Spouses Want to Work[13]

1. Contribute to the family finances
2. Financial security
3. Financial opportunity
4. Financial independence
5. Accrue benefits such as savings and retirement
6. Well-being
7. Employment continuity
8. Pay off general and student loan debt
9. Social support
10. Connect to their community

A number of companies and organizations across the United States recognize the value that military spouses bring to the workplace, and understand that the skills they have translate well into many of their businesses.

"QUOTABLE"

"Hiring is the number one pillar of our holistic and enterprise-wide La Quinta Salutes Military Initiative, and we are committed to being not only 'military friendly' but also 'military family friendly.' Understanding the employment challenges military spouses face and recognizing the untapped talent pool they represent, La Quinta strives to hire military spouses and caregivers into portable, flexible careers with the potential for advancement."

—Derek Blake, Vice President of Marketing and
Military Programs at La Quinta Inns & Suites

Our nation's military spouses are more educated than most working Americans, they often have significant leadership skills, and have proven quite adept at flourishing in the midst of changing environments.[14] A 2013 report found that 66 percent of military spouses had performed volunteer work in the preceding year, and because they relocate regularly they have often become proficient at building extensive networks across vast distances.[15] They are also often very tech savvy, comfortable with social media, and used to taking the initiative to accomplish the mission in front of them.[16]

 LEARNING POINT

A robust (and free!) resource from the Hiring Our Heroes program is the following PDF that your hiring managers can use for hiring both veteran and military spouses: https://www. vetemployerroadmap.org/new-blog/2017/3/27/recruiting-military-spouses.

BREAKOUT BOX

Business Case for Hiring Military Spouses[17]

1. **Resilient**—Military spouses face many challenges, including family separations, frequent relocation, separation from friends and family, and difficulty finding employment or finishing their education. Yet, despite juggling multiple responsibilities, they report better coping than the average civilian.

2. **Adaptable**—Military support infrastructure largely depends on at-home spouses relying on one another through social activities, help with childcare, and overall social support.

3. **Civically Engaged**—In their 2014 survey of military families, Blue Star Families found that 68 percent of respondents reported they had either formally or informally volunteered in the past year—significantly higher than the 21.8 percent of the general public who formally volunteered with an organization in 2015 as reported by the Department of Labor.

4. **Educated**—Eighty-four percent have some college education or higher, 25 percent have a bachelor's degree, and 10 percent have an advanced degree.

5. **Socially Aware**—Military spouses often interact with a variety of people of different cultures, backgrounds, ages, and ethnicities. The military exposes spouses to a variety of cross-cultural and social experiences, and interactions with VIPs and the press. Military spouses understand norms around operational security and safety.

6. **Multitasking Capable**—In a study of over 6,200 military spouses, despite juggling multiple responsibilities, 75 percent reported feeling confident in their ability to handle problems.

7. **Resourceful**—Military spouses learn to use the resources available to them, and they create unique and innovative solutions to problems despite obstacles or challenges.

8. **Diverse**—The active duty military spouse community has a larger proportion of ethnic and racial minorities than the broader civilian population.

9. **Entrepreneurial**—Twenty-eight percent of military spouse respondents have either been self-employed or operated their own business, and 34 percent indicated they had an interest in online or work-from-home opportunities.

10. **Adaptable**—Military families live with consistent uncertainty. Deployments may occur with little warning, families may be asked to move on short notice, and benefits and allowances frequently change unexpectedly. Despite these challenges, 68 percent of active duty spouses say they are satisfied with the military way of life.

MILITARY SPOUSE RÉSUMÉS AND INTERVIEWS

The typical résumé and application process may put military job candidates at a disadvantage or eliminate them from consideration before they even have a chance to compete. As discussed earlier, they often may have gaps in their résumés due to relocations demanded by the military. And you may not see the linear growth in responsibility and position titles that you expect from your civilian applicants. However, by understanding the challenges they often face and that their résumés do not necessarily reflect their skills and the value they can bring to you, you will benefit from giving them a chance to come in for that personal interview.

"QUOTABLE"

"Being a military spouse requires that one learn to go with the flow, to bend so as not to break. When we can't find jobs that align with our career goals, we translate our skills and transition ourselves into new professions. Military spouses are flexible."

—Deb Kloeppel, Founder and President of the Military Spouse Corporate Career Network (MSCCN)

Try not to make assumptions about length of time, pay expectations, résumé gaps, or periods of unemployment without discussing these issues with a potential job candidate. Where possible, focus on transferable skills and the ability to adapt and learn as opposed to specific job experience.

 **LEARNING POINT**

Common features of military spouse résumés often include short job duration, certifications in lieu of education, employment that is unrelated to educational background or level of education, an unclear demonstration of advancement or increasing responsibilities over time, and more volunteer rather than paid work experience. Give them a chance to explain these issues.

BREAKOUT BOX

Three Myths about Military Spouse Employment

Myth 1: Military spouses don't have job or employment experience.

Truth: Military spouses who do not have a typically linear résumé still have lots of skills that employers value. Spouses' extensive volunteer experience is usually indicative of lots of workplace skills.

Myth 2: Military spouses have employment gaps in their résumés because they lack commitment.

Truth: Just like civilians, there are often great reasons for these gaps and career shifts. You should certainly inquire about them—that might be the best question you ask during an interview! If a military service member has been on active duty long enough, they will have moved several times (military families typically move every three to four years).[18] Of course, each of these moves means that the spouse had to look for another job. Far from being a warning sign, these career changes demonstrate their resourcefulness and resilience and give military spouses a wide variety of experience that they bring with them to their new jobs.

Myth 3: Military spouses don't have strong educational backgrounds.

Truth: More than 85 percent of military spouses have completed some college coursework (higher than the national average),[19] 25 percent have attained a bachelor's degree, and 10 percent have an advanced degree.[20] Military spouses are actually commonly underemployed in regard to their educational qualifications.

Once you do decide to interview a military spouse, it is important to give them the opportunity to describe how hiring them will benefit your organization. Many spouses are not aware that they should list volunteer service on their résumés—even if none is listed, ask them what volunteer work they might have been involved with. Often, the volunteer services they have performed demonstrate the same skills required in many businesses (e.g., clear communication, organizational management, leadership, budgets).

Also, give them a chance to explain any gaps in their résumé. As previously discussed, military spouses typically face periods of unemployment when their families move to different bases, and without exploring that you may incorrectly assume they left their previous job because of poor work performance. Finally, inquire how your job opening fits their past experience and their future career goals. Military spouses have diverse backgrounds and are used to managing numerous projects at the same time, and they may be a great fit for your needs. Their transferable skills may become apparent, and even an asset, upon further discussion.

 LEARNING POINT

Questions you should consider when planning your military spouse hiring initiative include:

- How many spouses can you hire?
- What kind of positions will you hire for?
- Do you have remote, telecommute, or telework positions?
- How will you evaluate your military spouse job candidate?
- Will you create a military spouse employee resource group?

BREAKOUT BOX

La Quinta's Top Tips for Hiring Military Spouses[21]

1. Create a program that addresses and understands the employment challenges of military spouses as revealed in the Hiring Our Heroes spouse survey.

2. Promote career opportunities that provide flexibility, portability, career growth, and pay equity.

3. When participating in hiring fairs, have a conversation with job seekers: turn over the résumé or application and allow them to talk about their passion and ask you questions about your company. They want to know if your corporate culture is a good fit for them. Encourage them to talk about their volunteer experience, which may not be included on their résumé. Valuable talent and skills are often unveiled.

4. Educate and train your hiring managers and employees on the value of military spouses—an untapped talent pool that is highly educated, eager to work, adaptable, loyal, and dedicated. La Quinta has produced an internal military recruitment guide with a section specifically on why military spouses would be an asset to their team, as well as resources for where and how to find them.

5. Deployments and PCS moves create high levels of stress: set up a military business resource group (BRG; similar to our new La Quinta Salutes) for veterans and military spouses that provides civilian and military-affiliated team members opportunities to connect and receive support through social and professional activities.

6. La Quinta also recognizes the entrepreneurial spirit of military spouses and we encourage purchasing products and services from military spouse–owned businesses, for which we provide fifteen-day payment terms. (Of course, veteran-owned businesses are also included.)

7. By directly addressing military spouse challenges and concerns, La Quinta has earned the Military Friendly Spouse Employer designation from *Military Spouse* magazine for the sixth consecutive year and is ranked among the top ten for 2017. Our military spouse program also contributed to La Quinta being ranked #50 in *Military Times* Best for Vets: Employers 2017.

HIRING MILITARY SPOUSES IS A NATIONAL SECURITY ISSUE

As identified above, there is a plethora of reasons why military spouses are very likely great fits at your organization. At the same time, there is a much larger issue that you should understand. Many of your organizations already have veteran-hiring programs, and one reason why they are important is that if our veterans are not able to secure good careers after their service, future service members will be disinclined to volunteer for the military. For military spouses, we face a similar situation.

💡 LEARNING POINT

More than half of active duty personnel are married and a large majority of military spouses feel that they have a say in whether their spouses stay in the military.

Unlike private corporations that can hire new leadership teams or CEOs, the military develops its own leaders who are completely promoted from within. This development requires significant time and resources. The retention of trained personnel is a critical aspect of ensuring the success of our military and spouse employment certainly does affect whether service members decide to stay in or leave.

"QUOTABLE"

"Today's married service members have grown up in an environment where they expect to be 50 percent of the marital unit and it is often hard for them to imagine having a wife who doesn't work. Both are equal partners with equal responsibility in the relationship.

It creates great personal angst for the service member to stomach the idea that his spouse is foregoing gainful employment due to his employment choice."

—Brooke Goldberg, Director of Military Family Policy and Spouse Programs
at Military Officers Association of America (MOAA)

If a service member feels that his service is jeopardizing his wife's career or their ability to function as a family, he will certainly be less likely to stay in the military. Two incomes are often necessary for both civilian and military families, and there are intrinsic emotional and financial benefits to consistent employment. As identified by Hiring Our Heroes, 81 percent of military spouses and their service members have discussed the possibility of leaving the service, with the availability of career opportunities for both spouses cited as one of the of the top deciding factors.[22] Certainly, our military readiness will be affected if enough service members choose to leave the military because of the significant challenges their spouses face securing their own employment.

CASE STUDY

La Quinta's Efforts to Support Military Spouses When They Move

With over eight hundred hotels throughout the US, La Quinta Inns & Suites promotes portability, flexibility, and career advancement when encouraging military spouses to join its team. Many have been interviewed at Hiring Our Heroes military spouse networking events and hiring fairs, while others are recommended by their peers. An example of La Quinta's commitment to supporting military spouses occurred when a GM in San Antonio found out they were being transferred to Dallas where no GM positions were available; La Quinta placed them at a hotel as an assistant GM but kept their salary at the GM level.

HOW YOU CAN FIND MILITARY SPOUSES

If corporations sometimes struggle to find veterans, they certainly must need help locating military spouses in search of employment as well. To that end, there are four sources (and a fifth general recommendation) you should connect with as part of your search:

1. **JobPath,** a robust employment platform for all members of a military family. Tens of thousands of military spouses are looking for new careers on this site, which provides many resources for job seekers, including a mentorship portal (www.yourjobpath.com).

2. **The Military Spouse Employment Partnership (MSEP)**, a targeted recruitment and employment solution hosted by the Department of Defense. It provides companies with direct access to spouses seeking career opportunities. It currently has more than two hundred partners who have hired more than fifty thousand military spouses (msepjobs.militaryonesource.mil).

3. **The Military Spouse Corporate Career Network (MSCCN)**, which specializes in helping organizations find qualified military spouses. This private-sector, nonprofit organization offers spouses virtual and in-person meetings or webinars, helps them with résumés and other resources, and connects them with employers (www.msccn.org).

4. **Hiring Our Heroes Military Spouse Employment Program**, which each year hosts twenty fairs exclusively for spouses on military installations. The fairs feature spouse-focused employers and workshops geared toward spouses' unique challenges. In addition, Hiring Our Heroes also hosts networking receptions in selected locations to connect spouses with local business leaders, chamber of commerce representatives, and military installation staff in a social, relaxed setting (www.uschamberfoundation. org/hiring-our-heroes/military-spouse-program).

5. **Military Spouse professional organizations,** which focus on supporting military spouses in specific professions. These are a great way to reach a targeted audience of job seekers:
   - Military Spouse JD Network (www.msjdn.org)
   - Society of Military Spouses in STEM (SMSS; www.smsstem.org)
   - Military Spouse Behavioral Health Clinicians (www.msbhc.org)

BREAKOUT BOX

Ten Ways Corporations Can Support Military Spouses[23]

1. **Include military spouses** as part of an overall diversity strategy for sourcing, hiring, recruitment, and retention.

2. **Identify opportunities** for telework, flex work, part-time, or positions that can move across locations or geographies where possible.

3. **Train your recruiters, hiring managers, and HR professionals** on military cultural competence so they are familiar with the barriers that impact military spouse employment. These efforts should include efforts to reduce stigma with the goal of creating an environment where spouses feel safe to discuss impending moves.

4. **Identify training, mentorship, and educational opportunities** that can be leveraged to onboard military spouse hires so they can succeed, advance, and thrive in the workplace.

5. **Form military affinity groups in your organization** that enable military spouse employees to interact with and support one another, and provide and receive mentorship. Encourage military spouse employees to self-identify by proactively and visibly destigmatizing their military affiliation.

6. **Attend and participate on coalitions, task forces, and planning meetings** related to military spouse employees to interact with and support one another, and provide and receive mentorship.

7. **Prioritize hiring military spouses as a unique group** in addition to veterans and service members, and ensure that this priority is shared across the organization. Facilitate open communication about opportunities within the company if a spouse's current or desired position is location flexible.

8. **Highlight successful spouse employees** using a variety of channels so that their success and yours can be recognized and duplicated.

9. **Identify events, employee benefits, supportive employee services, and individual people** who can mentor a new military spouse employee on an individual basis.

10. **Leverage in-house or external childcare** to minimize childcare costs and ensure access to childcare; provide tax benefits for childcare to mitigate childcare costs.

• • • • • • • • • • •
CASE STUDY

Prudential and Military Spouses

The key part of any military spouse program is what happens when the inevitable happens: the dreaded PCS. A PCS for the service member is a vehicle for new responsibilities, varied experiences, and enhanced professional growth. For the spouse involved, it typically means an end of employment, an abrupt stop to career growth, and the start of a protracted search for new employment at the new duty station. And when the new job is found, a new iteration begins, starting from square one, no seniority, and starting-level wages. For the companies involved, it also means new recruiting and training costs, assimilation, and decreased productivity as the new employee finds their way in the organization.

Prudential's approach to addressing this challenge is a product of its commitment to veterans and military spouses and its organizational structure across the country. Prudential has relatively few corporate office locations in the United States—few of which are in close proximity to military bases. This led Prudential to commit to job portability. Rather than moving a spouse to a new corporate location near the next duty station as some companies can do, Prudential is allowing its military spouse workforce to take their current job with them and work remotely from their home in the new location. This is made possible by a robust telecommunication infrastructure already in place with the company and experience gained by some business units that have embraced remote work for specific types of jobs in the past.

The benefits to the military spouse are obvious. They avoid the need to start the job search all over, keep job continuity and continuity for the family in terms of finances and benefits. Prudential also benefits from the continuity in that the investment is not lost in training or experience. Increased employee loyalty that impacts retention is also a result. There are challenges to this approach, such as geographic differences that may impact salary and benefits, policies on leave time necessary for the family to relocate to the new duty station, and complexities that may result from moves to international locations with regulations that may impact remote work. Barbara Koster, global CIO and executive sponsor for all veterans initiatives at Prudential, says, "Our goal is to address head on the challenges that military spouses face every few years when they move. Our firm's commitment to providing them meaningful careers is not only a good thing for the spouses and families of our military service men and women, but also a great talent strategy for Prudential." Here are some things to consider when creating a military spouse talent strategy and allowing remote work:

- Geographic variations in cost of living from work location to work location,
- Policy on approved time off for PCS moves,

- Management readiness to work with employees in a remote work scenario,
- Regulatory concerns (state-by-state and international),
- Appropriateness of jobs for remote work, and
- Process to allow remote workers to acclimate to work culture and group dynamics.

MILITARY SPOUSE RESOURCE CENTER

If you are a military spouse, it is a fact of life that your active duty husband or wife will receive PCS orders and have to move to another base after one or two enlistment periods. And that sole issue is at the root of many of the challenges that you face when it comes to finding full-time employment. But your employment issues are gaining more traction—with the Department of Defense, corporate America, and the nonprofit sector—and there are a number of resources you should take advantage of.

BREAKOUT BOX

Advice from USAA on the Issue of State Certifications

Military spouses are encouraged to find portable careers, yet many of the most portable jobs come with a catch: you need to be state-certified to work in the field, and for many spouses, that turns out to be a recurring nightmare. Here are five tips from USAA on how to handle state certifications.

- **Save money.** Build up a cash cushion so that if there is a gap in time before you get hired at your next position, you have some cash to fill the gap.

- **Stay organized.** Keep a folder with your notes and names of people you spoke to and on what day. Don't let this certification lapse—especially certifications that you currently hold. You definitely don't know when you're going to end up back in that state.

- **Don't delay.** Get the ball rolling as soon as you find out you're moving. Start looking at different options and find out what the requirements are.

- **Remain flexible.** Look to get any experience where you can. Don't restrict yourself by only looking for a 9-to-5 job. Consider freelance work as a temporary fix.

- **Don't go it alone.** Many veterans and other military spouses online are willing to help you with advice and tips for dealing with the challenges you face.

BREAKOUT BOX

Advice about Licensure and Networking from the Military Spouse JD Network (MSJDN)

Utilize Military Spouse Specific Licensing Accommodations

Getting recertified each time you move can be expensive and time consuming. Fortunately, all fifty states have adopted legislation to reduce the burden of transferring your professional license as a military spouse. The implementation of these rules still varies from state to state, so check with the local agency, but don't be afraid to ask about special accommodations available to military families. This can include expedited processing, reduced fees, or a temporary permit while you wait for the permanent license. Teachers, medical occupations, and attorneys are often excluded from these laws, but groups like MSJDN are working to remove the remaining licensing barriers for these specialized occupations.

Tap into the Military Spouse Mafia

Military spouses are an incredible community, always willing to help out and lift someone up. But have you thought about tapping into that network for the job search at your next duty station? At MSJDN, our annual survey shows that 15 percent of our members have found a job through MSJDN—and that number goes up every year. Our members connect with each other and are able to establish relationships before they PCS into a location, and extend the local relationships they built to the next military spouse attorney coming into the location. Our members connect each other to local leaders and job opportunities. The most valuable asset you might have is your military spouse network!

—Libby Jamison, President of MSJDN

You are already familiar with your strongest resource—you! Your own personal networking will make an incredible difference for you, personally and professionally, when it is time for you to relocate. Take the time to write out a list of people who can help you, in your current location and where you are headed, and you may surprise yourself at the size of your list. Make sure to include your spouse and their close friends, neighbors, military spouse organizations, other career-minded spouses, friends from church and other groups, and past employers. Further, a formal mentor can provide guidance, direction, and insight in every aspect of the employment process. Consider working with someone who shares your values and is someone you respect.

LEARNING POINT

Some companies, such as U.S. Bank, give special consideration to employee requests for internal transfers made necessary by reassignments of spouses who are in the military.

BREAKOUT BOX

MOAA provides transition options other than quitting your current job and finding a new one:[24]

1. Before leaving your current position, approach your current employer about remote or telecommuting options. Present a package outlining your proposed arrangement and how the employer will benefit from this arrangement (continuity in the position with a proven employee who knows the job requirements and is familiar with the company, no difficult or costly searches for a replacement, and so on). Be sure to stress the value to the employer, not to yourself. Don't ignore the potential downside but offer reasons why the pros outweigh the cons.

2. Explore freelance work or contract consulting. Consider this an option to get your foot in the door by demonstrating your value to a potential employer.

3. Use strategic volunteer opportunities to enhance your skill set, demonstrate your commitments, build your network, fill résumé gaps, and open doors to paid work opportunities. Look for places where you can utilize the skills you want to strengthen or new skills you desire to develop. Skills obtained or fortified through volunteering are no less valuable than those gained through a salaried position.

4. Earn additional credentials or training. Go to school for an advanced degree, earn a certification, or pursue professional development opportunities through additional coursework, seminars, or workshops.

5. Explore entrepreneurship. A helpful resource might be Veteran Women Igniting the Spirit of Entrepreneurship (V-WISE), which enables female veterans and military spouses to find their passions and learn the business-savvy skills to turn their ideas or businesses into a growth venture. The program is hosted through IVMF.

HELPFUL RESOURCE LINKS FOR MILITARY SPOUSES

- JobPath's veteran and military spouse employment portal (www.yourjobpath.com)
- Hiring Our Heroes Military Spouse Employment Program résumé builder, job finder, interview prep, career tracking (www.mycareerspark.org)
- MOAA Spouse on Facebook (www.facebook.com/moaaspouse)

- Blue Star Families Military Spouse Resources (bluestarfam.org/milspouse-employment/)
- MOAA's LinkedIn Career Networking Group (www.moaa.org/linkedin)
- CareerOneStop's list of free and fee-based self-assessment tools and resources (www.careeronestop.org/explorecareers/selfassessments/findassessments.aspx)
- Military One Source Spouse Education and Career Opportunities (www.militaryonesource.mil/seco)
- MOAA Spouse on Twitter: @MOAA_MilLife
- Hiring Our Heroes InGear Career (http://ingearcareer.org/)
- Military Spouse Employment Partnership (MSEP; https://msepjobs.militaryonesource.mil/msep/)
- Childcare Aware for Military Families (https://usa.childcareaware.org/fee-assistancerespite/military-families/)
- The Military Spouse eMentor Program (https://www.ementorprogram.org/)
- Veteran Career Transition Program (VCTP; https://ivmf.syracuse.edu/veteran-and-family-resources/career-training/)
- Glassdoor (www.glassdoor.com)
- Your closest American Job Center (https://www.careeronestop.org/localhelp/find-american-job-centers.aspx)
- Julie M. Whittaker, "Unemployment Compensation (Insurance) and Military Service," Congressional Research Service, April 24, 2013, fas.org/sgp/crs/misc/RS22440.pdf
- US Department of Labor, "Noncompetitive Appointment of Certain Military Spouses Eligibility," www.dol.gov/oasam/doljobs/noncompetitive.htm
- USAJOBS, Special Hiring Options for Military Spouses (help.usajobs.gov/index.php/Special_Hiring_Options)
- MilSpouseFest hosted by MilitaryOneClick and presented by USAA (militaryoneclick.com/milspousefest2017/)

BREAKOUT BOX

Turning Jobs into Careers for Military Spouses: What Has Walmart Done, and How?

Walmart offers programs that provide military spouses job security, which can be a challenge when families receive transfer orders from the military. Through its Military Family Promise, Walmart guarantees a job at a nearby store or club for all military personnel and military spouses employed by the company who move to a different part of the country because they or their spouse have been transferred by the US military.

- - - - - - - - - - -
CASE STUDY

Military Spouses and Social Media

I used social media to establish my personal brand, bypass job applications, get noticed, and get hired (twice).

In the winter of 2015, I attended a job fair for veterans and military spouses. I met a regional manager of a pest control company. We exchanged information and connected on LinkedIn. At the time, I was working as a telemarketer. Some would say this role didn't use the full potential of my degree in chemistry. However, I decided to turn those lemons into lemonade. I wrote an article on LinkedIn: "Why You Should Value Your Job as a Telemarketer." I published this on April 2, 2015. No more than twelve hours after, the regional manager I met at the job fair several months prior sent me a message on LinkedIn. He said that a role became available and invited me in for an interview. I ended up with the job. If he and I weren't connected on LinkedIn, he wouldn't have gotten the notification about my article (I was able to see that he viewed my article) and may not have thought about me for the newly open role.

For my current job, I didn't rely solely on the job application. I used LinkedIn to make connections with employees holding the same role for which I applied—managers and the co-CEOs and founders of the company. I had ongoing Twitter conversations with my current manager about his favorite college football team. I created a Twitter list with current employees, managers, and the company account. I watched what was shared to learn more about the company culture and current projects. I shared the company's content and gave thoughtful replies. The above activities put me on their radar. After several weeks of submitting my application, their recruiter reached out to me for an interview. I ultimately became their first-ever hire from Twitter. They featured my story in the company blog.

—Sam P. Lark Jr., military spouse, Speaker,
and Social Media Relationship Strategist

• • • • • • • • • • •

ENDNOTES

1. Rosaline Maury and Brice Stone, *Military Spouse Employment Report* (Syracuse, NY: Institute for Veterans and Military Families, February 2014), 5, https://ivmf.syracuse.edu/wp-content/uploads/2016/06/MilitarySpouseEmploymentReport_2013.pdf.

2. Defense Manpower Data Center (DMDC), *2012 Survey of Active Duty Spouses*, June 2014, http://download.militaryonesource.mil/12038/MOS/Surveys/ADSS1201-Briefing-Support-Deployment-Reintegration-PCS-WellBeing-Education-Employment.pdf.

3. National Academy of Medicine, "Characteristics of the Deployed," in *Returning Home from Afghanistan: Assessment and Readjustment Needs of Veterans, Service Members, and Their Families* (Washington, DC: National Academies Press, 2013), https://www.ncbi.nlm.nih.gov/books/NBK206861/.

4. Hiring Our Heroes, *Military Spouses in the Workplace: Understanding the Impacts of Spouse Unemployment on Military Recruitment, Retention, and Readiness* (Washington, DC: Chamber of Commerce Foundation, June 2017), 4, https://www.uschamberfoundation.org/reports/military-spouses-workplace.

5. Department of Treasury and Department of Defense, *Supporting Our Military Families: Best Practices for Streamlining Occupational Licensing across State Lines*, February 2012, http://archive.defense.gov/home/pdf/Occupational_Licensing_and_Military_Spouses_Report_vFINAL.PDF.

6. Deborah A. Bradbard, Rosalind Maury, and Nicholas J. Armstrong, *The Force behind the Force: Employing Military Spouses* (Syracuse: Institute for Veterans and Military Families, July 2016), 4, https://ivmf.syracuse.edu/wp-content/uploads/2016/07/Prudential_Report_7.21.16_REVISED_digital.pdf.

7. Rosaline Maury and Brice Stone, *Military Spouse Employment Report* (Syracuse: Institute for Veterans and Military Families, February 2014), https://ivmf.syracuse.edu/wp-content/uploads/2016/06/MilitarySpouseEmploymentReport_2013.pdf.

8. Rosaline Maury and Brice Stone, *Military Spouse Employment Report* (Syracuse: Institute for Veterans and Military Families, February 2014), 6, 52, 90, https://ivmf.syracuse.edu/wp-content/uploads/2016/06/MilitarySpouseEmploymentReport_2013.pdf.

9. Hiring Our Heroes, *Military Spouses in the Workplace: Understanding the Impacts of Spouse Unemployment on Military Recruitment, Retention, and Readiness* (Washington, DC: Chamber of Commerce Foundation, June 2017), 8, https://www.uschamberfoundation.org/reports/military-spouses-workplace.

10. Hiring Our Heroes, 7.

11. Hiring Our Heroes, 11.
12. Hiring Our Heroes, 11.
13. Deborah Bradbard, Rosalind Maury, and Nicholas J. Armstrong, *The Force behind the Force: Training, Leveraging, and Communicating about Military Spouses as Employees* (Syracuse: Institute for Veterans and Military Families, December 2016), 9–10, https://ivmf. syracuse.edu/wp-content/uploads/2016/08/IVMF__standard_prudential_12.6.16_ FINAL_CLEAN-002.pdf.
14. "Military Spouses: A Hidden Pool of Talent," Veteran Employer Roadmap, Hiring Our Heroes, March 27, 2017, https://www.vetemployerroadmap.org/ new-blog/2017/3/27/military-spouses-a-hidden-pool-of-talent.
15. "Blue Star Spouse Employment Toolkit: Translating Military Spouses' Lived Experience into Strong Resumes," Hiring Our Heroes, February 2014, https://bluestarfam.org/ wp-content/uploads/2016/04/blue_star_spouse_employment_toolkit_feb2014.pdf.
16. "Military Spouse Employment Partnership," fact sheet, Department of Defense, http://download.militaryonesource.mil/12038/MOS/Factsheets/SECO/MSEP-Factsheet-Corporate.pdf.
17. Bradbard, Maury, and Armstrong, *Training, Leveraging, and Communicating about Military Spouses*, 9–10.
18. "All About DoDEA Educational Partnership," US Department of Defense Education Activity, accessed April 23, 2018, https://www.dodea.edu/Partnership/about.cfm; Mike Nagel, "Military Families, Moving, and Stress," *Care.com* (blog), June 2, 2010, https://www.care.com/c/stories/4354/military-families-moving-and-stress/; and W. Michael Hix, Herbert J. Shukiar, Janet M. Hanley, Richard J. Kaplan, Jennifer H. Kawata, Grant N. Marshall, and Peter J. E. Stan, *Personnel Turbulence: The Policy Determinants of Permanent Change of Station Moves*, (Santa Monica, CA: RAND, 1998), 5, https://www. rand.org/content/dam/rand/pubs/monograph_reports/2007/MR938.pdf.
19. "Military Spouses," Veteran Employer Roadmap.
20. "Military Spouse Employment Parternship," Department of Defense.
21. Hiring Our Heroes.
22. Hiring Our Heroes, 14.
23. Deborah A. Bradbard, Rosalind Maury, and Nicholas J. Armstrong, *The Force behind the Force: A Business Case for Leveraging Military Spouse Talent* (Syracuse: Institute for Veterans and Military Families, July 2016), 13, https://ivmf.syracuse.edu/wp-content/ uploads/2016/07/Prudential_Report_7.21.16_REVISED_digital.pdf.
24. Military Officers Association of America, *A Complete Guide to Military Spouse Employment*, MOAA Military Family Initiative (Alexandria, VA: Military Officers Association of America, 2017), 6, http://www.moaa.org/uploadedFiles/Content/Publications_and_ Media/MOAA_Publications/Publication_Downloads/2670_SpouseEmployment_ final2.pdf.

CHAPTER 9

Veteran Entrepreneurship and Supplier Diversity

*As an entrepreneur, having the freedom to cause your own failure
should be one of the chief motivators for your own success.*

—Scott Davidson, Managing Principal
of the GCO Consulting Group

Although this book is obviously focused on employment, as a veteran entrepreneur I wanted to include some basic guidance for other entrepreneurially minded veterans and for companies that want to support veteran-owned businesses. To that end, in this section I aim only to point you in the right direction if these ideas interest you—there are a number of other books and resources out there that focus specifically on these topics.[1]

FOR EMPLOYERS

One in seven veterans are self-employed or small business owners, and one-quarter of veterans say they are interested in starting or buying their own business.[2] As of June 2016, there were 2.5 million veteran-owned businesses in America, representing 9.1 percent of all US businesses. Together they generate about $1 trillion in revenue and employ nearly 6 million Americans. These numbers have risen over recent years despite a decline in the overall number of veterans in the population.[3] Needless to say, the health of the veteran-owned small-business industrial base has a sizable impact on the American economy. So when a large business commits to supporting the military or the veteran community, supply-chain diversity can be a part of that commitment.

Clearly, corporate America can have a huge impact on veteran-owned businesses by focusing on them and including them in their supplier diversity channels. Those veteran-owned companies have to provide top-quality service and products, but creating opportunities will certainly help them grown and, as often is the case, hire more veterans.

As discussed earlier in Chapter 6, there are a number of communities where businesses have banded together to exchange best practices around hiring veterans and military spouses and to share resources for doing so. That same phenomena does not exist quite so much regarding veteran-owned businesses. However, First Data and IVMF have spearheaded the Coalition for Veteran Owned Businesses (CVOB) to encourage large businesses to specifically include veteran-owned businesses as part of their supplier diversity initiatives. To join this coalition, or simply to learn more, please go to www.veteranbusinesscoalition.org.

BREAKOUT BOX

The Coalition for Veteran Owned Businesses

The CVOB is a coalition of industry leaders committed to providing innovative solutions and thought leadership to grow and support veteran-owned businesses in communities throughout the nation. The coalition provides economic opportunity to veterans, their families, and the communities in which they live by offering leadership and a national platform to support military spouse– and veteran-owned businesses, entrepreneurs, and suppliers. The coalition

- Increases access to opportunities and information for veteran and military spouse businesses within corporate supply chains;

- Drives awareness and commerce opportunities for veteran and military spouse businesses in the public marketplace;

- Creates networking opportunities for veteran-owned businesses and large companies;

- Provides educational resources on access to capital by veteran and military spouse businesses;

- Contributes to veteran and military spouse employment;

- Creates awareness of existing resources and connects small business owners with education, lending, and networks for entrepreneurs;

- Supports nationwide "buy veteran" campaigns; and

- Provides educational resources on pertinent business topics such as access to capital, certifications, and employment.

Participating Companies and Organizations:

American Express	KKR
BP America	La Quinta Inn & Suites
Enterprise Holdings Inc.	Lockheed Martin Corporation
First Data	Suntrust Banks Inc.
Fleishmanhillard	The Walt Disney Company
Institute for Veterans and Military Families at Syracuse University	USAA
	US Chamber of Commerce Foundation
Johnson & Johnson	Verizon Communications Inc.
JP Morgan Chase and Co.	Walmart and Sam's Club

—Ray Bermudez, Vice President and Head of Military Veteran Affairs at First Data Corporation

As you can see from the list of companies participating in the CVOB, they represent a wide variety of industries. If you are a large company and want to join their coalition, you can find out more information at their website. If you are a veteran–owned company, chances are that the work you do is a good fit for at least one of those companies, in some capacity or another. Take the time to learn more about the ones that interest you, register in their supplier diversity databases, and then contact them directly.

BREAKOUT BOX

Walmart and Veteran-Owned Businesses

Many veterans gain important skills and leadership abilities from their active duty experiences that lead to successful business ownership, such as strong work ethic, teamwork, and adaptability. In the fiscal year of 2017, we sourced hundreds of millions of dollars from veteran-owned businesses (VOBs). As a founding member of the CVOB, we aim to continue to not only source products and services from VOBs, but also help support their entrepreneurial training and provide much needed access to resources. That's why in September 2017, we hosted CVOB's first ever Vet Source, an event providing procurement and training opportunities for VOBs with *Fortune* 500 companies. The event went very well, and more are planned for 2018.

—Gary Profit, Senior Director of Military Programs for Walmart

---

FOR ENTREPRENEURS

 LEARNING POINT

According to the most recent data, there is about one veteran-owned firm for every ten veterans, and veteran-owned firms employ 5.8 million individuals. A recent SBA study also found that military service exhibits one of the largest marginal effects on self-employment, and veterans are 45 percent more likely to be self-employed than nonveterans.[4]

Because over 9 percent of small businesses are veteran–owned, we are clearly overrepresented in the world of small business.[5] There is something about what we learn in the military that not only makes us good employees in corporate America, but also encourages us to start our own businesses. I am not sure if it is confidence, subject matter expertise, a desire to prove ourselves, or a combination of all three, but this is certainly an area that is very familiar to many veterans and their families. There have never been more resources for veteran entrepreneurs than now, and if you are thinking about going down this road, you are doing yourself a disservice by not taking advantage of them.

BREAKOUT BOX

Guidance for Potential Entrepreneurs

1. If you can solve a problem, you can be an entrepreneur.

2. Even if you aren't successful in starting a business, it will likely expand your network far beyond anything else you could have done otherwise (and create great job opportunities).

3. Customers and revenue are all that matter in a startup—are you solving a real problem? Do people like your solution? Are they willing to pay for it?

4. Surround yourself with people who have done this before you. Entrepreneurship is not (contrary to popular opinion) a solo sport.

5. Be tenacious enough to charge forward, but smart and humble enough to know when it isn't working and ask for feedback.

—Todd Connor, CEO of Bunker Labs

BREAKOUT BOX

Eight Important Lessons for Veteran Entrepreneurs

1. Don't be afraid to subcontract. Some business is better than no business.

2. Be patient. Cultivate a relationship with large businesses—earn their business.

3. Do your research on the company you say you want to work with. No large corporation is like another.

4. Be prepared to articulate your business briefly—the elevator speech. Clear and concise language is imperative.

5. Veteran-owned suppliers help large companies be better. That's why they want to do business with you, but you still need the best widget.

6. Know your area—get connected to your local ecosystem.

7. Many companies use online platforms such as Ariba to find prospective suppliers. All suppliers in the platform are visible to all companies who subscribe to the system.

8. Private-sector spending on procurement dwarfs the amount spent by federal government and defense contractors.

—Coalition for Veteran Owned Businesses

💡 LEARNING POINT

Access this link to find a detailed list of resources related to veteran entrepreneurship: https://militaryonlinecolleges.org/veteran-entrepreneurship.

Five years ago, you would have been hard pressed to find more than a handful of veteran entrepreneurship programs. Now, there is a wide variety of courses across the country. Some are online, some are brick and mortar, and many are a combination of the two. Most courses are free, but some do have costs. I attended the Entrepreneurship Bootcamp for Veterans with Disabilities (EBV) at Syracuse University in 2009 (free) and the Stanford Ignite—Post-9/11 Veterans (paid) course in 2015. Both were great programs and very helpful to new entrepreneurs. Below is a list of a dozen programs and resources, in no particular order.

- **The Entrepreneurship Bootcamp For Veterans with Disabilities (EBV)**
  The EBV National Program organized by IVMF is a novel, one-of-a-kind initiative designed to leverage the skills, resources, and infrastructure of higher education to offer cutting-edge, experiential training in entre-preneurship and small business management to post-9/11 veterans with service-connected disabilities and a passion for entrepreneurship as well as to military family members who serve in a caregiver role to a vet-eran with a service-connected disability. This program is offered by a con-sortium of universities including Cornell, Syracuse, Florida State, UCLA, Texas A&M, Purdue, UConn, LSU, Saint Joseph's, and the University of Missouri. IVMF also has separate entrepreneurship training programs for veterans' families (called EBV-F) and one specifically for women veterans (V-Wise). (ebv.vets.syr.edu/)

- **Veteran's Business Outreach Center (VBOC)**
  The VBOC program is a one-stop shop for transitioning service mem-bers, veterans, and military spouses looking to start, purchase, or grow a business. Located nationwide, VBOCs provide transition assistance pro-grams and business development assistance such as training, counseling

and mentoring, and resource referrals. To learn more about them, including specific locations, visit (www.sba.gov/tools/local-assistance/vboc).

- **The Small Business Administration (SBA) Office of Veterans Business Development**
  The mission of the Office of Veterans Business Development (OVBD) is to maximize the availability, applicability, and usability of small business programs for veterans, service-disabled veterans, reserve component members, and their dependents or survivors. OVBD is SBA's liaison with the veteran business community; it provides policy analysis and reporting, and is an ombudsman for veteran entrepreneurs. OVBD has a number of programs and services to assist aspiring and existing veteran entrepreneurs such as training, counseling and mentorship, and oversight of Federal procurement programs for veteran-owned and service-disabled veteran-owned small businesses. (www.sba.gov/offices/headquarters/ovbd/resources)

- **NYU Tandon School of Engineering Veteran Entrepreneur Training (VET)**
  VET was designed for US military veterans and spouses who want to transition into entrepreneurship after completing their service. Program participants learn from startup companies and industry leaders through hands-on experiential learning, mentorship, and capstone projects. Through the program's business and technology training, participants are given the tools to turn aspirations into career opportunities and new ventures. Upon successful completion, graduates earn a VET Certificate from NYU Future Labs. (engineering.nyu.edu/business/future-labs/veteran-support/veteran-entrepreneur-training)

- **Patriot Boot Camp (PBC)**
  PBC is a nonprofit founded in 2012 to provide active duty service members, veterans, and their spouses with access to mentors, educational programming, and a robust community of experts and peers to help them innovate and build impactful businesses. PBC's core program is an intensive three-day technology entrepreneurship boot camp modeled after the Techstars accelerator to provide educational training and one-on-one mentoring to inspire and advance startup founders. PBC runs this program

twice per year, in Texas and Colorado, for cohorts of fifty tech entrepreneurs. (patriotbootcamp.org)

- **Bunker Labs**
  A national not-for-profit 501(c)(3) organization built by military veteran entrepreneurs to empower other military veterans as leaders in innovation. Through local chapters across the country, Bunker Labs provides educational programming, access to resources, and a thriving local network to help military veterans and their spouses start and grow businesses. (www.bunkerlabs.org)

- **National Veterans Entrepreneurship Program (VEP)**
  VEP is a rigorous entrepreneurial learning and development opportunity for veterans with service-connected disabilities and those who have uniquely distinguished themselves in the military. VEP is designed for veterans interested in starting a new venture as a means to be financially independent and for veterans who have an existing business whose profits they would like to increase. (warrington.ufl.edu/centers/cei/outreach/vep)

- **Stanford Ignite—Post-9/11 Veterans**
  This full-time program is exclusively for post-9/11 veterans and uses the same curriculum as their global Stanford Ignite offerings. It also features components such as career advising, visits to local Bay Area companies, and sessions with hiring managers. Stanford GSB alumni veterans will be actively engaged as mentors, guest speakers, and panelists evaluating student presentations. Stanford Ignite provides approximately 100 classroom hours and 100–150 project hours. (www.gsb.stanford.edu/programs/stanford-ignite/campus/post-9-11-veterans)

- **Boots to Business**
  This is another SBA program. It's a two-step entrepreneurial training program that includes a two-day classroom course and an eight-week online course that offer instruction on forming a business plan and other essential elements of early business ownership. (www.sba.gov/offices/headquarters/ovbd/resources/160511)

- **National Veteran Small Business Coalition (NVSBC)**
  This organization supports veteran-owned small businesses by promoting policies that encourage participation of veteran-owned businesses in federal contracting opportunities. Members receive access to resources related to federal contracting. (www.nvsbc.org)

- **Office of Small and Disadvantaged Business Utilization (OSDBU)**
  The VA's OSDBU site provides information about the Center for Verification and Evaluation's verification process for veteran-owned businesses looking to gain eligibility for the VA's Veterans First Contracting Program. Any veteran-owned business looking for VA contracts set aside for veterans must first go through the verification process. (www.va.gov/osdbu)

- **GI Go Fund**
  In partnership with Panasonic, PSEG, and the Kessler Foundation, GI Go Fund has opened its revolutionary Veterans Employment Center in Newark, New Jersey, where veterans receive job training, résumé writing, and career counseling from a dedicated team that works with them on whatever needs they may have. In addition to the job training, this center includes an Incubator Space, which will give veterans, primarily disabled veterans, a customized space to start or grow a small business. The Incubator also includes great amenities like conference room space and Internet access, along with shared space that entrepreneurial veterans can reserve to host meetings and conduct their business, all at no cost to the veteran. (www.gigo.org).

. . . .
CASE STUDY

The University of Connecticut Entrepreneurship Bootcamp for Veterans with Disabilities

Our model is based on the sea of good will. The UConn EBV program leverages relationships and local resources from more than forty organizations to help train and mentor veterans to start businesses and find full-time employment. Our metrics are the 3 *E*s:

Employment, Entrepreneurship, and Education. Although UConn is a public institution, we take no taxpayer money. Our program is funded by charitable grants, corporate philanthropy, and individual donations. Some of our prominent supporters include the Hughes Family Foundation, Persbacker Foundation, Bank of America, TicketNetwork.com, Pratt & Whitney UTC, SBM Charitable Foundation, Disabled American Veterans Charitable Service Trust, Newman's Own Foundation, Prudential, Synchrony Financial, Dell, and LinkedIn.

The program is in some ways very representative of the post-9/11 generation of combat veterans. The program is inclusive, and program graduates are diverse:

- Ethnically diverse: 49 percent non-Caucasian ethnic minorities;
- 25 percent female graduates, 10 percent LGBTQ, and two transgender veterans;
- 75 percent enlisted and 25 percent officer graduates;
- Educationally diverse: every level of educational attainment, from high school drop-outs, GEDs, and associate's degrees, through law school, medical school, and PhDs;
- Geographically diverse:
  - Represent twenty-five states and several foreign nations (for example, China, Belgium, and Ecuador),
  - 25 percent from Connecticut,
  - 50 percent from the Northeast United States,
  - 75 percent from I-95 corridor Boston to Virginia Beach, VA,
  - 90 percent from the East Coast from Maine to Florida;
- 15 percent have been awarded Purple Hearts;
- 20 percent have been decorated for combat or meritorious service in combat;
- 25 percent have diagnosed TBI or PTSD;
- 20 percent have multiple master's degrees;
- 10 percent are serial entrepreneurs;
- No particular service branch is overrepresented in the population of graduates; and
- We've had several veterans go on to other elite entrepreneurial programs, like Tech All Stars, Shark Tank, Bunker Labs, and the Stamford University tech accelerator program.

—Michael Zacchea, Director of UConn Entrepreneur
Bootcamp for Veterans with Disabilities

ENDNOTES

1. See for example, http://veteranentrepreneurship.org; Mark L. Rockefeller, "7 Free Resources Veteran Entrepreneurs Will Use to Crush It in 2017," *Forbes*, January 19, 2017, https://www.forbes.com/sites/marklrockefeller/2017/01/19/7-free-resources-veteran-entrepreneurs-will-use-to-crush-it-in-2017; Nyasha Boldon, Rosalinda Maury, Nicholas Armstrong, and Ryan Van Slyke, *The State of Veteran Entrepreneurship Research: What We Know and Next Steps* (Syracuse: Institute for Veterans and Military Families, November 2016), https://ivmf.syracuse.edu/article/the-state-of-veteran-entrepreneurship-research-what-we-know-and-next-steps/; and https://www.entrepreneur.com/topic/veterans.

2. "Veterans Fact Sheet," US Small Business Association, July 6, 2012, https://www.sba.gov/sites/default/files/Veterans%20fact%20sheet_7_6_12.pdf.

3. *Operation Boots to Business Veteran Entrepreneurship Assessment,* white paper (Syracuse: Institute for Veterans and Military Families, June 2016), https://www.sba.gov/sites/default/files/b2b_vet_entrepreneurship_assessment.pdf.

4. "Facts on Veterans and Entrepreneurship," US Small Business Administration, accessed April 23, 2018, https://www.sba.gov/content/facts-veterans-and-entrepreneurship.

5. Joseph Sobota, *Veteran-Owned Businesses and Their Owners: Data from the US Census Bureau's Survey of Business Owners* (Washington, DC: US Small Business Administration, April 2017), 23, https://www.sba.gov/sites/default/files/advocacy/435-veteran-owned-businesses-report.pdf.

CHAPTER 10

Women Veterans

"No woman joins the military to make a man of herself."

—Jas Boothe, former Army Officer, Inspirational
Leader, and Founder of Final Salute Inc.

There are two reasons I decided to include a chapter specifically dedicated to women veterans: (1) I fear that when many civilians think of veterans, they automatically think of men, and don't realize how many women are actually in the military and the types of things they do; and (2) women are obviously different than men and therefore do have unique focus areas that I wanted to highlight to employers and to women veterans looking for resources. That being said, I am not personally familiar with particular challenges that women veterans may face, so you will see in this chapter that I rely on information I have gathered from the VA, as well as two particular submissions by experts in this field.

As you will see in this chapter, women have been a part of our military since the founding of our nation, and now make up over 15 percent of the United States Armed Forces. Women in our military deploy to foreign soil to fight our nation's battles, fly attack helicopters, run convoys, lead troops and civil affairs missions, and suffer significant injuries and death in action, just like their male counterparts. That being said, some people in our country continue to belittle their contributions or simply do not understand that in today's military, with the exception of some special operation missions and some specific infantry roles, women are on the front lines and should not be considered any different than the men.

BREAKOUT BOX

Notable Statistics about Women Veterans

1. Women have formally been a part of the United States Armed Forces since the inception of the Army Nurse Corps in 1901, but have informally served since the inception of our nation's military. In 1948, Congress made women a permanent part of the military service.

2. Almost half of employed women veterans (49 percent) work in management, professional, or other related occupations, compared with 41 percent of nonveteran women.

3. Approximately two million veterans in the United States and Puerto Rico are women.

4. Only 21 percent of all women veterans had a high school diploma or less as their highest level of educational attainment in 2015, compared with 40 percent of nonveteran women. (To join the military now, candidates must have a high school diploma or GED, but that requirement was not always in place.)

5. More women veterans had some college as their highest level of education than nonveteran women (44 percent compared with 32 percent, respectively). Overall, a higher percentage of all women veterans (34.5 percent) than nonveterans (28.1 percent) had completed a bachelor's or advanced degree.

6. In 2015, working-age veteran women (i.e., those 17–64 years old) had a higher labor force participation rate (71.5 percent) than nonveteran women (70.1 percent).

7. Overall, women veterans were less likely than nonveteran women to be living in poverty in 2015. About 10 percent of all veteran women and 15 percent of all nonveteran women had incomes below the poverty threshold.

8. According to the Congressional Research Service, approximately 299,548 female service members were deployed for contingency operations, over 800 were wounded, and over 130 died in Iraq and Afghanistan between September 2001 and February 2013.

9. Women serve in every branch of the military, representing 15.5 percent of active duty military and 19.0 percent of National Guard and Reserve forces in 2015.

10. About two million (9.4 percent) of the total veteran population are women. Women are now the fastest growing cohort within the veteran community.

—Department of Veterans Affairs[1]

BREAKOUT BOX

Barriers to Employment for Women Veterans

1. Women veterans are nearly three times as likely to be homeless than nonveteran women.[2]

2. Compared to male service members, female service members are more likely to be single parents with one or more dependent children.[3]

3. Only one in six women veterans understand the healthcare benefits they earned through their service.[4]

4. Despite years of effort, sexual assault in the military remains a persistent and serious problem. Over 6 percent of women and 1 percent of men report unwanted sexual contact on DoD surveys.[5]

5. In 2015, nearly forty-eight thousand women veterans received compensation for PTSD. PTSD accounts for roughly 12 percent of all service-connected disabilities for women veterans.[6]

RESOURCES FOR WOMEN VETERANS

- **VA's Center for Women Veterans**
  They monitor and coordinate the VA's administration of benefit services and programs for women veterans. The Center advocates for a cultural transformation that recognizes the service and contributions of women veterans and women in the military, and also raises awareness of the responsibility to treat veteran women with dignity and respect. To learn more about the Center for Women Veterans, follow this link: https://www.va.gov/womenvet/.

- **National Women Veterans Summit**
  In 2017 the VA held the National Women Veterans Summit, which included a number of seminars specifically for veteran women. These included such topics as employment, entrepreneurship, health research, state and local resources, military sexual trauma, and reproductive health. For a complete listing of those seminars, and to watch the cyberseminars, please follow this link: https://www.va.gov/womenvet/acwv/summitNational2017.asp.

- **VA Health Care for Women Veterans**
  Women veterans may qualify for healthcare coverage through the VA, including (but not limited to) annual wellness exams, mammograms, prenatal care, and assistance with nursing. At each VA medical center and community-based outpatient clinic (CBOC) nationwide, a women veterans program manager (WVPM) is designated to advise and advocate for women veterans. The WVPM can help coordinate all the services you may need, from primary care to specialized care for chronic conditions or reproductive health. Women veterans who are interested in receiving care at the VA should contact the nearest VA medical center and ask for the WVPM. For more information, see https://www.benefits.va.gov/persona/veteran-women.asp.

- **Women Veteran Coordinators**
  There are women veteran coordinators (WVCs) located in every regional office who function as the primary contact for women veterans. WVCs

provide specific information and comprehensive assistance to women veterans and their dependents and beneficiaries concerning VA benefits and related non-VA benefits. They may assist you in the claims intake, development, and processing of military sexual and personal trauma claims.

- **VA Benefits for Survivors of Military Sexual Trauma**
  The VA has special services available to help women who have experienced military sexual trauma (MST), including free, confidential counseling and treatment for mental and physical health conditions related to MST. You do not need to have a service-connected disability or injury and may be able to receive this benefit even if you are not eligible for other VA care. You do not need to have reported the incidents when they happened or have other documentation that they occurred in order to receive MST services. Every VA facility has a designated MST coordinator who serves as a contact person for MST-related issues. This person is your advocate and can help you find and access VA services and programs, state and federal benefits, and community resources. Two VA websites where you can find more information and resources are https://www.ptsd.va.gov/public/types/violence/military-sexual-trauma-general.asp and https://www.mentalhealth.va.gov/msthome.asp.

- **Women Veterans' Services (NYS)**
  New York State's Division of Veterans' Affairs has a designated women veterans program coordinator (WVPC). Her job is the identification, development, planning, organization, and coordination of all statewide programs and services to ensure that they are meeting the needs of women veterans and that women veterans are receiving the full array of benefits that they have earned. She travels throughout the state to assist women veterans and to educate others in an effort to normalize the experience of women veterans. You can find more information at https://veterans.ny.gov/content/women-veterans'-services.

- **The Women Veterans Rock**
  This organization is a coalition of veteran women organizations and women advocacy organizations supporting women veterans and military families in the areas of housing, employment, education, financial stability,

and health and wellness. As part of Women Veterans Rock, the Women Veterans Civic Leadership Institute (WVCLI) is a fellowship program that teaches participants the fundamentals of civilian civic and community leadership. The institute is uniquely designed to aid today's military women in getting involved in community-based leadership opportunities. They assist veteran women in becoming positive agents of social change for military women and military families in today's post-9/11 world. For more information, see https://www.womenvetsrock.org.

- **The Service Women's Action Network (SWAN)**
  Founded in 2007, SWAN aims to be the voice of all military women—past, present and future. It is a member-driven community network advocating for the individual and collective needs of service women. SWAN is guided by the priorities of its members, who include thousands of women and men, service members, and civilians alike. It is committed to seeing that all service women receive the opportunities, protections, benefits, and respect they deserve. For more information, go to https://www.service women.org.

FOUR UNIQUE CHALLENGES FACING WOMEN VETERANS
by Kittie W. Watson, Melanie N. Joyce, and Lieutenant Colonel Wendy M. Perry

The percentage of women actively serving in the military continues to grow: women currently make up almost 17 percent of the United States Armed Forces as well as almost 20 percent of the Military Reserves. Increasing numbers of women veterans are entering civilian life: over two million women veterans make up 9.4 percent of the total veteran population. As veteran women transition to the civilian job market, many struggle to catch up with their nonveteran peers. Many find that they are overqualified in specific skills and disciplines because of their military training and leadership experience, yet lack the professional certifications required for desired civilian roles. Most also have difficulty translating military experiences to a civilian context. Like many women, women veterans often face additional family and childcare responsibilities that keep them from taking advantage of available VA benefits and education programs, such as the Post-9/11 GI Bill and Vocational Rehabilitation and Employment (VR&E), designed to help them prepare for, obtain, and maintain suitable employment.

While all veterans face transitional challenges when leaving the military, women also encounter at least four unique challenges that require government agencies, academic institutions, companies, and potential employers to acknowledge and ultimately change.

1. Inadequate VA Support for Women Veterans

It is well-documented that the VA is challenged to adequately meet the overall needs of veterans. The current VA system, enacted by Executive Order in 1930, was designed with male veterans in mind. With a system designed decades ago, it has not kept pace with changing military demographics. Women's healthcare, psychological, and childcare needs have not been a top priority or concern. However, with the number of veteran women seeking treatment and assistance having increased by 80 percent since 2002, this needs more immediate attention. While the VA has made strides in supporting the unique needs of women veterans, only recently has there been a focused effort on providing equity of services and resources to this underserved veteran population. Such efforts include the adoption of the Center for Women Veterans, National Association of Women Veteran Coordinators, and, within the VA healthcare system, the designation of WVPMs.

Despite these efforts, many military medical care providers within VA facilities have not been trained to provide basic medical services, such as prenatal care or gynecological care, for women. The *Wall Street Journal* reports that a third of VA medical centers do not have a gynecologist on staff. In addition, with 20 percent of women veterans reporting having experienced MSTs (including rape), most VA medical centers are not staffed to support the volume of women veterans presenting with a history of MST and lack the infrastructure to provide for the privacy and nonmale provider preferences of this veteran population. For example, a screening from the VA found that between 15 and 20 percent of female patients suffer from MST and are three times as likely to suffer comorbid mental health issues such as depression and PTSD. And while 20 percent of women veterans report being the victims of MST, many incidents go unreported, which confirms the male-dominated military culture into which nearly all veteran women have been indoctrinated, resulting in them feeling isolated, lacking support, and working to be invisible. The most staggering statistic, however, is that women veterans have a 250 percent higher risk for suicide than civilian women, and veteran women who do not use VA services have seen a 98 percent increase in rates.

While healthcare disparities for women veterans persist, a separate but equally lacking area of support is childcare. Without childcare support, women veterans, like all women who are divorced or single mothers, are challenged to find professional positions, continue their education, or make geographic moves for employment. And, with a divorce rate of 23.4 percent among women veterans (compared to 12.6 percent of non-military women), childcare support is a growing concern. These factors influence women veterans' ability to compete for desirable professional positions and sustain economic independence. Recent reports suggest that women veterans are twice as likely as civilian women to become homeless, and are the fastest-growing segment of the homeless veteran population.

2. **Civilian Misunderstanding about Women's Roles in the Military**
    Another challenge that women veterans face is that many civilians think of veterans as men. Civilians often learn about military experience from how it is depicted in the media and women have had limited exposure until recently. Many people simply forget there are women veterans. They discount women's military experience as less challenging than that of their male counterparts; however, since the wars in Iraq and Afghanistan, the ratio of female veterans who have served in combat or war zones compared to those who have not has increased dramatically: 30 percent since 9/11 (compare that to 57 percent of male veterans). Women also face biases about their expertise and leadership approach. When they acknowledge women in the military, most civilians mistakenly assume

that women serve in auxiliary or support roles. Many employers translate a woman's experience in the military differently than they would a man's. In addition, just as with civilian women, veteran women face a double-bind paradox: they are often trained to be assertive, and research results suggest that assertive women are more likely to be perceived as aggressive or having "harsh" leadership practices. When these women make a request for pay equity or promotion opportunities, they risk being labeled as domineering or overly ambitious.

3. **Transition Assistance Programs Are Designed for Men**

Decades ago, the Military Transition Assistance Program (TAP) was designed to help those transitioning out of the military into civilian roles. Unfortunately, not all TAPs are created equal. While there a few military installations in recent years that have adopted innovative strategies or are collaborating with corporate partners to better prepare transitioning service members, to date, there is no consistent operating company model for the process across all armed services. Many are led by military personnel, retired military members, and military spouses, who have had little personal experience working in the civilian or corporate environment themselves. In fact, in most cases, TAP classes are designed for the youngest and least experienced service members transitioning to civilian life. Participation in the program is a requirement for all military personnel separating from the service; however, program content and delivery is inconsistent in its approach to addressing the unique skills and circumstances of service members, especially women. Employers would be wise to realize that new veteran-hires have often received little to no training about the differences between military service and working for a civilian organization. Additionally, according to the VA, female veterans through the age of 34 have more children under 18 years of age than their civilian counterparts. Female service members often delay having children because of their military obligations and transition to civilian life as the primary caregivers of small children. This leads to complicated job searches in the civilian world because of childcare concerns and résumé gaps. TAP in its current form ignores this additional challenge that women veterans face.

4. **Underdeveloped Networking Skills: Social Isolation and Invisibility**
   Another challenge that influences veteran women's transition to civilian roles is the lack of training and experience with effective corporate networking. Depending on the specific roles and units in which a military woman has served, there may have been more exposure and interaction in predominantly male environments, which unfortunately can minimize social interaction and result in isolation. The situation is often compounded in situations perceived as unsafe or when veteran women have experienced or witnessed sexual harassment. In addition to providing limited opportunities for networking outside of the organic unit, the military culture does not foster skills for networking or navigating civilian work culture situations. Research suggests that women veterans are less likely to self-identify with their service when entering civilian roles. Military men build strong bonds and networks that translate into career opportunities within the military and help them when transitioning to civilian roles. Military women, on the other hand, usually report a lack of strong referral connections to build work opportunities. Some, in fact, struggle to identify references who really know them well for job applications. Most of their relationship networking comes from limited socializing that doesn't translate to furthering their careers.

WHAT CAN BE DONE TO BETTER SUPPORT VETERAN WOMEN?

1. Create a safe place for women veterans to be validated.
   - Provide resources to stabilize difficult circumstances using referrals to resources for housing, childcare, job training, and supportive counseling assistance.
   - Assist women veterans in getting connected to both medical and mental health care even if not provided by the VA.

2. Identify and match women veterans with sponsors or mentors who can model how to navigate the unwritten rules in civilian organizations.
   - Look for sponsors outside of VERGs.
   - Offer training and practice in professional rather than social networking. Demonstrate how strong networks can further their careers through the exchange of resources, ideas, and referrals.

3. Educate hiring managers and business leaders about the most pressing issues and challenges facing veteran women.
   - Provide information and training on how body language affects perception of empathy and authority. Women tend to portray empathy naturally but face a unique challenge showing authority without being perceived as overbearing.

4. Advocate with legislators for resources to provide women veterans with support and treatment.
   - Work to partner with local military units to provide practical training and information to transitioning female service members through the TAP program.

Authors

Kittie W. Watson, Ph.D., is president of Innolect, an executive leadership and organization development firm that prepares executives and their teams to succeed in the workplaces of the future. With over twenty-five years of strategic change management experience, her current research supports the successful recruitment, transition, and retention of military veterans. She serves as an advisory board member for VettedHeroes.

Melanie N. Joyce, MBA, served for over eleven years as a US Naval Aviator and flight instructor. She currently works for Canadian Aviation Electronics instructing advanced multi-engine flight students from the US

Navy, Marine Corps, and Coast Guard. She holds an airline transport pilot's license and multiple aircraft type ratings, and is a mother to three young boys.

Lieutenant Colonel Wendy M. Perry, MS, RN, US Army (Ret.) is a consultant with Innolect, lending focused expertise on veteran integration, women veterans, and military culture. She is an experienced healthcare leader, registered nurse, and educator with over twenty years of active duty service. She is currently appointed as an ambassador for the Women in Military Service for America Memorial Foundation for the state of Georgia.

BREAKOUT BOX

Addressing the Needs of Women Veterans at the Women Veterans Center

From the founding of our nation to present time, women in the military have been underrepresented heroines. Women veterans shine throughout history as examples for future generations by proudly securing our country's liberties and freedoms. Their persistence and service paved the way for the military women of today to join a traditionally male-dominated institution and serve their country, not only as women, but as Soldiers, Sailors, Airmen, Marines, and Coast Guardsmen.

Women veterans are the fastest growing minority demographic of the veteran population, with some estimates stating that by 2040 women will make up 18 percent of the veteran population. As a nation and across industry sectors, we must begin to embrace women veteran's dedication and sacrifices as unique and intrinsically valuable to the stability of our country.

Culturally, we place a great emphasis on a hero narrative that rarely invokes the female story. As employers, hiring managers, and folks within the human resource sector, we need to adapt our expectations and become more inclusive of the distinct needs and skill sets of our women veterans.

At the Veterans Multi-Service Center's Women Veterans Center (WVC), we pride ourselves on maintaining a facility tailored to the unique needs of women veterans and their families. In a separate space, the WVC offers help with immediate needs (meals, clothing, and toiletry products), and provides a robust calendar of fellowship activities. At the WVC, veteran women can utilize our computer lab, check out books from our lending library, help themselves to items from our clothing closet, and spend time in camaraderie with one another.

At the WVC we have tried to eliminate as many barriers to participation as possible. We have a child's play area attached to our computer lab. This allows women veterans to work on their résumés and look for jobs in a safe space that is inclusive of their kids. The furniture is arranged utilizing trauma-informed techniques so that all entrances and exits are always visible, and we created a private restroom. We also provide transportation help getting to and from the WVC as well as to our outside fellowship activities.

—Anna Stormer, Coordinator of the Women Veterans Center
at the Veterans Multi-Service Center

ENDNOTES

1. Office of Data Governance and Analytics, *Women Veterans Report: The Past, Present, and Future of Women Veterans* (Washington, DC: National Center for Veterans Analysis and Statistics, February 2017), vii–viii, 5–6, 8, 10, 19, 27, https://www.va.gov/vetdata/docs/SpecialReports/Women_Veterans_2015_Final.pdf.
2. Ann Elizabeth Montgomery et al., *Women Veterans and Homelessness, Homeless Evidence and Research Roundtable Series* (Philadelphia:VA National Center on Homelessness among Veterans, July 2016), 5, https://www.va.gov/homeless/nchav/docs/HERS-Womens-Proceedings.pdf.
3. Frances Murphy, Sherrie L. Hans, and Bradley J. Reina, *Women Veterans: The Long Journey Home* (Cold Spring, KY: Disabled American Veterans, 2015), 36, https://www.dav.org/wp-content/uploads/women-veterans-study.pdf.
4. Murphy, Hans, and Reina, *Women Veterans*, 9.
5. Murphy, Hans, and Reina, *Women Veterans*, 23.
6. Office of Data Governance and Analytics, *Women Veterans Report*, 29.

APPENDIX A

List of Reports

Throughout this book we cited numerous reports and thought you might appreciate a list of them (and several more). Needless to say, there are many other reports related to veteran employment, but the sources provided here offer a lot of very helpful information for any organization that wants to learn even more about hiring, onboarding, and retaining veterans and military spouses.

- George W. Bush Institute, *Confronting the Invisible Wounds of War: Barriers, Misunderstanding, and a Divide* (Dallas: George W. Bush Presidential Center, 2018), https://gwbcenter.imgix.net/Resources/ GWBI-invisiblewoundsperceptionssurvey.pdf.
- Institute for Veterans and Military Families, *Leading Practice: Measuring the Impact of Veterans in the Workplace*, (Syracuse: Institute for Veterans and Military Families, 2012), http://toolkit.vets.syr.edu/wp-content/ uploads/2012/12/LP-Tracking-Veterans.pdf.
- George W. Bush Institute, *I Am a Post 9/11 Veteran* (Dallas: George W. Bush Presidential Center), https://gwbcenter.imgix.net/Resources/ gwbi-msi-i-am-a-post-911-veteran.pdf.
- Phillip Carter, Amy Schafer, Katherine Kidder, and Moira Fagan, *Lost In Translation: The Civil-Military Divide and Veteran Employment* (Washington, DC: Center for a New American Security, 2017), www.cnas.org/ publications/reports/lost-in-translation.
- Rosalinda Maury, Brice Stone, and Jennifer Roseman, *Veteran Job Retention Survey Summary* (Washington, DC: Institute for Veterans and Military Families, 2016), https://ivmf.syracuse.edu/wp-content/ uploads/2016/10/VetAdvisor-ReportFINAL-Single-pages.pdf.

- Hiring Our Heroes, *Military Spouses in the Workplace: Understanding the Impacts of Spouse Unemployment on Military Recruitment, Retention, and Readiness* (Washington, DC: Chamber of Commerce Foundation, June 2017), https://www.uschamberfoundation.org/reports/military-spouses-workplace.
- Department of Treasury and Department of Defense, *Supporting Our Military Families: Best Practices for Streamlining Occupational Licensing across State Lines*, February 2012, http://archive.defense.gov/home/pdf/Occupational_Licensing_and_Military_Spouses_Report_vFINAL.PDF.
- Rosalinda Maury and Brice Stone, *Military Spouse Employment Report* (Syracuse: Institute for Veterans and Military Families, February 2014), https://ivmf.syracuse.edu/wp-content/uploads/2016/06/MilitarySpouseEmploymentReport_2013.pdf.
- Deborah Bradbard, R. Maury, and Nicholas J. Armstrong, *The Force behind the Force: Training, Leveraging, and Communicating about Military Spouses as Employees* (Syracuse: Institute for Veterans and Military Families, December 2016), https://ivmf.syracuse.edu/wp-content/uploads/2016/08/IVMF__standard_prudential_12.6.16_FINAL_CLEAN-002.pdf.
- Deborah Bradbard, R. Maury, and Nicholas J. Armstrong, *The Force behind the Force: A Business Case for Leveraging Military Spouse Talent* (Syracuse: Institute for Veterans and Military Families, 2016), https://ivmf.syracuse.edu/wp-content/uploads/2016/12/ForceBehindtheForce.BusinessCaseforLeveragingMilitarySpouseTalentACC_02.21.18.pdf.
- Margaret C. Harrell and Nancy Berglass, *Employing America's Veterans: Perspectives from Businesses* (Washington, DC: Center for New American Security, 2012), https://www.cnas.org/publications/reports/employing-americas-veterans-perspectives-from-businesses.
- William B. Caldwell and Crispin J. Burke, *America's Veterans: A Sound Investment* (Washington, DC: Center for New American Security, 2013), https://www.cnas.org/publications/reports/americas-veterans-a-sound-investment.
- McKinsey and Company, "How Companies Can Capture the Veteran Opportunity," presentation, September 2012, http://toolkit.vets.syr.

edu/wp-content/uploads/2012/11/Presentation-1-20120911-Veteran-opportunity.pdf.

- Institute for Veterans and Military Families, *The Business Case for Hiring a Veteran: Beyond the Clichés* (Syracuse: Institute for Veterans and Military Families, 2012), https://ivmf.syracuse.edu/wp-content/uploads/2016/06/The-Business-Case-for-Hiring-a-Veteran-3-6-12.pdf.
- CEB Corporate Leadership Council, "The Business Case for Hiring Veterans," presentation, https://www.cebglobal.com/human-resources/forms/military-hiring.html.
- Institute for Veterans and Military Families, *Guide to Leading Policies, Practices and Resources: Supporting the Employment of Veterans and Military Families* (Syracuse: Institute for Veterans and Military Families, 2016), https://ivmf.syracuse.edu/wp-content/uploads/2016/07/guidetoleadingpractices1.pdf.
- 100,000 Jobs Mission, *Leading Practice: Performance and Retention*, October 22, 2015, https://www.veteranjobsmission.com/sites/default/files/knowledge_exchange/Engagement%20and%20Retention.pdf.
- Institute for Veterans and Military Families, Workforce Readiness Research Series, https://ivmf.syracuse.edu/research/topics/employment/workforce-readiness.
- Phillip Carter and Katharine Kidder, *A Continuum of Collaboration: The Landscape of Efforts to Serve Veterans* (Washington, DC: Center for a New American Security, April 2017), https://www.cnas.org/publications/reports/a-continuum-of-collaboration.
- Institute for Veterans and Military Families, *Launching a Veteran Employment Program: Best Practices in Recruiting, Hiring, Onboarding and Retaining Veterans* (Syracuse: Institute for Veterans and Military Families, 2013), https://www.veteranjobsmission.com/leading-practices/launching-veteran-employment-program.
- J. Michael Haynie, *Revisiting the Business Case for Hiring a Veteran: A Strategy for Cultivating Competitive Advantage*, Employment Research Series (Syracuse: Institute for Veterans and Military Families, April 2016), https://ivmf.syracuse.edu/wp-content/uploads/2016/06/IVMF_WorkforceReadinessPaper2_April16_Report2.pdf.

- Angela Halvorson, *Understanding the Military: The Institution, the Culture, and the People*, SAMHSA white paper, 2010, https://www.samhsa.gov/sites/default/files/military_white_paper_final.pdf.
- Dori Meinert, "Hidden Wounds," *HR Magazine*, July 1, 2011, https://www.shrm.org/hr-today/news/hr-magazine/pages/0711meinert.aspx.
- Office of Data Governance and Analytics, *Women Veterans Report: The Past, Present, and Future of Women Veterans* (Washington, DC: National Center for Veterans Analysis and Statistics, February 2017), https://www.va.gov/vetdata/docs/SpecialReports/Women_Veterans_2015_Final.pdf.

Veteran Service Organizations

Plenty of veteran service organizations (VSOs) and military nonprofit organizations existed before the terrorist attacks of 9/11, and tens of thousands more have sprung up since that horrific day. While it is a good thing to have so many organizations that aim to help our veterans and their families, at the same time, it is overwhelming for those in need, as well as those who want to donate and contribute, to find the right fit.

It would be impossible for me to list all of the VSOs or even recommend the best ones—the list is far too expansive and subjective. But in order to at least point you in the right direction, I have listed here a number of the VSOs that I referenced throughout the book, as well as others that also make an impact in the veteran community. Although I have tried to categorize them (albeit somewhat broadly), please be aware that a number of these organizations provide a wide variety of services and could easily fit into several different categories.

What's the best way to find a good organization? Ask others around you, especially veterans and military spouses. The more specific you are in what you are looking for, the easier it will be to identify a good fit. In the meantime, this is a good list to get you started. Please note that organizations not listed here are not necessarily bad; I am simply limited by space and my own knowledge. For a more detailed of VSOs provided by the Department of Veterans Affairs, please visit www.va.gov/vso/VSO-Directory.pdf.

Community Supportive Services and Collaboration

1. America's Warrior Partnership (AWP; www.americaswarriorpartnership.org)
2. Swords to Plowshares (www.stp-sf.org)
3. National Veterans Legal Services Program (www.nvlsp.org)
4. Focus Marines Foundation (www.focusMarines.org)
5. Blue Star Families (www.bluestarfam.org)
6. National Association of State Directors of Veterans Affairs (www.nasdva.us)
7. GI Go Fund (www.gigo.org/)
8. Bob Woodruff Foundation (www.bobwoodrufffoundation.org)
9. National Military Family Association (www.nmfa.org)
10. Team Rubicon (www.teamrubiconusa.org)
11. Team Red, White & Blue (www.teamrwb.org)
12. Soldiers' Angels (www.soldiersangels.org)
13. Military Warriors Support Foundation (www.militarywarriors.org)
14. Gary Sinise Foundation (www.garysinisefoundation.org)
15. Hope for the Warriors (www.hopeforthewarriors.org)
16. Mission United (www.unitedway.org/mission-united)

Emergency Financial Assistance for Veterans

1. USA Cares (www.usacares.org)
2. Operation Homefront (www.operationhomefront.org)
3. Navy Mutual Aid Association (www.navymutual.org)
4. Defenders of Freedom (www.defendersoffreedom.us)
5. American Red Cross (community referrals; www.redcross.org/get-help/military-families/services-for-veterans)

Branch- and Unit-Focused Organizations

1. Marine Corps League (www.mclnational.org/)
2. Air Force Association (www.afa.org)
3. Navy League of the United States (www.navyleague.org)
4. Reserve Officers Association of the United States (ROA; www.roa.org)
5. Association of the United States Army (www.ausa.org)

6. Association of the United States Navy (www.ausn.org)
7. The Retired Enlisted Organization (www.trea.org)
8. Fleet Reserve Association (www.fra.org)
9. Green Beret Foundation (www.greenberetfoundation.org)
10. Navy Seal Foundation (www.navysealfoundation.org)

Congressionally Chartered (and Similar) Veteran Service Organizations

1. The American Legion (www.legion.org)
2. Gold Star Wives (www.goldstarwives.org)
3. American Red Cross (www.redcross.org)
4. AMVETS (www.amvets.org)
5. Blinded Veterans Association (BVA; www.bva.org)
6. Disabled American Veterans (DAV; www.dav.org/)
7. Military Officers Association of America (MOAA; www.moaa.org)
8. Military Order of the Purple Heart (MOPH; www.mophhq.org/)
9. Paralyzed Veterans of America (PVA; www.pva.org)
10. Veterans of Foreign Wars of the United States (www.vfw.org)
11. Vietnam Veterans of America (www.vva.org)
12. Wounded Warrior Project (www.woundedwarriorproject.org)
13. United Services Organization (www.uso.org)

Mental Health and Tragedy Assistance

1. Tragedy Assistance Program for Survivors (TAPS; www.taps.org)
2. American Gold Star Mothers (www.goldstarmoms.com)
3. Give An Hour (giveanhour.org/)
4. Vets4Warriors (vets4warriors.com/)
5. Cohen Veterans Network (www.cohenveteransnetwork.org)
6. Marcus Institute for Brain Health (www.ucdenver.edu/anschutz/patientcare/marcusinstitute/Pages/marcusinstitute.aspx)
7. Injured Marine Semper Fi Fund (semperfifund.org)
8. Boulder Crest Retreat (www.bouldercrestretreat.org)
9. 22 Kill (www.22kill.com)
10. PsychArmor (psycharmor.org)

Employment and Networking

1. JobPath (www.yourjobpath.com)
2. Veteran Success Resource Group (www.veteransuccessgroup.org)
3. FourBlock (www.fourblock.org)
4. US Chamber of Commerce Foundation, Hiring Our Heroes (www.hiringourheroes.org)
5. Hire Heroes USA (www.hireheroesusa.org)
6. Veterati (www.veterati.com)
7. American Corporate Partners (www.acp-usa.org)
8. The Mission Continues (www.missioncontinues.org)
9. Goodwill (www.goodwill.org)
10. Warriors Ethos (www.warriorsethos.org)

Recreational Therapy and Adaptive Sports

1. Disabled Sports USA and Warfighter Sports (www.disabledsportsusa.org)
2. Adaptive Sports Foundation (www.adaptivesportsfoundation.org)
3. Project Healing Waters (www.projecthealingwaters.org)
4. Salute Military Golf Association (www.smga.org)
5. Tee It Up for the Troops (www.teeitupforthetroops.org)
6. R4 Alliance (www.r4alliance.org)
7. Vacations for Veterans (www.vacationsforveterans.org)
8. Sierra Club Military Veterans (content.sierraclub.org/outings/military)
9. Warriors and Quiet Waters (www.warriorsandquietwaters.org)
10. Vail Veterans Program (www.vailveteransprogram.org)

Fifteen Things Veterans Want You to Know

1. We are not all Soldiers.

- Each branch of the military has its own mission.
- Each has different services, different rank structures, different uniforms, and each expertly performs different missions.
- Each has its own microculture.
- Only Army personnel are Soldiers, so you need to state "military personnel" or "veterans" as reference, and not generalize all as "Soldiers."

2. Reserves are part of the military.

- There are two ways to serve in uniform in our country:
  - Active Duty—full-time job is to serve in the active duty forces of the military.
  - Reserves—trained to serve but have day-to-day civilian jobs; may have previously served as active duty.
  - Active duty and Reserves members balance and complement each other.
- Training is one weekend per month and two weeks per year.
- Reserves remain ready and serve together as a unit.
- They are mobilized as needed.
- Mobilization can be disruptive to work and family life.
- Reserves often don't have the same resources and support when they return back from missions that active duty military personnel do.

- All branches of the military have reserves.
- Some military personnel make the choice to stay in the reserves after leaving active duty to stay ready and remain in the military.
- Reserves members have their own unique challenges related to living day-to-day as a civilian, then immediately and abruptly being deployed, then returning to their community, where they may not be understood.

3. Not everyone in the military is infantry (in tanks, on patrol, etc.).

- Active duty is made up of 1.4 million Americans among the five branches.
- The Reserves have more than eight hundred thousand members ranging from infantry to technicians, mechanics, cooks, administrators, lawyers, doctors, and musicians.
- Many service members are expertly trained for months and years to get specialty ratings.
- Military jobs have different physical and mental requirements and demands.

4. The military has leaders at every level in the chain of command.

- Each branch has a different rank structure.
- Each rank level has leadership in place.
- Military culture prides itself on its leadership.
- Being responsible and accountable for others is what gives service members pride.
- It is less important to know what rank someone is than it is to know that they followed orders and were responsible for others.

5. Military is always on duty.

- Service members live their work 24/7.
- Readiness is a full-time, around-the-clock job.
- This takes its toll on military personnel and their families.
- There are no off days.

- Even when they are on leave, service members can be called immediately, at a moment's notice.

6. Service members take pride in appearance and conduct.

- All military services have standards for the way people look in uniform.
- The military takes physical fitness seriously.
- Service members are held to a standard of conduct and are held accountable.

7. Not all service members have killed someone.

- Those who have do *not* want to talk about it.
- This is a question that should not be asked *ever*.

8. Not all service members have PTSD, and PTSD probably isn't what you think.

- Combat can be traumatic and can cause PTSD, which requires treatment.
- PTSD also occurs in civilians who have lived through something traumatic.
- PTSD is caused by many different types of trauma, including combat, sexual violence, abuse, and terrible vehicle accidents.
- Most people who experience a trauma do not go on to develop PTSD; this is why it is considered "disordered" and not a normal reaction.
- Many who were diagnosed with PTSD recover and lead entirely functional lives.
- There will be individual difference in how people with PTSD respond.
- Inquire about the individual's worst day in military service and their best day (for healthcare providers *only*).

9. Service members who do have invisible wounds of war are not dangerous or violent.

- Invisible combat wounds include
  - PTSD,

- ○ TBI,
- ○ Depression, and
- ○ Substance use disorder.
- Invisible wounds are real—and are injuries.
- Not all are mental illnesses or psychiatric conditions.
- Invisible wounds deserve the same treatment as visible injuries.
- The majority of people with invisible wounds are not prone to being dangerous or violent.

10. It's sometimes hard for service members to ask for help.

- The military has long-standing history of requiring emotional and physical perfection.
- Stigma is decreasing, and invisible wounds are more validated now.
- Just by understanding that it is hard to ask for help, you are one step closer to them.

11. Military service changes people.

- The military changes people. The change is permanent and that's okay.

12. Veterans differ in how much they identify with the military after they leave active duty.

- How much military service affects veterans' day-to-day lives is different from person to person.
- Ask a veteran: *How do you define yourself now? How has your military service shaped you?*
- Service members integrate their military experiences in different ways.

13. Service members' families serve with them.

- The military family's experience is unique and challenging.
- The family is frequently separated from loved ones.

- Some military families move every two or three years.
- The moves make it difficult to establish school and employment.
- Family dynamics and responsibilities are constantly changing.
- Here's the good part: military families are resilient, adaptive, and flexible.
- Stop and think about the sacrifice these families have made.

14. Service members would die for each other and their country.

15. All service members made these sacrifices for one reason: to serve something more important than themselves.

- This idea defines military culture.
- Service members choose honor, commitment, and duty every day.

FIVE QUESTIONS YOU SHOULD ASK

1. Did you serve in the military?

- Veterans want to be asked about their service.
- It starts the conversation.

2. If yes, which branch?

- Asking this question shows that you know there is a difference.
- You don't need to know all the specifics of each branch; it's most important to know that there *are* differences and not to generalize.

3. What was your job in the military?

- There are literally hundreds of things a person could have done during their military service.
- This question acknowledges and validates all the different things a person could have done in the military.
- This question helps make the gap smaller.

4. **What was your worst day in your military service or on deployment? (For healthcare providers only.)**

5. **What was your best day in your military service or on deployment? (For healthcare providers only.)**

For more information about the PsychArmor Institute and to view other courses, visit https://psycharmor.org.

Reprinted with permission from PsychArmor Institute.

Bibliography

America's Heroes at Work. "Accommodating Employees
with Traumatic Brain Injury." *Brainline*, May 21, 2012.
http://www.brainlinemilitary.org/content/2012/05/
accommodating-employees-with-traumatic-brain-injury-.

Bergland, Christopher. "Exposure to Natural Light Improves Workplace
Performance." *Athlete's Way* (blog), *Psychology Today*, June 5, 2013.
https://www.psychologytoday.com/blog/the-athletes-way/201306/
exposure-natural-light-improves-workplace-performance.

Bradbard, Deborah, R. Maury, and Nicholas J. Armstrong. *The Force
behind the Force: Training, Leveraging, and Communicating about Military
Spouses as Employees.* Syracuse: Institute for Veterans and Military
Families, December 2016. https://ivmf.syracuse.edu/wp-content/
uploads/2016/08/IVMF__standard_prudential_12.6.16_FINAL_
CLEAN-002.pdf.

Caldwell, William B., and Crispin J. Burke. *America's Veterans: A
Sound Investment.* Washington, DC: Center for New American
Security, 2013. https://www.cnas.org/publications/reports/
americas-veterans-a-sound-investment.

Carter, Phillip, Amy Schafer, Katherine Kidder, and Moira Fagan. *Lost
in Translation: The Civil-Military Divide and Veteran Employment.*
Washington, DC: Center for a New American Security, 2017. www.
cnas.org/publications/reports/lost-in-translation.

CEB Corporate Leadership Council. "The Business Case for Hiring
Veterans." Presentation. https://www.cebglobal.com/human-
resources/forms/military-hiring.html.

Chairman of the Joint Chiefs of Staff. *DOD Dictionary of Military and Associated Terms.* Washington, DC: The Joint Staff, February 2018. http://www.jcs.mil/Portals/36/Documents/Doctrine/pubs/dictionary.pdf.

Curry Hall, Kimberly, Margaret C. Harrell, Barbara A. Bicksler, Robert Stewart, and Michael P. Fisher. *Veteran Employment: Lessons from the 100,000 Jobs Mission.* Santa Monica: RAND Corporation, 2014. https://www.rand.org/pubs/research_reports/RR836.html.

Department of Treasury and Department of Defense. *Supporting Our Military Families: Best Practices for Streamlining Occupational Licensing across State Lines.* February 2012. http://archive.defense.gov/home/pdf/Occupational_Licensing_and_Military_Spouses_Report_vFINAL.PDF.

Department of Veteran Affairs. *VA Handbook 0802: Federal Recovery Coordination Program.* Washington, DC: Department of Veteran Affairs, 2011. https://www.va.gov/vapubs/viewPublication.asp?Pub_ID=537&FType=2.

Disabled American Veterans. *The Veteran Advantage: DAV Guide to Hiring and Retaining Veterans with Disabilities.* Cold Spring, KY: Disabled American Veterans, 2018. https://www.dav.org/wp-content/uploads/HiringGuide.pdf.

Force Planning Requirements Directorate, *Defense Manpower Requirements Report, Fiscal Year 2015.* Washington, DC: Office of the Assistant Secretary of Defense for Readiness and Force Management, June 2014. http://prhome.defense.gov/portals/52/documents/RFM/TFPRQ/docs/f15%20DMRR.pdf.

George W. Bush Institute. *I Am a Post 9/11 Veteran.* Dallas: George W. Bush Presidential Center, n.d. https://gwbcenter.imgix.net/Resources/gwbi-msi-i-am-a-post-911-veteran.pdf.

Goode, Shelton, and Isaac Dixon. "Are Employee Resource Groups Good for Business?" *HR Magazine*, August 25, 2016. https://www.shrm.org/hr-today/news/hr-magazine/0916/pages/are-employee-resource-groups-good-for-business.aspx.

Hamblen, Jessica. "PTSD 101: PTSD Overview." Education course, Department of Veteran Affairs. https://www.ptsd.va.gov/professional/continuing_ed/flash-files/ptsd-overview-course/launcher.html#.

Harrell, Margaret C., and Nancy Berglass. *Employing America's Veterans: Perspectives from Businesses.* Washington, DC: Center for New American Security, 2012. https://www.cnas.org/publications/reports/employing-americas-veterans-perspectives-from-businesses.

Hiring Our Heroes. "Accommodating Veterans with Disabilities." Employer Roadmap, 2017. https://www.vetemployerroadmap.org/wounded-veterans/2017/3/27/accommodating-veterans-with-disabilities.

———. *Military Spouses in the Workplace: Understanding the Impacts of Spouse Unemployment on Military Recruitment, Retention, and Readiness.* Washington, DC: Chamber of Commerce Foundation, June 2017. https://www.uschamberfoundation.org/reports/military-spouses-workplace.

———. *Veterans in the Workplace: Understanding the Challenges and Creating Long-Term Opportunities for Veteran Employees.* Washington, DC: Chamber of Commerce Foundation, 2016. https://www.uschamberfoundation.org/sites/default/files/Veterans%20in%20the%20Workplace_0.pdf

Institute for Veterans and Military Families. *The Business Case for Hiring a Veteran: Beyond the Clichés.* Syracuse: Institute for Veterans and Military Families, 2012. https://ivmf.syracuse.edu/wp-content/uploads/2016/06/The-Business-Case-for-Hiring-a-Veteran-3-6-12.pdf.

————. *Guide to Leading Policies, Practices and Resources: Supporting the Employment of Veterans and Military Families.* Syracuse: Institute for Veterans and Military Families, 2016. https://ivmf.syracuse.edu/wp-content/uploads/2016/07/guidetoleadingpractices1.pdf.

————. *Leading Practice: Measuring the Impact of Veterans in the Workplace.* Syracuse: Institute for Veterans and Military Families, 2012. http://toolkit.vets.syr.edu/wp-content/uploads/2012/12/LP-Tracking-Veterans.pdf.

Job Accommodation Network. *Accommodation and Compliance Series: Employees with Post Traumatic Stress Disorder.* October 8, 2015. https://askjan.org/media/downloads/PTSDA&CSeries.pdf.

Maurer, Roy. "This Is Why Finding Talent Is Getting Tougher in 2016." Society for Human Resource Management, June 20, 2016. https://www.shrm.org/hr-today/news/hr-news/pages/recruiting-gets-harder-in-2016.aspx.

Maury, Rosalinda, and Brice Stone. *Military Spouse Employment Report.* Syracuse: Institute for Veterans and Military Families, February 2014. https://ivmf.syracuse.edu/wp-content/uploads/2016/06/MilitarySpouseEmploymentReport_2013.pdf.

Maury, Rosalinda, Brice Stone, and Jennifer Roseman. *Veteran Job Retention Survey Summary.* Syracuse: Institute for Veterans and Military Families, 2016. https://ivmf.syracuse.edu/wp-content/uploads/2016/10/VetAdvisor-ReportFINAL-Single-pages.pdf.

McCausland, Tracy C., Michael G. Shanley, Chaitra M. Hardison, Anna Rosefsky Saavedra, Angela Clague, James C. Crowley, Jaclyn Martin, Jonathan P. Wong, and Paul S. Steinberg. *What Veterans Bring to Civilian Workplaces.* Santa Monica: RAND Publications, 2017.

Meindert, Dori. "Hidden Wounds." *HR Magazine,* July 1, 2011. https://www.shrm.org/hr-today/news/hr-magazine/pages/0711meinert.aspx.

Menna, Amy. *Post Traumatic Stress Disorder and the Workplace: What Employers and Coworkers Need to Know*. Camden, ME: A Gift from Within, August 24, 2012. http://www.giftfromwithin.org/html/PTSD-Workplace-What-Employers-Coworkers-Need-To-Know.html.

Military Officers Association of America. *A Complete Guide to Military Spouse Employment*, MOAA Military Family Initiative. Alexandria, VA: Military Officers Association of America, 2017. http://www.moaa.org/uploadedFiles/Content/Publications_and_Media/MOAA_Publications/Publication_Downloads/2670_SpouseEmployment_final2.pdf.

Montgomery, Ann Elizabeth, Tom Byrne, Alison B. Hamilton, and Rani A. Hoff. *Women Veterans and Homelessness*. Homeless Evidence and Research Roundtable Series. Philadelphia: VA National Center on Homelessness among Veterans, July 2016. https://www.va.gov/HOMELESS/nchav/docs/HERS-Womens-Proceedings.pdf.

Murphy, Frances, Sherrie L. Hans, and Bradley J. Reina. *Women Veterans: The Long Journey Home*. Cold Spring, KY: Disabled American Veterans, 2015. https://www.dav.org/wp-content/uploads/women-veterans-study.pdf.

National Center for PTSD. "How Common Is PTSD?" Department of Veteran Affairs, October 3, 2016. http://www.ptsd.va.gov/public/ptsd-overview/basics/how-common-is-ptsd.asp.

Nebraska Department of Veteran's Affairs. "What Is PTSD (Posttraumatic Stress Disorder)?" 2007. http://www.ptsd.ne.gov/what-is-ptsd.html.

Office of Data Governance and Analytics. *Women Veterans Report: The Past, Present, and Future of Women Veterans*. Washington, DC: National Center for Veterans Analysis and Statistics, February 2017. https://www.va.gov/vetdata/docs/SpecialReports/Women_Veterans_2015_Final.pdf.

Whittaker, Julie M. "Unemployment Compensation (Insurance) and Military Service." Congressional Research Service, April 24, 2013. http://fas.org/sgp/crs/misc/RS22440.pdf.

Wounded Warrior Project. "Make the Connection: Writing Effective Position Descriptions." 2015. https://www.woundedwarriorproject. org/media/1579/make-the-connection-writing-effective-position-descriptions_rev-5615.pdf.

Wounded Warrior Project. "Warriors to Work: A Resource for Employers." 2015. https://www.woundedwarriorproject.org/media/1581/ warriors-to-work-a-resource-for-employers_rev5615.pdf.

About the Author

Justin Constantine retired from the US Marine Corps at the rank of lieutenant colonel. He is now an inspirational speaker and veteran advocate. He speaks at numerous corporate, educational, and military institutions about leadership, the upside of change, teamwork, and overcoming adversity. Justin is also a partner at JobPath, a robust veteran employment platform that provides a variety of solutions to corporations, government agencies, and nonprofit organizations that hire veterans.

Justin deployed to Iraq in 2006, serving as a civil affairs team leader attached to an infantry battalion. While on a routine combat patrol, Justin was shot in the head by a sniper. Although the original prognosis was that he had been killed in action, Justin survived thanks to risks taken by his fellow Marines and a courageous Navy Corpsman. For his service in Iraq, he earned the Purple Heart, Combat Action Ribbon, and Navy-Marine Corps Commendation Medal.

After recovering from his injuries in 2007, Justin worked at the US Department of Justice and then as counsel for the Senate Veterans' Affairs Committee. In 2011, the Secretary of Defense appointed him to a four-year term on the Task Force for Recovering Warriors. Justin also worked for several years with the FBI as an attorney on a counterterrorism team. He now sits on the board of directors of a number of national nonprofit organizations, and cofounded his own in 2015.

In 2015, he completed his first book, *My Battlefield, Your Office*, which applies military leadership skills to the private sector. His writing on military and leadership issues has been featured by such outlets as *CNN*, *Time*, the *Washington Post*, the *Atlantic*, *Forbes* magazine, *USA Today*, *Business Insider*, *Stars and Stripes*, and the *Huffington Post*.

Justin graduated from James Madison University in 1992 with a double major in English and Political Science and a minor in German. He joined the US Marine Corps while in law school at the University of Denver

School of Law, and graduated from there in 1998. Justin was the Honor Graduate of his class at the Marine Corps Command and Staff College in 2009. In 2015, he graduated on the Dean's List from Georgetown University with a Master of Laws degree focusing on national security.

In 2012, the Virginia legislature passed a commending resolution highlighting Justin's continued support of veterans and other wounded warriors. Justin is a Presidential Leadership Scholar, has been named a Champion of Change by the Obama White House, and was also awarded the prestigious inaugural 2014 Lincoln Award recognizing his outstanding achievements and excellence in providing opportunities and support to our nation's veterans and military families. Justin was also one of the wounded warriors painted by President George W. Bush in his book *Portraits of Courage*.

Index

Other SHRM Titles

A Manager's Guide to Developing Competencies in HR Staff
Tips and Tools for Improving Proficiency in Your Reports
Phyllis G. Hartman, SHRM-SCP

California Employment Law: A Guide for Employers
Revised and Updated 2018 Edition
James J. McDonald, Jr., JD

Digital HR
A Guide to Technology-Enabled HR
Deborah Waddill, Ed.D.

From Hello to Goodbye: Second Edition
Proactive Tips for Maintaining Positive Employee Relations
Christine V. Walters, JD, SHRM-SCP

Go Beyond the Job Description
A 100-Day Action Plan for Optimizing Talents and Building Engagement
Ashley Prisant Lesko, Ph.D., SHRM-SCP

The HR Career Guide
Great Answers to Tough Career Questions
Martin Yate, CPC

HR on Purpose!!
Developing Deliberate People Passion
Steve Browne, SHRM-SCP

Mastering Consultation as an HR Practitioner
Making an Impact on Small Businesses
Jennifer Currence, SHRM-SCP

Motivation-Based Interviewing
A Revolutionary Approach to Hiring the Best
Carol Quinn

The Practical Guide to HR Analytics
Using Data to Inform, Transform, and Empower HR Decisions
Shonna D. Waters, Valerie N. Streets, Lindsay A. McFarlane, and Rachel Johnson-Murray

The Power of Stay Interviews for Engagement and Retention
Second Edition
Richard P. Finnegan

Predicting Business Success
Using Smarter Analytics to Drive Results
Scott Mondore, Hannah Spell, Matt Betts, and Shane Douthitt

The Recruiter's Handbook
A Complete Guide for Sourcing, Selecting, and Engaging the Best Talent
Sharlyn Lauby, SHRM-SCP

The SHRM Essential Guide to Employment Law
A Handbook for HR Professionals, Managers, and Businesses
Charles H. Fleischer, JD

The Talent Fix
A Leader's Guide to Recruiting Great Talent
Tim Sackett, SHRM-SCP

Books Approved for SHRM Recertification Credits

107 Frequently Asked Questions About Staffing Management, Fiester (ISBN: 9781586443733)

47 Frequently Asked Questions About the Family and Medical Leave Act, Fiester (ISBN: 9781586443801)

57 Frequently Asked Questions About Workplace Safety and Security, Fiester (ISBN: 9781586443610)

97 Frequently Asked Questions About Compensation, Fiester (ISBN: 9781586443566)

A Manager's Guide to Developing Competencies in HR Staff, Hartman (ISBN: 9781586444365)

A Necessary Evil: Managing Employee Activity on Facebook, Wright (ISBN: 9781586443412)

Aligning Human Resources and Business Strategy, Holbeche (ISBN: 9780750680172)

Applying Advanced Analytics to HR Management Decisions, Sesil (ISBN: 9780133064605)

Applying Critical Evaluation: Making an Impact in Small Business, Currence (ISBN: 9781586444426)

Becoming the Evidence Based Manager, Latham (ISBN: 9780891063988)

Being Global: How to Think, Act, and Lead in a Transformed World, Cabrera (ISBN: 9781422183229)

Black Holes and White Spaces: Reimagining the Future of Work and HR, Boudreau (ISBN: 9781586444617)

Business Literacy Survival Guide for HR Professionals, Garey (ISBN: 9781586442057)

Business-Focused HR: 11 Processes to Drive Results, Mondore (ISBN: 9781586442040)

Calculating Success, Hoffman (ISBN: 9781422166390)

California Employment Law, Revised and Updated, McDonald (ISBN: 9781586444815)

Collaborate: The Art of We, Sanker (ISBN: 9781118114728)

Deep Dive: Proven Method for Building Strategy, Horwath (ISBN: 9781929774821)

Defining HR Success: 9 Critical Competencies for HR Professionals, Alonso (ISBN: 9781586443825)

Destination Innovation: HR's Role in Charting the Course, Buhler (ISBN: 9781586443832)

Developing Business Acumen, Currence (ISBN: 9781586444143)

Developing Proficiency in HR: 7 Self-Directed Activities for HR Professionals, Cohen (ISBN: 9781586444167)

Digital HR: A Guide to Technology-Enabled Human Resources, Waddill (ISBN: 9781586445423)

Diverse Teams at Work: Capitalizing on the Power of Diversity, Gardenswartz (ISBN: 9781586440367)

Effective Human Resource Management: A Global Analysis, Lawler (ISBN: 9780804776875)

Emotional Intelligence 2.0, Bradberry (ISBN: 9780974320625)

Financial Analysis for HR Managers, Director (ISBN: 9780133925425)

From Hello to Goodbye, 2e, Walters (ISBN: 9781586444471)

From We Will to at Will: A Handbook for Veteran Hiring, Constantine (ISBN: 9781586445072)

Give Your Company a Fighting Chance, Danaher (ISBN: 9781586443658)

Go Beyond the Job Description, Lesko (ISBN: 9781586445171)

Got a Minute? The 9 Lessons Every HR Professional Must Learn to Be Successful, Dwyer (ISBN: 9781586441982)

Got a Solution? HR Approaches to 5 Common and Persistent Business Problems, Dwyer (ISBN: 9781586443665)

Handbook for Strategic HR: Best Practices in Organization Development, Vogelsang (ISBN: 9780814432495)

Hidden Drivers of Success: Leveraging Employee Insights for Strategic Advantage, Schiemann (ISBN: 9781586443337)

HR at Your Service: Lessons from Benchmark Service Organizations, Latham (ISBN: 9781586442477)

HR on Purpose: Developing Deliberate People Passion, Browne (ISBN: 9781586444259)

HR Transformation: Building Human Resources from the Inside Out, Ulrich (ISBN: 9780071638708)

HR's Greatest Challenge: Driving the C-Suite to Improve Employee Engagement …, Finnegan (ISBN: 9781586443795)

Investing in People: Financial Impact of Human Resource Initiatives, 2e, Boudreau (ISBN: 9780132394116)

Investing in What Matters: Linking Employees to Business Outcomes, Mondore (ISBN: 9781586441371)

Leading an HR Transformation, Anderson (ISBN: 9781586444860)

Lean HR: Introducing Process Excellence to Your Practice, Lay (ISBN: 9781481914208)

Linkage Inc.'s Best Practices for Succession Planning: Case Studies, Research, Models, Tools, Sobol (ISBN: 9780787985790)

Looking to Hire an HR Leader, Hartman (ISBN: 9781586443672)

Manager 3.0: A Millennial's Guide to Rewriting the Rules of Management, Karsh (ISBN: 9780814432891)

Manager Onboarding: 5 Steps for Setting New Leaders Up for Success, Lauby (ISBN: 9781586444075)

Manager's Guide to Employee Engagement, Carbonara (ISBN: 9780071799508)

Managing Employee Turnover, Allen (ISBN: 9781606493403)

Managing the Global Workforce, Caligiuri (ISBN: 9781405107327)

Managing the Mobile Workforce: Leading, Building, and Sustaining Virtual Teams, Clemons (ISBN: 9780071742207)

Managing the Older Worker: How to Prepare for the New Organizational Order, Cappelli (ISBN: 9781422131657)

Mastering Consultation as an HR Practitioner, Currence (ISBN: 9781586445027)

Measuring ROI in Employee Relations and Compliance, Phillips (ISBN: 9781586443597)

Motivation-Based Interviewing: A Revolutionary Approach to Hiring the Best, Quinn (ISBN: 9781586445478)

Multipliers: How the Best Leaders Make Everyone Smarter, Wiseman (ISBN: 9780061964398)

Negotiation at Work: Maximize Your Team's Skills with 60 High-Impact Activities, Asherman (ISBN: 9780814431900)

Nine Minutes on Monday: The Quick and Easy Way to Go from Manager to Leader, Robbins (ISBN: 9780071801980)

One Strategy: Organizing, Planning and Decision Making, Sinofsky (ISBN: 9780470560457)

People Analytics: How Social Sensing Technology Will Transform Business, Waber (ISBN: 9780133158311)

Perils and Pitfalls of California Employment Law: A Guide for HR Professionals, Effland (ISBN: 9781586443634)

Point Counterpoint II: New Perspectives on People & Strategy, Vosburgh (ISBN: 9781586444181)

Point Counterpoint: New Perspectives on People & Strategy, Tavis (ISBN: 9781586442767)

Practices for Engaging the 21st-Century Workforce, Castellano (ISBN: 9780133086379)

Predicting Business Success: Using Smarter Analytics to Drive Results, Mondore (ISBN: 9781586445379)

Proving the Value of HR: How and Why to Measure ROI, Phillips (ISBN: 9781586442316)

Reality Based Leadership, Wakeman (ISBN: 9780470613504)

Rethinking Retention in Good Times and Bad, Finnegan (ISBN: 9780891062387)

Social Media Strategies for Professionals and Their Firms, Golden (ISBN: 9780470633106)

Solving the Compensation Puzzle: Putting Together a Complete Pay and Performance System, Koss (ISBN: 9781586440923)

Stop Bullying at Work, 2e, Daniel (ISBN: 9781586443856)

Talent, Transformation, and the Triple Bottom Line, Savitz (ISBN: 9781118140970)

The ACE Advantage: How Smart Companies Unleash Talent for Optimal Performance, Schiemann (ISBN: 9781586442866)

The Big Book of HR, Mitchell (ISBN: 9781601631893)

The Crowdsourced Performance Review, Mosley
(ISBN: 9780071817981)

The Cultural Fit Factor: Creating an Employment Brand That Attracts …, Pellet
(ISBN: 9781586441265)

The Definitive Guide to HR Communication, Davis
(ISBN: 9780137061433)

The E-HR Advantage: The Complete Handbook for Technology-Enabled Human Resources, Waddill (ISBN: 9781904838340)

The Employee Engagement Mindset, Clark
(ISBN: 9780071788298)

The EQ Interview: Finding Employees with High Emotional Intelligence, Lynn
(ISBN: 9780814409411)

The Global Challenge: International Human Resource Management, Evans
(ISBN: 9780073530376)

The Global M&A Tango, Trompenaars
(ISBN: 9780071761154)

The HR Answer Book, 2e, Smith
(ISBN: 9780814417171)

The HR Career Guide: Great Answers to Tough Career Questions, Yate
(ISBN: 9781586444761)

The Manager's Guide to HR, 2e, Muller
(ISBN: 9780814433027)

The Performance Appraisal Tool Kit, Falcone
(ISBN: 9780814432631)

The Power of Appreciative Inquiry: A Practical Guide to Positive Change, Whitney
(ISBN: 9781605093284)

The Power of Stay Interviews for Retention and Engagement, 2e, Finnegan
(ISBN: 9781586445126)

The Practical Guide to HR Analytics, Waters
(ISBN: 9781586445324)

The Recruiter's Handbook, Lauby
(ISBN: 9781586444655)

The SHRM Essential Guide to Employment Law, Fleischer (ISBN: 9781586444709)

The Talent Fix: A Leader's Guide to Recruiting Great Talent, Sackett (ISBN: 9781586445225)

Touching People's Lives: Leaders' Sorrow or Joy, Losey (ISBN: 9781586444310)

Transformative HR: How Great Companies Use Evidence-Based Change …, Boudreau
(ISBN: 9781118036044)

Transformational Diversity, Citkin
(ISBN: 9781586442309)

Up, Down, and Sideways: High-Impact Verbal Communication for HR Professionals, Buhler
(ISBN: 9781586443375)

View from the Top: Leveraging Human and Organization Capital to Create Value, Wright (ISBN: 9781586444006)

What If? Short Stories to Spark Diversity Dialogue, Robbins (ISBN: 9780891062752)

What Is Global Leadership? 10 Key Behaviors that Define Great Global Leaders, Gundling
(ISBN: 9781904838234)

Winning the War for Talent in Emerging Markets: Why Women are the Solution, Hewlett
(ISBN: 9781422160602)